READINGS FROM

THE LU-WANG SCHOOL
OF NEO-CONFUCIANISM

Larry

READINGS FROM

THE LU-WANG SCHOOL OF NEO-CONFUCIANISM

Translated, with Introductions and Notes, by
Philip J. Ivanhoe

Hackett Publishing Company, Inc.
Indianapolis/Cambridge

14 13 12 11 10 09   1 2 3 4 5 6

For further information, please address:

Hackett Publishing Company, Inc.
P.O. Box 44937
Indianapolis, IN 46244-0937

www.hackettpublishing.com

Cover design by Abigail Coyle
Text design by Carrie Wagner
Composition by SNP Best-set Typesetter Ltd., Hong Kong
Printed at Sheridan Books, Inc.

Library of Congress Cataloging-in-Publication Data

Readings from the Lu-Wang school of Neo-Confucianism / translated, with
introductions and notes, by Philip J. Ivanhoe.
   p. cm.
   Includes bibliographical references and index.
   ISBN 978-0-87220-960-2 (pbk.)—ISBN 978-0-87220-961-9 (cloth)
   1. Neo-Confucianism.   2. Philosophy, Chinese—960-1644.   I. Lu,
Jiuyuan, 1139-1193.   II. Wang, Yangming, 1472-1529.   III. Ivanhoe, P. J.
IV. Huineng, 638-713. Liuzu da shi fa bao tan jing. English. Selections.
   B127.N4R43 2009
   181'.112—dc22
                          2008052826

The paper in this publication meets the minimum requirements of American
National Standard for Information Sciences—
Permanence of Paper for Printed Library Materials,
ANSI Z39.48-1984

∞

For Lee H. Yearley—

> *Whose work teaches us to wonder, inquire, and appreciate much that is hidden;*

> *Whose example inspires us to practice and refine the art of our vocation.*

CONTENTS

Acknowledgments   ix

Preface   xi

PART ONE: The *Platform Sutra* (*Tanjing* 壇經)   1

Introduction   3

The Dunhuang Version of the *Platform Sutra* (Selections)   14

PART TWO: Lu Xiangshan 陸象山 (1139–1193)   27

Introduction   29

Letters   44

Recorded Sayings   76

Expository Essays   79

Short Meditations   89

Poetry   93

PART THREE: Wang Yangming 王陽明 (1472–1529)   99

Introduction   101

Letters   116

A Record for Practice (*Chuanxilu*)   131

Questions on the Great Learning (*Daxue wen*)   160

Essential Instructions for Students at Longchang   173

Poetry   178

Suggested Readings   185

Index   189

ACKNOWLEDGMENTS

Thanks to Sing-chen Lydia Chiang, Erin M. Cline, Eirik L. Harris, Eric L. Hutton, Jiang Hong, Paul Kjellberg, David W. Tien, and Mark T. Unno for corrections, comments, and suggestions on earlier drafts of this volume. Special thanks to the Department of Public and Social Administration, City University of Hong Kong, for generously supporting this work and to Melanie J. Dorson and Justin Tiwald for carefully reading through and commenting on the entire manuscript.

PREFACE

This volume contains three sets of selected translations; the first is from the Tang dynasty (618–906) Buddhist classic the *Platform Sutra*, the second from the writings of the Song dynasty (960–1127) neo-Confucian Lu Xiangshan, and the third from the Ming dynasty (1368–1644) neo-Confucian Wang Yangming. Lu and Wang came to be regarded as the founders of the Lu-Wang School or "Learning of the Heart-Mind," a philosophical perspective and movement that challenged many of the views espoused by the orthodox Cheng-Zhu School or "Learning of Principle," which was named after the Song dynasty philosophers Cheng Yi (1033–1107) and Zhu Xi (1130–1200). A short introduction is provided for each set of translations, sketching important features of the history, biography, and philosophy of the authors and exploring some of the main features and qualities of these works. The introductions are not intended to provide complete accounts of these thinkers or texts; their aim is to present the reader with some of the primary themes—both philosophical and stylistic—that inform these writings in order to set the stage for the translations that follow. I have chosen selections that, as much as possible, present complete or at least substantial and consistent samples of these texts, which, at the same time, represent each author's overall philosophy and approach. Any such selection will necessarily leave out important passages and ideas, and readers are encouraged to pursue further study of these texts and thinkers, beginning with the Suggested Readings on page 185 of this book.

PART ONE
The *Platform Sutra* (*Tanjing* 壇經)

Introduction to
the *Platform Sutra*

We begin this volume of translations from the Lu-Wang School with selections from the Buddhist classic the *Platform Sutra* primarily because of the tremendous, poorly understood, and often overlooked influence Chinese Buddhism in general and this text in particular has had upon neo-Confucian thought.[1] I will sketch some of the core features of this early Chan (J. Zen) Buddhist classic and note ways in which these influenced the content, shape, and style of Lu Xiangshang's and Wang Yangming's philosophies; this sketch will give general claims about philosophical influence more substance and specific form. I have used the Dunhuang 敦煌 manuscript of the text, which dates from the late ninth century, because it provides a version of the *sūtra* closer to what Lu would have seen and not significantly philosophically different from what Wang would have read.[2] The text opens with a brief "biography" of Huineng 惠能 (638–713), the man destined to become the Sixth Patriarch of the Southern School of Chan. While not a reliable record of historical events, Huineng's biography offers us historically important information about the ways in which figures like the Sixth Patriarch were

---

1   I have argued for this point in Philip J. Ivanhoe, *Ethics in the Confucian Tradition: The Thought of Mengzi and Wang Yangming,* rev. 2d ed. (Indianapolis: Hackett, 2002). The most thorough and revealing study of this aspect of Chinese culture to date is the recent dissertation by David W. Tien, "Discursive Resources and Collapsing Polarities: The Religious Thought of Tang Dynasty Scholar-Officials" (University of Michigan, 2009).

2   For a study and translation of this text, see Philip B. Yampolsky, trans., *The Platform Sutra of the Sixth Patriarch: The Text of the Tun-huang Manuscript* (New York: Columbia University Press, 1967).

understood.³ We shall discuss both the content and style of Lu's and Wang's official biographies when I introduce their respective philosophies; these works also offer revealing insights into aspects of their thought and lives.

We are told that Huineng's father died while he was still a child and his mother raised him on her own.⁴ They were commoners and poor; he did not receive any formal education and made a living by peddling firewood. One day he happened to hear someone chanting the *Diamond Sutra* and later recounted, "hearing it my mind became clear and I was awakened." After questioning the man, Huineng "realized" he was "predestined" to go study with the Fifth Patriarch, a monk named Hongren 弘忍 (601–674); so, off he went. Many elements of this story are significant, but for our purposes Huineng's commoner status and lack of education are key. Despite lacking social status and formal schooling, Huineng understood the highest truths of Buddhism. Among other things, this shows spiritual wisdom is not the result of any form of privilege; it is not the result of learning or acquiring anything new; rather, it flows spontaneously out of an original and perfectly pure and innocent nature shared by all people—as well as all creatures and things. In Buddhist texts such as the *Platform Sutra,* this common endowment is called "Buddha-nature" (*foxing* 佛性).

The implications of this claim are many and profound, but perhaps the greatest is an absolute spiritual and moral equality among human beings.⁵ All people are fundamentally Buddhas and would act as Buddhas do if only they could get in touch with and manifest their true natures;

---

3   For our purposes, it matters little whether the details of Huineng's biography report historical events. In my view, they clearly do not. Nevertheless, they tell us important things about how people thought of Huineng and spiritual virtuosi like him.

4   Huineng shared the misfortune of losing his father in childhood with the early Confucian sage Mengzi 孟子 (also called Mencius; 391–308 B.C.E.), whose mother is renowned for raising and educating him on her own. In this regard, Huineng's early life resonates with a cherished story in traditional Chinese culture and differs dramatically from that of the historical Buddha.

5   While it would be difficult to overstate the importance of Buddha-nature in *Mahāyāna* Buddhism, one should keep in mind that like all teachings, this idea of a pure, innate nature is an example of skillful means (*upaya*). More than simply stating some fact of the matter, Buddha-nature is metaphorical, analogical, evocative, and expressive.

unfortunately, the Buddha-nature of most people is hidden or obscured by selfish desires. As the text goes on to explain, such desires ultimately arise and are reinforced by a fundamentally mistaken view about the self, a view that fails to see that the self is (not) isolated and separate from the world but in fact shares the very same fundamental nature as all people, creatures, and things. This general point of view is an important foundation for the great compassion (*mahākaruna*) that is one of the most distinctive features of *Mahāyāna* Buddhism; it also makes sudden enlightenment (*dunwu* 頓悟), the signature event of Chan Buddhism, possible and in some sense an inevitable feature of their philosophy.[6] For if in fact we all possess a pure and perfect nature that reveals our underlying connection to the universe, all that remains is for us to "wake up" to this fact. One cannot *intend* to wake up: one either is awake or in the process of awakening—or one is asleep. One cannot intend to be enlightened: it simply must happen.[7]

Lu and Wang adopted much of the form and structure of this set of characteristically Chan Buddhist beliefs concerning the nature of people and the rest of the world. As will be clear, though, they fill in these general claims about an underlying shared nature with distinctively Confucian content and go on to shape their versions of these claims into the familiar themes and aims of the Confucian tradition. Of course, the kind of influence we see here and elsewhere did not go in only one direction—the traditions of Confucianism, Daoism, and Buddhism continually interacted and influenced one another—but the extent to which neo-Confucian thinkers were affected by Buddhist ideas is our present concern. That such influence occurred should come as no surprise, for Buddhism had become a fundamental part of Chinese culture

---

6   For a discussion of *mahākaruna* and its role within *Mahāyāna* Buddhism, see Paul Williams, *Mahayana Buddhism: The Doctrinal Foundations* (London: Routledge, 1989). For a collection of essays on the topic of sudden enlightenment, see Peter N. Gregory, ed., *Sudden and Gradual: Approaches to Enlightenment in Chinese Thought* (Honolulu: University of Hawaii Press, 1987). Like the notion of Buddha-nature, the idea of sudden enlightenment must be understood against the background of skillful means. See note 5.

7   As we shall discuss later, one can prepare the ground for enlightenment by engaging in certain practices, and good teachers can play an important role in bringing forth enlightenment. Like midwives, though, they can only help with the birth; enlightenment must arise in and come forth from the individual.

in the more than one thousand years separating neo-Confucians from their classical forebears, in many ways dominating elite culture and profoundly affecting almost every aspect of Chinese life. Even before one comes to recognize particular examples of such influence, it should strike one as wildly implausible that the contributions Buddhism had upon indigenous Chinese ways of thinking could be anything less than deep and pervasive. Let us, however, continue to identify and discuss specific features of the *Platform Sutra* that find clear parallels—thematic, philosophical, and stylistic—in the thought of Lu and Wang.

One of the central events in the *Platform Sutra* is the spirit verse "competition" Hongren initiates in order to choose his successor.[8] The best and most advanced pupil at the monastery and the obvious favorite to win the competition is a monk named Shenxiu 神秀 (606?–706). Shenxiu represents the traditional educated monk; in contrast, Huineng, who is unable to read or write, is a spiritual Cinderella—relegated to the kitchen during the initial competition. But like his Western fairy-tale counterpart, Huineng finds a way to join the festivities; a series of clever developments in the plot allow him to compose his own verses, which someone writes for him on the wall of one of the halls in the monastery. Hongren immediately recognizes these compositions as manifesting enlightenment. He then calls Huineng to him and secretly passes on his teaching and authority.[9]

Huineng's poems take everything a little further than Shenxiu's: instead of there being a "tree of enlightenment" (i.e., the self) as in Shenxiu's composition, Huineng makes clear that there is no self. Instead of insisting on the need for "polishing one's mirror" (i.e., working to make oneself better), Huineng emphasizes the need for realizing that one's fundamental nature is perfectly pure, and that it will remain so: all dust (i.e., all defilements) are self-inflicted wounds, delusions we generate

---

8   This event and most importantly the poems presented by its two central participants are included in this volume.

9   Here and especially later in the *Platform Sutra*, we see a different side of Huineng. In addition to being an iconoclastic, Daoist-like character, he was, at the same time, an abbot and master. These different faces of Huineng represent not only two important features of the Chan tradition but also the complementary tension between the sudden and gradual methods.

through our own misapprehension of the true state of things. What is needed is a profound and transforming insight. We do not need to acquire and accumulate new knowledge, nor do we need to cultivate new and improved psychological states. We simply must recognize that things are perfect the way they are. The highest spiritual attainment does not involve gaining anything new, but rather losing all that is false. It is finding relief from self-deception, not developing a radically new and unknown state of mind. As we shall see, all of these ideas appear, in distinctively Confucian garb, in the thought of Lu and Wang.

The *style* of philosophizing we see in the *Platform Sutra* is another important type of influence. For example, the reliance on poetry is significant. Poetry communicates through images and rhythms that evoke mental and affective states, not through discrete claims and discursive arguments. Its message and effect are more direct and spontaneous than ordinary speech. Lu and Wang both relied upon and showed a preference for poetic expression over systematic essays or commentaries, and selections of their philosophical poetry are included in this volume. The style of the personal exchanges we see between Hongren and his disciples also influenced the way Lu and Wang taught and interacted with their students. Like Chan Buddhist masters, these later Confucian teachers served not only as inspiring exemplars but also as spiritual coaches for their students: they taught, led, coaxed, cajoled, frustrated, and at times even frightened their disciples, explicitly employing a broad, therapeutic method of instruction. Another important influence is captured in the idea that the highest level of spiritual attainment is a kind of knack "not residing in words or letters."[10] Lu and Wang regularly imply that traditional knowledge and even the classics themselves are as much impediments as aids to self-cultivation. Wise teachers know enlightenment when they see it and can coach their students toward it, but even the most gifted cannot directly impart it to another person. Enlightenment is something one must find for oneself and in one's own life; one cannot discover it by looking at what others have written, said,

---

10   This line is from a famous description of Chan Buddhism. See note 26 in this part of the volume. The idea finds clear early precedents in Daoist texts such as the *Zhuangzi* 莊子 and offers a good example of how indigenous Chinese thought influenced and transformed Buddhism.

or done.[11] This idea is illustrated in the traditional Chinese cautionary tale warning those who seek the beauty of the moon not to focus on the finger pointing to the moon or they will miss all the moon's Heavenly glory.

Chan Buddhism was profoundly influenced by what is known as the perfection of wisdom (*prajñā pāramitā*) literature, a movement within Buddhism that tends to see wisdom or insight as both necessary and sufficient for enlightenment.[12] People holding this view believe that proper insight into the way the world really is will result in, in part constitutes, or is itself enlightenment. Few ever held the most radical versions of such a position; however, many strongly emphasized "insight" over other forms of religious practice.

On the opposite side of the spectrum were thinkers who advocated the attainment of certain ideal meditative states. This influence goes back to India and traditions of various yogic practices. The core idea is that what one needs to attain enlightenment is a state of complete meditative stability (*samādhi*), and this state can only be achieved through proper meditative practices, particularly those designed to settle the mind and "eliminate thoughts."[13] The word *chan* 禪, which provides the name of the Chan School of Buddhism, is an approximation of the Sanskrit word for meditation (*dhyāna*).

Huineng, in his sermon previously discussed, seeks to abolish the dichotomy between insight (*hui* 惠) and stability (*ding* 定),[14] arguing that these present a false choice. There is no such thing as meditative stability apart from proper insight; proper insight involves a state of meditative stability. The *Platform Sutra* rejects a number of standard conceptions of what meditative stability and insight involve. One way

---

11   When compared with the thought of classical Confucians such as Mengzi or Xunzi 荀子, such a view significantly diminishes the role that environment plays in moral development, especially in the early stages of life.

12   For an introduction to the *prajñā pāramitā* tradition, see note 22 in this part of the volume.

13   See the commentary to Section 13 and the text of Section 14. Compare Wang Yangming's remarks on meditation in his "For My Students in Chen Zhou," presented in this volume.

14   The most important discussion of this pair of concepts is found primarily in Sections 13 and 14.

of looking at the position the text recommends is that a proper understanding (i.e., "insight") of the nature of self and the world will produce
a certain affective state (i.e., "meditative stability") and that this mental
state cannot be produced except through such insight. Those who really
understand always have this calm and stable state of mind; they do not
need to be engaged in formal (traditionally) seated meditation in order
to be in a state of meditative calm. Seen from another angle, since meditation is being in the right state of mind, everything the enlightened
person does is meditation. This expands the scope of "right practice" to
include every action and thought one undertakes, and followers of Chan
insist that this kind of "mindfulness" is what the Buddha practiced. These
ideas about the relationships between understanding, right disposition,
and proper practice deeply influenced thinkers such as Lu and Wang and
find clearest expression in their refusal to countenance any form of moral
knowledge that lacked the proper and corresponding affective and behav-
ioral dimensions. There is not a great deal of distance between insisting
on the relationship between understanding and disposition and Wang's
signature teaching concerning the unity of knowing and acting, which
we shall explore in a later portion of this work. Both Lu and Wang also
manifest the open and flexible attitude toward what constitutes right
practice that is part and parcel of this general Chan Buddhist approach:
anything rightly done is proper; every good thought is meditation.

In Section 15, Huineng discusses two vitally important terms of art:
body (*ti* 體) and function (*yong* 用) and illustrates their meaning with
the example of a lamp and its light.[15] The lamp, being an actual, substantial thing—a body—is an example of *ti*. When the lamp is lit, it
produces light, the *yong* of this particular *ti*. These concepts, which
originated with the neo-Daoist thinker Wang Bi 王弼 (third century),
were used to make a number of points in the *Platform Sutra,* and they
became central terms of art among neo-Confucians. The *Platform Sutra*
claims that the lighted lamp and its light form an inseparable unity.
While one can logically conceive of a lighted lamp and its light as

15   For a discussion of the use of these concepts—commonly translated as "substance"
and "function," respectively—in neo-Confucianism, see Angus C. Graham, *Two Chinese
Philosophers: The Metaphysics of the Brothers Ch'eng* (La Salle, IL: Open Court, 1992), pp.
39–40; for a historical account, see my entry "TI/YONG" in Edward Craig, ed., *Routledge Encyclopedia of Philosophy* (London: Routledge, 1999), vol. 9, p. 400.

separate, they never actually occur apart from each other. (Aristotle makes a similar point about concave and convex surfaces.) Applying this point to meditative stability and insight, we see that while we can think of them as distinct things, actually they can never be found apart from each other. They are one body (*yiti* 一體). The idea of what it is for various phenomena to be "one body" becomes extremely important in Chan Buddhism and throughout the later Confucian tradition. In different and distinctive ways, both traditions insisted that at the deepest level every human being is one body with the universe. As we shall see later, Wang's ultimate ideal and spiritual goal was to regard Heaven, earth, and the myriad things as one body, to care for each part of the universe as if it were a part of one's own body. Such a view offers a dramatic contrast with early Confucian accounts of the Way.

As noted earlier, another philosophical dimension of the notions of *ti* and *yong,* and one that is equally important, is the notion that each and every "body" has a characteristic "function." In other words, there is a normative dimension to these ideas. The proper thing for a lighted lamp to do is to shine. If it is not broken or malfunctioning, it will shine, and if it is not covered over, for example, hidden under a basket, its light will illuminate whatever is nearby. Things (i.e., various "bodies") function naturally and only fail to function when somehow deprived of their natural state. Both Lu and Wang made broad use of such ideas, insisting that the various virtues of Confucianism are simply the natural functions of human nature: when our true nature is operating without obstruction, the result is perfect virtue. One of Wang's favorite illustrations of *ti* and *yong* is the eye and its power of sight, which he invoked to make a number of related points: (1) the eye is the "body" of sight, in that vision is embodied in the eye, (2) seeing is the eye's natural function, and (3) the only thing that will prevent a healthy (open) eye from seeing is some foreign substance that interferes with its natural operation.

Notice how such a view assumes not only that there is something like a natural function to each and every thing but also that things will operate according to their function as long as they are free of interference. As noted previously, according to the *Platform Sutra,* as long as our Buddha-nature is not impeded by selfish desires, we all will act like the Buddhas we really are. According to Lu and Wang, if we simply manifest the full and unadulterated functioning of our original nature, we all will be in fact the sages we really are. As Wang was fond of saying, the streets are full of sages.

To "fix" things that are not properly functioning (e.g., a person who acts improperly), one must work to eliminate some interference, not add something more to the self. For Buddhists, the interferences (i.e., selfish human desires) are not *real;* they are powerful and pernicious delusions that we generate by embracing false ideas about the self and the world. So, the spiritual task is for us to shed these false beliefs, relieve our delusions, and restore ourselves to spiritual health. Wang adopted or more properly adapted many of these ideas in fashioning his own point of view; this is clear from the following passage, which employs his favored metaphor of the eye and seeing:

> The Master once said to his disciples, "No thought should stick to the mind in itself, just as not the least bit of dirt should stick to the eye. It requires very little dirt to cover the eye and blot out Heaven and earth."

> He also said, "The thought need not be a selfish thought. Even good thoughts should not become stuck in any way. It is like putting gold or jade dust in the eye; just the same, the eye cannot open."[16]

When this general perspective is applied to a Confucian point of view, our innate moral sense comes to be seen as a naturally functioning faculty, which, as we shall see, is precisely how Wang Yangming described pure knowing (*liangzhi* 良知). Moral failure is regarded as aberrant, the result of an obstruction of the normal operation of this faculty, in much the same way as illness is a loss of good health—our normal state of being. In general, neo-Confucians agree with Buddhists in describing such interference primarily in terms of selfish desires and in seeing self-cultivation largely in terms of eliminating selfishness, in whatever forms

---

16   The quotation is my translation from a portion of *A Record for Practice* (*Chuanxilu*) not included in this volume. Compare Wing-tsit Chan, trans., *Instructions for Practical Living and Other Neo-Confucian Writings by Wang Yang-ming* (New York: Columbia University Press, 1963), pp. 256–57.

it takes. They tend to part company with Buddhists, though, concerning
the nature of selfish desires, seeing them as *real* but not *true* or authentic
parts of our original nature. Neo-Confucians tend to explain selfish
desires in terms of interfering *qi*, which obscures our sense of being connected with the rest of the world, by distorting and blocking the natural
functioning of the principles (*li* 理) that constitute our original or fundamental nature.[17]

Such a view, carried to its logical conclusion, results in a remarkable
concern with any and all forms of consciousness, particularly "self"-
consciousness, which in improper forms leads to selfish desires. Even
concern about one's own spiritual welfare can manifest selfishness and
become a major impediment if it leads to excessive concern for one's own
moral purity. This is clear in the quotation discussed previously, in which
Wang Yangming talks about "putting gold or jade dust in the eye."
Anything added to the original nature—even the "gold" or "jade" of
good intentions—can only interfere with the nature's spontaneous functioning. We find clear precedents for this set of ideas in the *Platform
Sutra* where it warns against the dangers of "viewing the mind" and
"viewing purity."[18]

The problem at the core of such discussions reflects an older and
characteristically, though not exclusively, Daoist conundrum about cultivating unselfconscious, natural spontaneity. Crudely put, the more we
work at being spontaneous, the more contrived we become; the more we
try, the greater our failure.[19] Chan and neo-Confucians such as Lu and
Wang want us to take something like the "Nike approach" as a way to
avoid this apparent problem: (Don't try)—*just do it*! But this is not quite
right, for such effort would involve individual willing and striving, which
are foreign to the ideal of spontaneity Lu and Wang espouse. According

---

17   For a more thorough analysis of these aspects of neo-Confucian philosophy, see
the parts on Lu and Wang in this volume.

18   See the discussion of these ideas in Sections 14 and 18.

19   For analyses of this set of ideas, see my "Spontaneity as a Normative Ideal," in
Yu Kam-por, Julia Tao, and Philip J. Ivanhoe, eds., *Taking Confucian Ethics Seriously:
Contemporary Theories and Applications* (Albany, NY: SUNY Press, forthcoming) and
Philip J. Ivanhoe, "The Theme of Unselfconsciousness in the *Liezi*," in Ronnie Littlejohn
and Jeffrey Dippmann, eds., *Riding the Wind with Liezi: New Essays on the Daoist Classic*
(Albany: SUNY Press, 2008): 129–52.

to Lu and Wang, enlightenment is something we cannot directly try to attain, but we can prepare the ground for this natural event to take place. Among other things, we can look toward and benefit from the advice and stimulation of wise teachers, who serve as spiritual coaches preparing us for play. Ultimately, though, the play in which we are to engage is the play of the Dao (the Way). The *Platform Sutra* tells us that "the Way must be allowed to flow freely."[20] This, too, is a theme both Lu and Wang sounded, often perplexing and frustrating their disciples, in a carefully orchestrated effort to elicit a transforming insight.

---

20   See Section 14.

THE DUNHUANG VERSION OF THE *PLATFORM SUTRA* (SELECTIONS)

Presented here are translations of selected passages from the opening sections of the *Platform Sutra of the Sixth Patriarch* (*Liuzu tanjing* 六祖壇經). Following most of the passages is a brief commentary.

4

One day, suddenly and quite unexpectedly, the Fifth Patriarch asked that all his disciples come to him. When they had gathered together, he said, "I say to you that birth and death are great affairs (*dashi* 大事) for the people of the world.[21] You disciples practice self-cultivation all day long, but all you seek is [rebirth in] blessed realms. You do not seek to escape from the bitter sea of birth and death. Your self-nature deludes you regarding the gateway to blessings; how can it possibly save you? All of you ponder this; return to your rooms and look within yourselves. Those with understanding and insight will grasp for themselves the *prajñā*-wisdom[22] of their original nature. Each of you, write a poem for me. I will look at your compositions, and if there is one among you who is enlightened regarding the great insight,[23] I will grant him the robe and the *dharma*[24] and make him the Sixth Patriarch. Quickly now, make haste!"

---

21   Compare Part Two, note 85.

22   *Prajñā* is the special, liberating wisdom that sees and appreciates that all things ultimately are "empty." For a helpful discussion of this idea, see the index entries in Heinrich Dumoulin, *India and China,* vol. 1 of *Zen Buddhism: A History* (New York: Macmillan, 1988).

23   The "great insight" is the truth of emptiness, which constitutes enlightenment.

24   *Dharma* is a Sanskrit word, usually translated as *fa* 法 in Chinese. It refers to Buddhist teachings or the Way in general, but its more technical senses include an object of consciousness or consciousness itself. Compare the terms "phenomenon" and "environment" discussed in notes 30 and 35.

*[This section lays out the fundamental challenge of Buddhism: deliverance from the "great affairs" of birth and death. Those who seek merely to improve their lot in this or some future life inadvertently doom themselves to remain in the cycle of birth, sickness, old age, and death; the very idea that one has a self keeps that "self" in the suffering state of cyclic existence (*samsāra*). To help oneself, one must abandon one's self.]*

6

[. . .] That evening, at the third watch [midnight], without anyone's knowledge, the head monk, Shen Xiu, took up a candle and by its light wrote a poem on the middle of the wall in the south corridor. His poem read:

> The body is the tree of insight (*prajñā*);
> The mind is like a clear mirror.
> Always clean and polish it;
> Never allow dirt or dust!

[The head monk Shen Xiu writes his verse anonymously, thereby showing admirable humility. His poem offers a good description of the Buddhist view of things, but it does not manifest the highest form of understanding. The illiterate monk Huineng asks someone to read Shen Xiu's verse to him; he admires it, pays homage to it, but also sees it for what it is. This leads Huineng to grasp the "great insight," and he dictates two verses of his own, which a young man writes for him on the wall of the west corridor. (The "west corridor" perhaps alludes to the direction from which Bodhidharma came when he first brought Buddhism from India to China.)]

8

[. . .] I, Huineng, also composed a poem and asked someone who was literate to write it down for me on the wall of the west corridor as a manifestation of my original mind (*benxin* 本心).[25] Unless one

---

25   This term finds one of its earliest uses in *Mengzi* 6A10, where it referred to one's innate, nascent moral sensibilities. It was taken up and used extensively by neo-Confucians. Here, it refers to an innate and perfect Buddha-mind or Buddha-nature. Throughout the portions on neo-Confucianism in this volume, I translate the Chinese word *xin* 心 as "heart-mind" to indicate that it was thought to contain faculties of cognition and emotion as well as intention or volition. In some contexts, one or another of these various senses may dominate, but often all are present to some degree. The reader is advised to judge by context where the emphasis falls in a given case.

recognizes one's original mind, studying the *dharma* will result in no benefit. If one recognizes one's original mind and sees one's nature, one will be enlightened regarding the great insight.[26] My poem went:

> Insight originally has no tree;
> The bright mirror has no stand.
> Buddha-nature is always pure and clean;
> How could there ever be dirt or dust?

Another verse went:

> The mind is the tree of insight;
> The body is the bright mirror's stand.
> The bright mirror originally is pure and clean;
> How could it be stained by dirt and dust?

[The Platform Sutra *makes clear and often repeats the fact that Huineng was uneducated and illiterate. On the one hand, this offers a polemic against the more entrenched and well-educated monastic elite, but its philosophical point is to affirm that insight (*prajñā*) is wholly innate, not acquired through learning. Huineng's verses correct and complete Shen Xiu's earlier verse and attest to Huineng's higher spiritual state. The passage concludes by noting that the other students were amazed by Huineng's verses and that the Fifth Patriarch secretly confirmed him as the rightful heir to the* dharma.*]*

12

[. . .] Good and learned friends, perfect understanding and insight are inherently within every person. But because of the delusion of their [conditioned] minds, they are unable to attain their own enlightenment. They must seek out a great and learned friend who will show them the

---

26   These lines are reminiscent of the famous four-line description of Chan, traditionally attributed to Bodhidharma but actually composed sometime in the Tang dynasty:

> A separate teaching, outside the tradition;
> not residing in words or letters.
> Directly pointing to the mind;
> see one's nature and become a Buddha.

For a discussion, see Dumoulin, *India and China,* pp. 85–86.

way and help them see their true nature. Good and learned friends, enlightenment *is* the completion of wisdom.

[Here we see the turn away from reliance on one's own power (zili 自力), characteristic of early Buddhism, toward a reliance on other power (tali 他力), characteristic of Mahāyāna. But in keeping with the Chan tradition, the aid one requires comes from a teacher not a savior; it is not the grace of a Buddha (e.g., Amitābha) or the compassion of a bodhisattva, but the help of a spiritual coach.]

13

Good and learned friends, this teaching of mine takes stability (*ding* 定) and insight (*hui* 惠) as its basis. Never be deluded into saying that insight and stability are separate. Stability and insight are one body (*ti* 體)—not two. Stability is the body of insight; insight is the function of stability. Where there is insight, stability is within the insight. Where there is stability, insight is within the stability. Good and learned friends, this is the principle of the identity of stability and insight.[27]

Students of the Way take heed! Do not say that stability precedes and gives rise to insight or that insight precedes and gives rise to stability. This is to regard stability and insight as separate. Those who embrace such a view profess a dualistic teaching. If what one says is good but one's mind is not good, there is no identity of insight and stability. If one's mind and what one says both are good, then internal and external are one, and there is identity of stability and insight. The practice of enlightening oneself does not lie in verbal arguments. If one argues about which comes first [stability or insight], one will never settle the matter. Instead, one will generate [false notions of] things and the self and will never escape the Four States.[28]

[The central issue in this section is the relationship between "stability" and "insight." This is an important debate within Buddhist thought and practice (it mirrors the tension between "quietism" and "activism" discussed in the commentary to Section 18). Basically, some Buddhists tend to describe the goal of

27 Wang's teaching regarding the unity of knowing and acting owes much to this view about the identity of stability and insight.

28 The Four States are birth, sickness, old age, and death.

their practice as attaining and maintaining complete meditative stability or calm (samādhi). Critics of such a view argue that this can become a selfish desire in its own right and can lead to insentience or even death (see the warnings about "cutting off thoughts" in Section 17). Instead, these critics advocate cultivating a saving "insight" (prajñā) into the true nature of self and world, as the path to liberation. The Platform Sutra *insists that these are simply two aspects of the enlightened mind.*

The primary message of this section is that right practice is the goal. This is similar to Suzuki's refrain throughout his classic work, Zen Mind/Beginner's Mind.[29] *In this section, particularly in the final line, we see a clear statement of the text's soteriological concern (escape from samsāra).]*

14

Universal *samādhi* is to act with a straightforward mind at all times: in motion or at rest, sitting or lying down. The *Vimalakīrti-nirdesa Sūtra* says, "A straightforward mind is the field of the Way (*dao* 道). A straightforward mind is the Pure Land." Do not falsely flatter the true Way by paying lip service to straightforwardness. One who talks about universal *samādhi* but does not act with a straightforward mind is not a disciple of the Buddha. Only the practice of a straightforward mind—not clinging to any attachment—can be called universal *samādhi.*

Deluded individuals are attached to phenomena;[30] they cling to universal *samādhi* and to the notion that having a straightforward mind is a matter of sitting motionless, eliminating delusions, and not allowing thoughts to arise. They think this is universal *samādhi.* But if one follows this kind of practice, one becomes like an insentient thing. In fact, this kind of practice is an impediment to the Way. The Way must be allowed to flow freely. Why would one impede it? As long as the mind does not abide in phenomena, the Way flows freely. If the mind abides, then it is

---

29   See Shunryu Suzuki, *Zen Mind/Beginner's Mind*, ed. Trudy Dixon (New York: Weatherhill, 1970).

30   "Phenomena" is my translation for the Chinese character *xiang* 相, which is often translated as "mark" in other contexts. It is that by which we take a thing to be the thing it is, something like a given thing's defining characteristic. As one might imagine, in Buddhist material, this has a strong negative connotation. Compare the terms *dharma* and "environment" discussed in notes 24 and 35.

fettered. If sitting motionless (constitutes right practice), it would have been wrong for Vimalakīrti to scold Sariputra for sitting in the forest.[31] Good and learned friends, I have seen those who teach people to sit viewing the mind and viewing purity, to remain motionless and to not allow thoughts to arise. Exerting themselves in this manner, deluded individuals fail to become enlightened, and clinging to this [method] can even cause them to go insane. There have been several hundred cases in which this has happened. Therefore, to teach in this way is a grave mistake.

[In this section we again see the claim that right practice is wisdom and enlightenment. We also see the first but not the last warning against heresies; these help us both to understand certain doctrinal issues and to appreciate the text's polemical dimensions. Wrong teachings not only do not help, they do positive and pernicious harm. This makes good sense. If the problem with us is wrongheaded thinking, the more systematic our wrongheaded thinking and the more tightly we embrace it, the lower our spiritual state and the more difficult our self-cultivation. Some teachings (e.g., Shen Xiu's verse) are less harmful; they help one to avoid accruing bad karma but must be abandoned if one is to achieve enlightenment.]

15

Good and learned friends, in what way do stability and insight form an identity? [They form an identity] in the same way that a lamp and its light [form an identity]. Where there is a lamp, there is light. Without the lamp, there is no light. The lamp is the embodiment of the light; the light is the function of the lamp. Though there are two names (i.e., lamp and light), there are not two bodies. Stability and insight are like this.

16

Good and learned friends, in the *dharma* there is no such thing as sudden or gradual. (However,) among people there are those with sharp and

---

31   This refers to an incident described in the *Vimalakīrti-nirdesa Sūtra*, which is the single most important text for understanding the *Platform Sutra*. See Robert A. F. Thurman, trans., *The Holy Teaching of Vimalakīrti: A Mahāyāna Scripture* (University Park: Pennsylvania State University Press, 1976).

those with dull spiritual capacity.[32] Deluded individuals pursue the gradual [method]. Enlightened individuals follow sudden cultivation. To realize one's original mind is to see one's original nature. Those who are enlightened realize that from the very start there is not the slightest difference.[33] Those who are unenlightened remain forever in the cycle of transmigration.

[The Platform Sutra advocates only sudden enlightenment, but what this means is not particularly clear (at least to those of us who remain unenlightened). The sūtra says that the only kind of practice one should engage in is the practice of enlightenment (i.e. being enlightened). One should not simply practice becoming enlightened, for this would be like taking as one's goal studying rather than mastering a discipline (e.g., to aim at continually practicing but never performing on the violin). However, because people have different karmic inheritances, their individual practice must be tailored to their particular capacities (one of the primary reasons for the central role of the teacher). But such "sudden practice" seems to amount to a kind of gradual method, designed to remove bad karma. (Consider the practice of the disciples of the Fifth Patriarch as described in the text.) What Huineng articulates is not so much an absolute choice between sudden and gradual as a presentation of the gradual within the larger and spiritually commanding framework of the sudden.

The sudden practice does not guarantee everyone immediate enlightenment (the sūtra never makes such a claim), but it is the only way to "realize" enlightenment. Other kinds of practice will never bring one to enlightenment because such practices require one to add something to one's innate enlightenment. The sudden practice deepens one's awareness and allows one to see more clearly, by removing the impediments of obscuring delusions, until, in a flash, one actually is enlightened. The final step is when the inherent Buddha-nature shines forth, unimpeded and hence unblemished. This is enlightening oneself (often

---

32   Sharp (*li* 利) and dull (*dun* 鈍) refer to the different spiritual states individuals can be in as a result of past karmic inheritance. Wang used something like this distinction when he talked about those with sharp roots (*li gen* 利根), who could be taught the highest truths in a direct and straightforward manner, but Wang simply meant those born with exceptional abilities. See the discussion of his famous "Four Sentence Teaching" in my *Ethics in the Confucian Tradition*, 2nd ed. pp. 80–81. For a complete translation and discussion, see Chan, *Instructions for Practical Living*, pp. 241–45. Note that Chan translates *li gen* as "sharp intelligence."

33   That is, no difference between the original mind and original nature of those who follow the sudden method and those who follow the gradual method.

mentioned in the text); it comes from within. In some ways it is like finding one's way out of a profound form of self-deception. This helps us to understand the Fifth Patriarch's reaction to the verses of Shen Xiu and Huineng. Shen Xiu's verse is not wrong; it will not lead people astray, but it will not lead to enlightenment either. Huineng's verse is superior not because it explains how one should practice or what enlightenment is but because it exhibits or manifests Huineng's enlightenment. The Chan tradition is one of enlightened teachers, not good expositors or careful analyzers of propositions.

The last line is aimed at those who simply seek to improve their karmic inheritance and enhance future rebirths. This itself is a karma-generating desire and will work to keep one within saṃsāra. Compare Section 4.

The modern Chinese scholar Hu Shi sees in this section and other parts of the text a strong put-down of the Northern School and its gradual method of cultivation, part of a general, highly polemical stance.[34] I do not believe that the polemical aspect is quite as strong as he and others claim (at least in the core of the sūtra). The gradual method is inadequate. However, the Platform Sutra advocates that one should not become obsessed with putting it down, just get things right. See the end of Section 18 for some remarks that support this reading.]

17

Good and learned friends, this teaching of mine has been handed down from long ago and all [who have taught it] have taken no-thought as its cardinal doctrine, no-phenomena as its substance, and nonabiding as its basis. [What do we mean by these?] No-phenomena is to be among phenomena yet separate from them. No-thought is to have thoughts yet not think them. Nonabiding is the fundamental nature of human beings.

Successive thoughts should not abide. Past, present, and future thoughts should succeed one another without being cut off. If a single thought is cut off, the Dharma Body separates from the physical body. As successive thoughts arise, they should not abide in any *dharma*. If a single thought abides, then successive thoughts will abide. This

---

34 See Hu Shih, "Ch'en (Zen) Buddhism in China: Its History and Method," *Philosophy East and West* 3 (1953): 3–24.

is called being fettered. If succeeding thoughts do not abide in any
dharma, then there will be no fettering. This is to take nonabiding as
the basis.

Good and learned friends, [no-phenomena means] to separate from
all phenomena. Just be able to separate from all phenomena and the
substance of your nature [will remain] clean and pure. This is why we
take no-phenomena as the substance.

To remain unstained in every environment[35] is called "no-thought."
In one's thoughts, one should separate from every environment and not
give rise to thoughts of any *dharma*. If one stops thinking about everything, one will eliminate all thoughts. [But] if even a single thought is
cut off, one will die and be reborn somewhere else.[36] Followers of the
Way take heed! Do not be obsessed with thoughts of the *dharma*. It is
bad enough if you yourself go astray, [but] to lead others into delusion,
unaware of one's own delusion, is to slander the *sūtras* and the *dharma*.
This is why no-thought is the cardinal doctrine [of our teaching].
Deluded individuals have thoughts about their environment, and based
upon these thoughts they generate false views. All passions and erroneous
thoughts arise in this way. This is why no-thought is taught as the cardinal doctrine of this teaching.

People of the world! Separate yourselves from phenomena and do not
generate thoughts. If one is without [such] thoughts then even [the
thought of] no-thought will not be established. What [thoughts] should
one be without? What are (true) thoughts? To be (without) thoughts is
to be separate from all the passions of dualism. Thusness[37] is the embodiment of thought; thought is the function of Thusness. If thoughts arise

35   "Environment" is my translation for the Chinese character *jing* 境, which refers
to the objects of perception (sometimes including a sixth sense—mental perception).
The aggregate of the objects of each of our senses in turn constitutes a "field" or "environment." Compare the terms *dharma* and "phenomenon" discussed in notes 24
and 30.

36   For a discussion of the problem of cutting off thought, see Paul J. Griffiths, *On
Being Mindless: Buddhist Meditation and the Mind-Body Problem* (La Salle, IL: Open
Court Press, 1986).

37   "Thusness" is *tathātā,* or Buddha-nature.

from one's true nature, then one's seeing, hearing, and sensing will be unstained in every environment and one's (true) self will always be present. The *Vimalakīrti-nirdesa Sūtra* says, "Externally, skillfully distinguishing the phenomena of various *dharmas*. Internally, remaining unmoved within the first principle."

[The central message of this section is that one is not to cut off thoughts. To work at cutting off thoughts is to "add something to the mind" and corrupt its original nature.[38] Rather, one is to allow Thusness (i.e., Buddha-nature) to function spontaneously. Compare Section 14, which warns us to not become insentient things and to let the Way flow freely.

The separation of the Dharma Body (dharma kaya) from the physical body (rupa kaya) is an oblique reference to death (which is made explicit a bit further on in this section). These two "bodies" are two aspects of the Buddha. Given our form as human beings, the only way we can manifest Buddha-hood is to realize both these aspects of the Buddha, together.[39]

"Followers of the Way take heed!" is another warning against heresy. It is bad enough if one practices this wrong teaching oneself, worse still if one leads others astray. Not only will you fail to help them (for if they succeed in "cutting off thoughts" they will die and simply be reborn and hence will still be in samsāra), but in the process you will also slander the dharma and the sūtras. This leads to direct rebirth in a particularly nasty Buddhist hell. Again, we see the soteriological goal—escape from samsāra—as a central theme in the text.

In the final paragraph, the Platform Sutra, like the Vimalakīrti-nirdesa Sūtra, is saying that one must be in the world but not of it. We must make effort, but only of the right sort. We are like flies caught in a spider's web. To try to flee the world is simply to indulge a futile, selfish, and karma-generating desire. The proper life is found in the "middle way," in neither complacency nor struggle. One is to allow one's inherent, pure Buddha-nature to function spontaneously, regardless of where one is.]

---

38   The idea that to add anything to one's original or natural state distorts and corrupts one can be traced to early Daoism. For example, see the closing section of *Zhuangzi*, chap. 5. Compare Wang's teaching that anything added to the mind obstructs and interferes with its operation: even good things should not be added.

39   There is a helpful discussion of this by Geshe Rabten in *Echoes of Voidness*. (London: Wisdom, 1983), p. 21.

18

Good and learned friends, in this teaching, sitting in meditation has never involved viewing the mind or viewing purity, nor should one remain motionless. Suppose one advocates viewing the mind. [Such a] mind is, from the very start, a delusion. And since delusions are illusory, there is really nothing to view. Suppose one advocates viewing purity. [But] one's nature, in itself, is pure. Only because of deluded thoughts is Thusness covered over and obscured. Apart from deluded thoughts, one's nature is pure. If one does not see the fundamental purity of one's own nature and instead stirs up one's mind to view purity, this will only generate delusions of purity. This delusion is without a basis [in reality]; therefore, we know that those who view it are viewing a delusion. Purity lacks a phenomenal form, yet some establish a phenomenal form of purity and call this [right] practice. Those who do this obstruct their own fundamental nature and end up being fettered by purity.

If one is motionless, one does not take note of the errors and faults of others. This is the nature [of being] motionless. Deluded individuals keep their physical bodies motionless, but as soon as they open their mouths, they speak of the right and wrong others have done.[40] [This is to] stray from and turn one's back on the Way. Viewing the mind and viewing purity are in fact great obstructions to the Way.

[In this section we see themes that are common throughout the text. The Platform Sutra *often is reminiscent of the "middle path" of Madhyamaka in its notion of emptiness and even in its use of a kind of negative dialectic.[41] One is not to seek a forced quietude, but one is to avoid attachment to phenomena.*

Some scholars see a deep tension in the text between (1) viewing one's nature (quietism) and (2) acting out Buddhist virtues in the world (activism). While these can be very helpful as heuristic categories, such dichotomies can obscure as well as reveal. The text can be read simply as insisting that we see our innate purity in our spontaneous, everyday actions—"hauling firewood and

40   Compare Kongzi's (also called Confucius) remark to his disciple Zigong in *Analects* 14.29.

41   For a helpful discussion of the "middle path" of Madhyamaka, see Richard H. Robinson and Willard L. Johnson, *The Buddhist Religion: A Historical Introduction* (Encino, CA: Dickenson, 1977), pp. 70–71.

carrying water."[42] *Such a view relies on a very strong assumption about the innate purity of an inherent Buddha-mind or Buddha-nature. Daoists and neo-Confucians make similar and equally strong assumptions about our inherent nature, but they fill in the content—i.e., our nature's structure, substance, and initial tendencies—in very different ways. The kind of tension noted previously can be seen, for example, in the* Platform Sutra's *use of the mind-as-mirror metaphor (a metaphor it inherited from the* Zhuangzi *and which it shares with many neo-Confucian texts).*[43] *We are urged to make our minds like a mirror: calm and unattached, reflecting but not storing. A mirror is "calm" and "unattached"; it accurately reflects the world without retaining images of what it reflects, which then would distort its future "functioning." But mirrors do not act. An enlightened Buddhist's "reflections" of the world entail acting in and responding to it in characteristic ways.*[44]*]*

19

Now that we know this to be the case, what do we, who follow this teaching, call "sitting meditation"? In our teaching, [sitting meditation] is to be completely without obstructions. Externally, not to allow thoughts to go out to any environment is "to sit." [Internally], to see one's original nature and maintain one's composure is "to meditate." What do we call meditative stability? Externally, to separate from phenomena is meditation. Internally, to maintain one's composure is stability. If externally there is some phenomenon, internally one's nature remains composed.

Fundamentally, one is pure and stable. One's composure is upset only if one is affected by the environment. If one separates from phenomena and maintains one's composure, then there is stability. Externally, to separate from phenomena is meditation. When internally [and externally] one maintains one's composure, there is stability. What we call "meditative stability" is to be externally meditating and internally stable.

---

42   This quotation is a line from a famous *gatha* (hymn) by the Tang dynasty Buddhist layman Pang Yun: "Spiritlike understanding and marvelous functioning; Carrying water and hauling firewood." For more on Pang, see Ruth Fuller Sasaki, Yoshitaka Iriya, and Dana R. Fraser, trans., *The Recorded Sayings of Layman Pang: A Ninth Century Zen Classic* (New York: Weatherhill, 1971).

43   For a thorough and revealing exploration of this metaphor, see Erin M. Cline, "Mirrors, Minds, and Metaphors," *Philosophy East and West* 58:3 (July 2008): 337–57.

44   For a discussion of this issue in regard to Wang's thought, see the index entries for "mirror (metaphor)" in my *Ethics in the Confucian Tradition*.

The *Vimalakīrti-nirdesa Sūtra* says, "Suddenly and completely, one regains one's original mind." The *Discipline of the Bodhisattva*[45] says, "Fundamentally, one's nature is clean and pure." Good and learned friends, see your own nature and your own purity. Cultivate and practice your own nature. If you put into practice the Dharma Body and carry out the practice of the Buddha, you will perfect the Buddhist Way.

45   For the complete name of and reference for this text, see Yampolsky, *The Platform Sutra*, page 141, note 83.

Part Two
Lu Xiangshan 陸象山
(1139–1193)

Introduction to Lu Xiangshan

Lu Jiuyuan 陸九淵 (1139–1193), whose courtesy name (*zi* 字) was Zijing 子靜 and style (*hao* 號) Xiangshan 象山, was born in the town of Jinxi 金谿 in Jiangxi Province.[1] He was the youngest of six brothers, two of whom, fourth brother Jiushao 九紹 (fl. twelfth century; courtesy name Zimei 子美, style Suoshan 梭山) and fifth brother Jiuling 九齡 (1132–1180; courtesy name Zishou 子壽, style Fuzhai 復齋), were impressive philosophers in their own right. As we shall discuss later, Jiuling was present at and participated in the extended discussion and exchange Jiuyuan had with Zhu Xi 朱熹 (1130–1200) at Goose Lake Temple (*E hu si* 鵝湖寺) in 1175; Jiushao initiated an important and extended scholarly debate with Zhu over the interpretation of a number of metaphysical issues central to neo-Confucian philosophy at the time.[2]

Jiuyuan passed the highest civil service exam and obtained the presented scholar (*jinshi* 進士) degree in 1172.[3] He held a number of posts,

---

1   For more detailed accounts of Lu's life and philosophy, see Lyman V. Cady, *The Philosophy of Lu Hsiang-shan* (Taipei: Pacific Cultural Foundation, 1939), Siu-chi Huang, *Lu Hsiang-shan: A Twelfth Century Chinese Idealist Philosopher* (New Haven, CT: American Oriental Society, 1944), and Carsun Chang, *The Development of Neo-Confucian Thought*, vol. 1 (New York: Bookman Associates, 1958).

2   For a study that describes the meeting at Goose Lake Temple, the later debate between Jiushao and Zhu Xi, and the relationship between Jiuyuan and Zhu, see the relevant sections of Julia Ching, *The Religious Thought of Chu Hsi* (New York: Oxford University Press, 2000).

3   Lu's examination essay was highly praised by Lü Zuqian 呂祖謙 (1137–1185), a friend of the great Zhu Xi and with him co-compiler of *A Record for Reflection* (*Jinsilu* 近思錄). For an English translation of this work, see Wing-tsit Chan, trans., *Reflections on Things at Hand* (New York: Columbia University Press, 1967). Zuqian was the one responsible for suggesting and facilitating the meeting between Jiuyuan and Zhu at Goose Lake Temple.

the highest of which was magistrate of what is now Jingmen 荊門 County in Hubei Province. He distinguished himself as magistrate by strengthening local military defenses, cutting through and eliminating bureaucratic red tape, settling legal cases, and implementing just and benevolent policies.[4] In all these endeavors, his administrative style was to encourage cooperation, treat others with humanity, and lead by example. Jiuyuan also served for four years as a member of the Imperial Academy (Guoxue 國學), where he and his ideas attracted a wide and enthusiastic following.

Beginning in 1187, he withdrew from public office and spent roughly five years in his hometown in Jiangxi, devoting the majority of his time and energy to teaching. His students, now numerous and devoted, built him a lecture hall on nearby Elephant Mountain (Xiangshan 象山). As his fame grew, Jiuyuan came to be associated with this place, eventually adopting the name "The Elder of Elephant Mountain" (Xiangshan weng 象山翁).[5] He died while serving as magistrate of Jingmen County, succumbing to a lifelong ailment, probably tuberculosis. According to his *Chronological Biography* (*Nianpu* 年譜), Lu faced his death with great calm and dignity. As he felt his time draw near, he announced to his family, "I am about to die." This led one among them to reply, "Why speak such inauspicious words? How are we to deal with this?" Seeking to comfort them and relieve their anxiety, Lu replied, "It [i.e., my death] is only natural."[6] His illness waxed and waned over the next few days. When his condition had improved, he met with a number of colleagues and talked with them about the principles of government. He then made sure that proper arrangements were in place for his funeral. After one more day, he passed away in silence.[7]

---

4   Like Wang Yangming, Jiuyuan was keenly interested and skilled in military matters. He was committed to the goal of regaining the territory lost to earlier invasions by the Jin Tartars. His biography informs us that when the sixteen-year-old Jiuyuan read an account of the sacking of Kaifeng and the carrying off of the imperial household, which occurred in 1126, he "cut off his fingernails and began to practice archery and horsemanship." See the entry for the year 1155 in Lu's *Chronological Biography* (*Nianpu* 年譜).

5   As a result, Jiuyuan is often referred to by his style, Xiangshan.

6   See the entry for the winter of 1193 in Lu's *Chronological Biography*.

7   This account of Lu's passing is a good example of an important genre that emerged in neo-Confucian biography describing last moments of life. For a revealing study of

One of the deepest and most vivid impressions one gains from study-ing the life and works of Lu Jiuyuan concerns his style and effectiveness as a teacher. Both he and his writings attracted a broad and devoted fol-lowing; we are told that in the course of his residence at Elephant Mountain, several thousand admirers came to study with him. His remarkable success as a teacher reflects the strength of his personal cha-risma, but it also stems from his idea that self-cultivation must focus on the intuitions and inclinations of each individual as these arise, develop, and take shape in the context of his or her actual life. Such an approach focused Jiuyuan's attention on developing teachings and a pedagogical style that offered students more of a therapy than a theory, and we can imagine that this played a significant role in the attractiveness and success of his message. The form of his written legacy expresses this central feature of his philosophy; unlike Zhu Xi, he did not write substantial, thematic essays or careful and comprehensive commentaries on the clas-sics. His writings were all in one way or another occasional or sharply focused thematically, and most of what we know about his philosophy comes from recorded conversations between him and his disciples. This sense of philosophical writing marked a break from what had become the norm among neo-Confucians, but from a historical perspective it can and should be seen as a return to the origin of the Confucian tradi-tion. Most of what we know of Kongzi's thought comes down to us in the *sayings* of the *Analects* (*Lunyu* 論語).[8] This text consists of short comments, reports, and at times quite poignant dialogues between the master and various disciples as well as other interlocutors; it contains no sustained, systematic essays of any kind. The one apparent exception to this claim about Kongzi's legacy consisting in aphorisms is the "Ten Wings" ("Shiyi 十翼"), a set of commentaries on the *Book of Changes*

---

this interesting phenomenon, see Peng Guoxiang, "Death as Ultimate Concern in the Neo-Confucian Tradition: Wang Yangming's Followers as an Example," in Amy Olberd-ing and Philip J. Ivanhoe, eds., *Mortality in Traditional Chinese Thought* (Albany, NY: SUNY Press, forthcoming). See also the discussion of Wang Yangming in Part Three of this volume.

8   My claim here takes no stand on whether the *Analects* in fact reflects the views of the historical Kongzi. Clearly, substantial parts of it do not. The point, though, is that thinkers such as Jiuyuan took this text as an authority and model.

(*Yijing* 易經) traditionally ascribed to Kongzi.[9] However, a consideration of these commentaries shows that the generalization holds firm, for the "Ten Wings" contains no sustained or systematic expositions of any kind. The text consists of terse, cryptic, and highly suggestive passages that offer sketches and suggestions, often cast in vivid and complex imagery and metaphor. This text, which deeply influenced Jiuyuan as well as every other neo-Confucian, also offered a distinctive paradigm for philosophical writing.

Lu's biography contains stories about his youth, similar to those told about most influential thinkers of his day, that reveal his remarkable abilities and presage his later accomplishments. For example, his biography tells us that when he was eight years old, "He heard someone reciting the sayings of Cheng Yichuan 程伊川 [1033–1107] and asked, 'Why don't the teachings of Yichuan accord with those of Kongzi and Mengzi?'"[10] This precocious remark offers a clear hint of Jiuyuan's future radical break with the Cheng-Zhu School, also known by the name "Learning of Principle" (*lixue* 理學), and the establishment of what eventually would come to be known as the Lu-Wang School, also called "Learning of the Heart-mind" (*xinxue* 心學). Moreover, five years later, when Jiuyuan was thirteen years old, we are told that he had a dramatic insight into the nature of the universe and its relationship to the human heart-mind:

> While reading some ancient texts, he came upon the word "universe" (*yuzhou* 宇宙)[11] and explained it by saying, "The four cardinal directions, together with up and down, are called space. The past to the present is called time." He then had a great and sudden insight, saying, "The past and future are infinite! Human beings along with Heaven, earth, and the myriad things all exist within the infinite!"

---

9   This attribution, which no contemporary scholar accepts, did not go unchallenged in the Chinese tradition. In the early Song dynasty, Ouyang Xiu 歐陽修 (1007–1072) repeatedly argued that Kongzi could not possibly have written the "Ten Wings."

10   See the entry for 1147 in Lu's *Chronological Biography*. Cheng Yichuan was the younger of the two famous Cheng brothers; they developed many of the defining themes of orthodox neo-Confucian thought, which, when further elaborated by Zhu Xi, came to be known as the Cheng-Zhu School.

11   The Chinese word for "universe" is composed of two characters, one meaning space (*yu* 宇) and one meaning time (*zhou* 宙).

He then took up his brush and wrote, "The affairs of the universe are my own affairs. My own affairs are the affairs of the universe." He further wrote, "The universe is my heart-mind. My heart-mind is the universe [. . .]"[12]

Even if we take these events to be greatly exaggerated or even wholly fabricated, they convey important information about the way people of Jiuyuan's time thought about human nature and moral insight, as well as the genre of biography. Such stories reveal a strong belief in the innate abilities of even extremely young children. This belief is in keeping with widely held neo-Confucian assumptions concerning a shared endowment of principles constituting or being contained within the heart-mind. This feature of neo-Confucian biography is philosophically interesting because it shows that metaphysical assumptions about the nature of the heart-mind made it possible and plausible to have ethical prodigies such as Jiuyuan.[13] If such wisdom must be *acquired* and can only be gained through broad, concerted, and prolonged experience and reflection, it would seem wildly improbable that any young person could possess it to such a degree. Rosalind Hursthouse aptly describes this latter kind of perspective, which is represented by any form of Aristotelianism or early Confucianism: "There are youthful mathematical geniuses but rarely, if ever, youthful moral geniuses, and this shows us something significant about the sort of knowledge that moral knowledge is."[14]

I shall next focus on some of Lu's core philosophical doctrines and teachings in order to clear away some mistaken claims commonly made about his philosophy and to offer a sketch of its basic parts, structure, tenor, and aims. Lu was not a formally systematic thinker, in the sense of presenting a step-by-step, carefully coordinated scheme or method of philosophy, but his various teachings hang together and form a coherent, interrelated, and mutually supporting whole. While he does make direct

---

12 See the entry for 1152 in Lu's *Chronological Biography*. Very similar lines are found in "Assorted Explanations," which can be found in this volume.

13 As I have argued in other work, it also makes the sudden enlightenment experience or the "discovery model" of self-cultivation possible. See my *Ethics in the Confucian Tradition: The Thought of Mengzi and Wang Yangming*, rev. 2d ed. (Indianapolis: Hackett, 2002).

14 See Rosalind Hursthouse, "Virtue Theory and Abortion," in Roger Crisp and Michael Slote, eds., *Virtue Ethics* (Oxford: Oxford University Press, 1997), p. 224.

and dramatic appeals to his own and his readers' intuitions, this aspect of his philosophy is hardly unique and often is significantly overstated; his writings offer careful and at times quite persuasive textual, historical, and philosophical arguments. At the core of his thought lies a constellation of metaphors and images, which he musters to invoke a range of related ideas that together compose his distinctive philosophical vision.

Almost every modern scholar who has written about Lu describes him as an "idealist" and, as we shall see, there is something right and important about this claim, but without going on to explain what one means by idealism, such descriptions tend to be unhelpful if not misleading. Idealism can refer to a number of mutually exclusive philosophical views about the nature of the mind, the world, and the relationship between them; some versions of idealism are quite plausible, while others involve metaphysical commitments that most contemporary philosophers regard as heroic and many take to be rash. In a number of cases in which modern interpreters have followed up by saying at least a little about what they mean by idealism, what they say, unfortunately, is clearly and dramatically wrong. For example, it is not uncommon to find modern scholars claiming that Lu's idealism denies the existence of a mind-independent world.[15] This would make Lu an advocate of a form of panpsychism in which the world is simply the sum total of the thoughts of all minds or some single, universal mind. Bishop Berkeley held something like this view, maintaining that what individual minds take to be the phenomenal or material world in fact exists merely as the object of contemplation in the divine mind of God. One might see a vague resemblance to Berkeley's view in some of Lu's claims about the heart-mind. Lu did believe that the heart-mind embodies all the principles (*li* 理) that give structure, shape, and meaning to the phenomenal world. But such a claim does not in any way entail a denial of the mind-independent existence of the world, and he surely never doubted or questioned the existence of the material world. Lu saw a metaphysically seamless universe in which the principles of the heart-mind and those of the world

---

15   For example, "Zhang Zai based his theories entirely on *qi*, whereas Zhu Xi's contemporary Lu Jiuyuan (1139–1193) asserted that *li* alone exists." See Conrad Schirokauer and Miranda Brown, eds., *A Brief History of Chinese Civilization* (South Melbourne, AU: Wadsworth, 2006), p. 161.

corresponded to and perfectly cohered with each other. The heart-mind is the unique site where a full understanding of the world can take place; it is where all principles can come to consciousness and be known. This is the main point of his famous teaching that "the universe is my heart-mind. My heart-mind is the universe."[16] Lines such as these have led some to infer that Jiuyuan thinks there is no world outside of the heart-mind. Such passages, though, must be read carefully and within the greater context of Lu's teachings; their meaning will then become clear. Consider the following: "This principle fills up and extends throughout the universe! Not even Heaven, earth, ghosts, or spirits can fail to follow this principle—how much less can human beings afford to do so?"[17] Another example: "The principles of the Dao simply are right in front of your eyes. Even those who perceive the principles of the Dao and dwell in the realm of the sages see only the principles of the Dao that are right in front of your eyes."[18] Such passages cannot be read as implying a reduction of the universe to the principles of the heart-mind; they point the way to a proper understanding of Lu's philosophy.

For Lu, coming to understand the world is not a process of taking it in or thinking about it through a set of categories but a process of tallying or matching up the principles inherent in the heart-mind with the various phenomena of the world.[19] Understanding always involves a subjective, introspective dimension: one discovers how things are by coming to see each truth *for oneself*. But "subjective" here does not imply any sense of an idiosyncratic interpretation; it only refers to the nature of the experience of understanding, to the individual, subjective consciousness wherein understanding takes place. The heart-mind is "shared" by all human beings in the sense of being a common inheritance, and the principles it contains are the same throughout the universe and across time. One implication of such a view is that when my heart-mind is rightly ordered, it will track and reveal the very same truths that the greatest sages first discovered. Jiuyuan put this notion in a typically

---

16   See the previous quotation in this part (and note 12).

17   See "(Eighth) Letter to Wu Zisi" in this volume.

18   See Section 3 of Lu's *Recorded Sayings* in this volume.

19   This view about what constitutes understanding is reflected in the modern Chinese word *lihui* 理會, which means a "meeting" or "joining" of "principles."

dramatic fashion: "If one understands the fundamental root or basis, the six classics are all one's footnotes!"[20] Our shared endowment of principles led Lu, like most neo-Confucians, to believe in a remarkably powerful ability to understand others—even people removed from one's experience by great expanses of space and time. The human heart-mind connects us in a profound and intimate way not only with other human beings but also with all other things in the world.

> Tens of thousands of generations ago, sages appeared within this universe and had this same heart-mind and this same principle. Tens of thousands of generations to come, sages shall appear within this universe and will have this same heart-mind and this same principle. Anywhere within the four seas, wherever sages appear, they will have this same heart-mind and this same principle.[21]

We are capable of tremendous degrees of empathy, but only if we work assiduously to remove all the impediments that block our natural sympathetic response; the greatest, most tenacious and fundamental obstacle to overcome is an excessive concern with oneself. As noted previously, the subjective dimension of understanding ensures that it always is in some sense personal, and this is particularly important when the knowledge being sought is ethical in nature. Thinkers such as Lu insist that moral knowledge involves not only cognition but also emotion and volition. Comprehending a moral truth—grasping an ethical principle— consists of seeing, feeling, and being properly disposed to act in a certain fairly specific way.

Like many neo-Confucians, Lu shared Hegel's drive to find a comprehensive unity underlying the diverse phenomena of the world: a unity that not only explains but justifies a universal scheme subsuming both the social and political order and the individual. Like Hegel, Lu sought an account that would bring all the parts into a sensible, normative whole that hangs together, eliminates all sense of alienation between the self and the world, and reveals an identity between what we think and what there is. But while Hegel believed in a world-historical process that

---

20   See Section 5 of Lu's *Recorded Sayings* in this volume.
21   See "Assorted Explanations" in this volume.

still was coming into being, as noted earlier, Lu believed each person already has within all the principles of the universe. The Way (*dao* 道) is complete and available within every human heart-mind. Perfect understanding is always at hand and involves the unfolding of an inherent endowment. This immediate availability has a number of important and distinctive consequences. For one thing, it means that *enlightenment* is a live and ever-present possibility, something each individual can pursue. Since a kind of selfishness is the major impediment to the free functioning of one's innate moral endowment, in a number of senses moral failure is "self" *imposed*. We fail to understand, act, and be moral because we fail to understand, act out of, and realize our true nature; we ourselves impose a distorted and excessively self-centered understanding of ourselves upon ourselves and the world around us. We suffer from a complex, severe, and virulent form of self-deception. This cluster of beliefs helps us understand why Lu places such great emphasis on starting and grounding the process of self-cultivation in *one's own* intuitions, responses, and inclinations. The sources of moral failure as well as the only genuine access to moral knowledge are to be found in each person's heart-mind; this must be the focus of one's ethical attention, effort, and activity. To look for moral knowledge "outside" of the heart-mind is fundamentally to misunderstand the nature of such knowledge and to perpetuate and deepen one's moral delusion.

This brief account of Lu's philosophy and ways in which it resembles and differs from that of important Western thinkers is aimed at providing a sketch of some of his most famous and influential claims. Even such a brief sketch should suffice to show how misleading it can be to uncritically apply terms from the Western philosophical tradition to a thinker such as Lu. At the same time, when properly focused, qualified, and supplied with sufficient nuance, such comparisons and contrasts help us to understand several key features of Lu's philosophy and set the stage for a discussion of some of the most dramatic and important differences between his views and those of Zhu Xi.

Lu met Zhu and explored differences between their respective philosophies on two separate occasions.[22] During their first meeting, which

---

22   For a study of these meetings, see Ching, *The Religious Thought of Chu Hsi*, pp. 132–51.

occurred at Goose Lake Temple in the summer of 1175, he was joined by his brother Jiuling. Lu and Zhu also exchanged a number of long letters, which subsequently were circulated among friends and other scholars. Jiuyuan's brother Jiushao began the most well-focused and sustained exchange of correspondence when he wrote to Zhu challenging his interpretation of the terms "ultimate-less" (*wuji* 無極) and "supreme ultimate" (*taiji* 太極). Jiuyuan took up and developed his brother's objections and responded to Zhu's attempts to defend his views in separate letters to Zhu. In the following, I will sketch the exchange of views that took place during the meeting involving Jiuyuan, Jiuling, and Zhu at Goose Lake Temple and then relate some of the themes that emerged in this discussion to the disagreements about *wuji* and *taiji* that served as the focus of the letters exchanged among Jiuyuan, Jiushao, and Zhu in the years 1188 and 1189.

Jiuyuan and Jiuling spent several pleasant days together with Zhu and a fellow scholar named Lü Zuqian at Goose Lake Temple exchanging poems and engaging in discussions focused on the nature of the heart-mind and the implications of their contrasting views on the process of self-cultivation. Jiuyuan expressed their core differences clearly and elegantly—though subtly and indirectly—in his poem "Written at Goose Lake to Rhyme with My Brother's Verse," which he wrote for and recited in the opening round of this meeting.[23] The Lu brothers' most fundamental objection concerned Zhu's teaching that the heart-mind exists in two forms: a pure heart-mind of the Way (*daoxin* 道心) and an adulterated human heart-mind (*renxin* 人心). Zhu argued that *daoxin* is an ideal state of the heart-mind, one that exists apart from and prior to the actual, existing things and affairs of the world, while *renxin* is the way this ideal becomes manifest as the heart-minds of people living in the world. According to Zhu, the heart-mind of the Way consists of pure principle (*li* 理) and so is completely good in every respect, while the human heart-mind is composed of vital energy (*qi* 氣) in addition to principle and so can never be purely good and often falls considerably short of the ideal.

The interfering influence of *qi* leads us to feel cut off from one another and the rest of the world and obscures the true nature of the principles

---

23   See the poetry selections from Lu's work in this volume.

that should guide us; it is the original and primary source of an excessive concern with and for oneself. Given that our original, pure natures remain mired in *qi*, no matter how hard or how long we work at self-cultivation, we never can fully escape the limitations of *renxin*. As a result, our ethical status remains in a "precarious" state, and we are "prone to error." These aspects of Zhu's philosophy led him to view the human heart-mind with a significant level of distrust and to look to the heart-mind of the Way as his absolute standard and guide. Those seeking to cultivate themselves are ill-advised to follow or even look directly to their own heart-minds for ethical guidance. They are much better served by focusing their attention and efforts outside the self; they should study the classics and rely upon the beneficial effects of ritual practice, working from the outside in to educate, reshape, and refine the self. This describes Zhu's primary path for self-cultivation or learning: pursuing inquiry and study (*dao wen xue* 道問學).[24] In contrast, Jiuyuan and his brother advocated honoring the virtuous nature (*zun de xing* 尊德性) as the proper way to cultivate the self. In their view, the first and greatest imperatives in the task of self-cultivation are gaining an awareness of and fully engaging the heart-mind, the font of ethical wisdom "never effaced throughout the ages."[25] Only such "easy and simple spiritual practice in the end proves great and long lasting." This is because the only genuine source for gaining and sustaining true understanding is the heart-mind. If one directs one's attention at the source, the results will flow forth and inform all that one does. In stark and utter contrast, "fragmented and disconnected endeavors leave one drifting and bobbing aimlessly." If one follows Zhu and looks for understanding "outside" the heart-mind—in books, rituals, and the advice of others—one simply will accumulate discrete bits of information that lack any overall coherence or sense. Such knowledge does not have the power to orient and move one toward the Way and in the end will only exhaust one's energy, resources, and spirit. Such an approach will yield neither deeper understanding nor proper action.

---

24   For a more detailed discussion of Zhu Xi's method of self-cultivation, see the chapter on Zhu in my *Confucian Moral Self Cultivation*, (Indianapolis: Hackett, 2000). Compare the discussion of Wang's method of self-cultivation in the later chapter on Wang in the same work.

25   This and the following quotations all are from Lu's poem, "Written at Goose Lake to Rhyme with My Brother's Verse," mentioned previously.

In a series of letters circulated among Jiuyuan, Jiushao, and Zhu, these themes reappear, in a different but recognizable form, in a debate about neo-Confucian metaphysics. The starting point is Zhu's claim that the terms *wuji* and *taiji* refer to two different aspects of the same thing, the highest and most comprehensive principle governing the Dao. His account of *taiji* is less controversial and shares several features with that of the Lu brothers. All agree that the term, which finds its locus classicus in the *Great Appendix to the Book of Changes* (*Xici zhuan* 繫辭傳), refers to the highest and most comprehensive principle governing the actual things and events of the world. Differences, though, arise in regard to the nature of this principle and its place in neo-Confucian ontology. Zhu takes *taiji* to be both the sum and organizing structure of all the principles of the world. At the same time, he thinks that there is something beyond or prior to *taiji* that serves as the ultimate source and ground of *taiji*, a kind of esoteric predecessor to the more exoteric *taiji*. Borrowing from the writings of Zhou Dunyi 周敦頤 (1017–1073), Zhu called this *most* ultimate principle *wuji*.[26]

Zhu argued for the importance of *wuji* on two interrelated grounds. First, he was concerned that people would mistakenly think of *taiji* as some sort of physical thing. Second, he thought such a conception would lead them to ignore the underlying unity *among* the different things of the world. Such concerns are not wholly unwarranted. Since *taiji* is the sum and organizing structure of all the principles of the world, *taiji* itself seems to exist in the realm of phenomena and risks being reified in much the same way as "the world" lends itself to being seen as a kind of physical entity rather than the comprehensive aggregation of everything (physical and nonphysical) that interrelates in complex ways and thereby makes up the world. Such a conception of the universe does seem to underemphasize if not efface a sense of it as a complex collection of discrete, interrelated elements, organized and given meaning by an underlying principle: *taiji*. In order to avoid these mistaken and inappropriate implications, Zhu argued that behind *taiji* was *wuji*, an inchoate yet pregnant and productive form of the supreme ultimate, in which all principles were present but not yet manifested. While not quite a

---

26   Zhou Dunyi, also called Lianxi 濂溪 after his place of residence, was one of the founding figures of the Song dynasty's neo-Confucian revival.

noumenal *realm, wuji* does seem to be a sphere of some kind, one that represents a distinctive and imperceptible *state* of the world. It is helpful to notice that Zhu's distinction between *wuji* and *taiji* echoes and reflects his views about *daoxin* and *renxin*, discussed previously. In both cases, the former (*wuji/daoxin*) stands as a pure, absolute form of and standard for the latter (*taiji/renxin*), which exists above and prior to the actual phenomena of the world.

Jiushao and Jiuyuan rejected Zhu's view for a number of interlocking reasons.[27] First, they argued on purely textual grounds that the term *wuji* lacked any precedent among the classics of Confucianism. Since the classics purportedly contained all the fundamental truths of Confucianism, this fact alone offered a strong prima facie reason for doubting the need for or importance of this concept. In addition, the Lu brothers raised further objections about the pedigree and value of this concept. Zhu borrowed the term *wuji* from Zhou's *Explanation of the Diagram of the Supreme Ultimate* (*Taiji tushuo* 太極圖說), one of his relatively early works. Jiushao argued that Zhou either was not the author of this work or, if he was the author, it represented an early and unrefined stage of his philosophy. To support the first claim, Jiushao noted that a number of reputable scholars argued that the *Explanation of the Diagram of the Supreme Ultimate* can be traced to Chen Xiyi 陳希夷 (906–989), an important thinker of the rival Daoist school. Moreover, no one disputed the fact that the term *wuji* does find an earlier, classical Daoist precedent in the twenty-eighth chapter of the *Laozi* (also called the *Daodejing*). To support the second argument, Jiushao notes that the term *wuji* does not appear anywhere in Zhou's later and more authoritative *Comprehending the Book of Changes* (*Tongshu* 通書) and infers from this fact that even if Zhou had used the term in the earlier work, he later repudiated it when he wrote his mature and definitive philosophy.

In addition to providing these textual and historical arguments, Jiuyuan argues that Zhu's explanation of the need for the concept *wuji* is not philosophically compelling. He sees no great threat in the possibility of reifying *taiji* in the way that Zhu fears and points out that none of the early sages expressed the slightest hint of any such concern. Contrary to what Zhu suggests, it is adding *wuji* on top of *taiji*, which Jiuyuan likens

---

27   See the letters from Jiuyuan to Zhu in this volume.

"to stacking a bed on top of one's bed,"[28] that poses the real risk. Such a theory can easily lead people to look away from the world of real things and actual affairs and to search in the insubstantial and imaginary realm of what does not exist (*wu* 無) for the ultimate principle of the Way. This is to fall into the error of Daoists and Buddhists: becoming lost in the speculative heavens rather than working to order the more mundane yet pressing affairs of earth. There is simply no need for such abstract and potentially misleading speculation and no evidence that the early sages embraced this esoteric metaphysical doctrine. According to Jiuyuan, the supreme ultimate neither is in the realm of what does not exist nor is some reified thing; it is the ideal state of the world and can be found among and only among the things of the world, whenever they attain their harmonious and perfect state. The highest principle governing and ordering the world is not complex, hidden, or esoteric. Instead, it is "right in front of your eyes" in everyday things and events, etched upon and revealed through the workings of our heart-minds.

In both the conversations at Goose Lake Temple and later correspondence, one can see many of the distinguishing features of Jiuyuan's philosophy as well as his differences from Zhu. Roughly put, Jiuyuan thought Zhu presented an excessively complex, highly speculative, and overintellectualized account of the Way, which threatened to lead people astray. From Lu's point of view, Zhu's teachings urge people to look outside the heart-mind for moral knowledge and to distrust their spontaneous intuitions and inclinations in favor of an established and codified moral standard found in the classics and traditional norms and practices. In contrast, and like many Chan Buddhists, Lu advocated more direct and immediate attention to the heart-mind, a way "not residing in words or letters." While one must be vigilant and on guard against the intrusion of self-centered thoughts, the greatest imperative is to look toward and trust in the heart-mind as one's true light and guide. The Way is found by heeding one's heart-mind as it leads one through the unique and ever-changing situations and events of daily life: there is no Way apart from the unencumbered activity of the heart-mind.

The concise message and telegraphic style—often relying upon evocative and enchanting poems, metaphors, and turns of phrase—seen in

---

28   See Lu's "Second Letter (to Zhu Xi)" in this volume.

both Jiuyuan's conversations and letters are characteristic of his philosophical writings. One can imagine that these aspects of his teachings impressed, challenged, and frustrated colleagues such as Zhu and perhaps some admirers as well, for Lu offers a set of gestures and a series of suggestions rather than clear directions or a full picture. Lu had a rare gift for opening up unexplored intellectual and spiritual horizons and inspiring others to follow him into new territory, but he never worked at carefully mapping much less settling the terrain he discovered. The vision he sketched is both coherent and powerful, but many details remained to be provided and many questions called out for answers. This work of filling in, extending, and greatly enriching Lu's original insights waited for and was taken up by Wang Yangming. In the process, Wang transformed Lu's initial vision into his own distinctive philosophy.

LETTERS[29]

Letter to Zeng Zhaizhi[30]

[. . .] In regard to your exchange of views with Zhang Taibo 章太博,[31] your ideas are perfectly correct, but the way in which you recite my theories in the beginning and then go on repeatedly to adduce evidence and illustrations to support them precisely illustrates your problem. By simply reciting other people's theories, you lose the point of their views. Memorizing what other people have said is very difficult, but it is not the same as understanding what they mean; often one fails to grasp the point [of what others have said]. In earlier ages, many [teachers] warned their disciples about recklessly recording what they were saying.[32] Because these disciples were incapable of understanding what was meant, would listen with their own point of view in mind, which inevitably led them to miss the point. If one is far removed [from a

---

29   This segment presents selections from eight different letters Lu Xiangshan wrote. Letters of this kind were not only a way for an author to correspond with the specific colleague to whom they were addressed but also a way to circulate the author's views to a wider audience. Important letters such as the ones translated here were often copied and passed around among a much larger group of interested readers.

30   Zeng Zhaizhi's 曾宅之 (n.d.) given name was Zudao 祖道, and he hailed from Luling 盧陵 (now Jian 吉安) in Jiangxi Province. He began as a student of Zhu Xi's, studied with Lu Xiangshan, but later returned to Zhu and compiled Zhu's literary works. This letter was written while Lu was residing at Elephant Mountain, the most prominent peak in the Dragon-Tiger Mountain Range (Longhushan 龍虎山).

31   We do not know more about this man than his name.

32   One can find such references in a number of scholars' works. For example, Cheng Yi once warned two disciples who were composing a record of his conversations, "While I am still here, what need is there for reading this book? If you do not grasp my heart-mind, what you write down will only be a record of your own ideas." See the later preface to the *Extant Works of the Two Cheng Brothers* (*Er Cheng yishu* 二程遺書; in *Siku quanshu* 四庫全書 Shanghai: Shanghai guji chubanshe, 1987), vol. 698, p. 5. For a later example of this kind of warning, see "Xu Ai's Preface" to Wang Yangming's work in Part Three of this volume.

speaker] and unable to meet with him [or her] face-to-face, then this is much worse than situations in which one can regularly ask questions via letters and meet with the person to whom one is writing. [In the latter case,] one can discuss and inquire about each other's views and appeal to evidence in exploring differences. If one debates in such a manner, one will avoid major errors.

For example, the two phrases "preserve integrity" (*cun cheng* 存誠) and "maintain reverential attentiveness" (*chi jing* 持敬) naturally are not the same; how could one talk about them together? One finds precedents for the phrase "preserve integrity" in ancient texts; while "maintain reverential attentiveness" is attested to only later in the written record. The *Book of Changes* says, "Keep out perversity and preserve integrity."[33] The *Mengzi* says, "Preserve your heart-mind."[34] Some in the past have used the word "preserve" (*cun* 存) to name their study or library.[35] The *Mengzi* says, "The average person lets it [i.e., the heart-mind] go; the cultivated person preserves it."[36] He [Mengzi] also said:

> If in one's life, one works to make few one's desires, then though there may be some respects in which one does not preserve [one's heart-mind], these will be few. If in one's life, one allows one's desires to proliferate, then though there may be some respects in which one does preserve [one's heart-mind], these will be few.[37]

With just this one word "preserve," one can naturally lead people to understand principle.[38] This principle originally is something granted to

---

33 See the "Elegant Words" ("Wenyan 文言") commentary to the first hexagram, *Qian* 乾, in the *Book of Changes*.

34 *Mengzi* 7A1.

35 This word also appears in the names of books, for example, *Preserving Learning* (*Cunxuepian* 存學篇) by the Qing dynasty Confucian Yan Yuan 顏淵 (1635–1704).

36 *Mengzi* 4B19.

37 *Mengzi* 7B35.

38 The "principle" (*li* 理) here is the term that in other contexts I have translated as "ethical principle" or "the principles that govern the world." The term has a long and rich history. Neo-Confucians such as Lu used it in both descriptive and normative senses. Roughly, it refers to the underlying patterns and processes of the world. Neo-Confucians believed that all human beings are endowed with a complete allotment of principles and that these constitute, in part or whole, the heart-mind. For more on this important term, see my *Confucian Moral Self Cultivation*, esp. pp. 46–57.

me by Heaven. It is not something welded onto me from outside.[39] If one truly understands that this principle is the core and master of the self and really makes it so, then outside things cannot move one and perverse doctrines cannot sway one.

Your affliction, my friend, is simply that you do not understand this principle; you have no master within. So whenever you encounter some frivolous theory or vague view, your only recourse is to rely on some idea you picked up from someone else to serve as your master. [In doing so,] the endowment that Heaven has granted to you becomes a guest and the positions of master and guest are inverted. You become lost and cannot find your way back, confused and unable to sort things out. These simple and clear principles can be taught to women and young children, but they are lost on and confound dedicated scholars who devise and in turn become wrapped up within their own irrelevant theories. They spend their years and end their days without ever attaining any grand insight. Are they not profoundly pathetic?

Had you been born in the orderly and flourishing age of antiquity and received the nurturing influence of the former sage-kings, you certainly would not suffer from this affliction. Even dedicated scholars will suffer from this kind of misfortune and harm if born in a later age, when true learning is cut off, the Dao has declined, and [the world] is filled and overflowing with heterodox doctrines and perverse theories, which spread and block up [the Dao]. They will sink into the same depraved state as ordinary men who indulge their feelings and follow every desire. Is this not using the pursuit of learning to slaughter the world?

Those in later ages who talk about the *Book of Changes* take its teachings to be supremely mysterious and profound. Students dare not speak lightly about what it says. And yet, when Kongzi commented upon the *Book of Changes*, he said:

> Through ease, *Qian* 乾 understands; through simplicity,
> *Kun* 坤 gains ability.[40] Those who attain the ease of *Qian*
> are easy to understand. Those who attain the simplicity of
> *Kun* are easy to follow. Those who are easy to understand

---

39   The last two sentences are close paraphrases of *Mengzi* 6A15 and 6A6, respectively.

40   *Qian* and *Kun* are the first two of the sixty-four hexagrams.

win the favor of adherents. Those who are easy to follow achieve success. Those who win the favor of adherents long endure. Those who achieve success are great. To long endure is the Virtue of the worthy. To be great is the heritage of the worthy. Those who attain ease and simplicity grasp the principles of Heaven and earth.[41]

Mengzi said, "The great Dao is like a wide road. Is it difficult to understand?"[42] Kongzi said, "Is benevolence far away? If I desire benevolence, *this alone* will bring benevolence."[43] Kongzi also said, "If for one day you can overcome yourself and return to ritual propriety, the whole world will ascribe benevolence to you."[44] He also said, "He was not thinking of her; [had he thought of her,] what distance would there have been between them?"[45] Mengzi once said, "The Dao is nearby but is sought in things far away; one's task lies in what is simple but is sought in what is difficult."[46] He also said:

> The Dao of Yao and Shun is nothing more than filial piety and respect for elder brothers. To walk sedately behind one's elders shows respect for elder brothers; to walk in an agitated fashion preceding one's elders fails to show such respect. Is walking sedately something people *cannot* do? [The answer is no!] It is something they simply *do not* do.[47]

He also said, "If people can fill out the disposition not to harm others, their benevolence will be more than ever can be used. If people can fill

---

41 See the first part of the *Great Appendix*.

42 *Mengzi* 6B2.

43 *Analects* 7.30.

44 *Analects* 12.1.

45 *Analects* 9.30. Kongzi here is commenting on the male and female subjects of a line of poetry.

46 *Mengzi* 4A12.

47 *Mengzi* 6B2. Lu moves the last line of the original to the front of the passage, as it appears here. For the difference between what one cannot do and what one does not do, see *Mengzi* 1A7. For an essay that explores this topic, see David S. Nivison, "Mengzi: Just Not Doing It," in Liu Xiusheng and Philip J. Ivanhoe, eds., *Essays on the Moral Philosophy of Mengzi* (Indianapolis: Hackett, 2002), pp. 132–42.

out the disposition not to transgress propriety, their righteousness will be more than ever can be used."[48] He also said, "Since people [all] possess these four sprouts [of virtue], if they say that they are unable [to act properly], they are selling themselves short. If they say that their rulers are unable, they are selling their rulers short."[49] Mengzi also said, "If I am unable to dwell in benevolence and act out of righteousness, this is called casting my self away."[50] For the most part, the words of the ancient sages and worthies all tally and accord with one another.

In general, the heart-mind is one and principle is one. "In the final analysis these form a unity; in their essence, they are one."[51] This heart-mind and this principle actually do not admit any duality. This is why Kongzi said, "My Dao has one thread running through it."[52] Mengzi said, "The Dao is simply one."[53] He also said, "There are only two Daos: benevolence and lack of benevolence."[54] "Benevolence" is none other than this heart-mind and this principle. [When Mengzi says] "seek and you shall have it,"[55] what you "shall have" is this principle. [When he talks about] "those who are first to understand," what they "understand" is this heart-mind. [When he talks about] "those who are first to awaken,"[56] what they awaken to is this principle. [When he talks about how all young children know] "to love their parents," it is this principle. [When he talks about how, as they grow, they all know] "to respect their elder brothers,"[57] it is this principle. [When he claims that anyone who suddenly] "sees a child about to fall into a well will have a feeling of alarm and concern [for the child],"[58] it is this principle. The reason that we are ashamed of shameful things and despise what is despicable is this

---

48   *Mengzi* 7B31.

49   *Mengzi* 2A6.

50   *Mengzi* 4A11.

51   Lu is quoting the Tang dynasty emperor Xuan Zong's 玄宗 (r. 712–56) preface to the *Classic of Filial Piety* (*Xiaojing* 孝經).

52   *Analects* 4.15.

53   *Mengzi* 3A1.

54   *Mengzi* 4A2.

55   *Mengzi* 6A6 and 7A3.

56   *Mengzi* 5A7.

57   *Mengzi* 7A15.

58   *Mengzi* 2A6.

principle. The reason we approve of what is right and disapprove of what is wrong is this principle. The reason we yield when it is proper to yield and defer when it is proper to defer is this principle. Reverence is this principle; righteousness also is this principle. What is inside is this principle; what is outside also is this principle.[59] This is why the *Book of Changes* says, "Being straight and square, he is great. Then without practice, he attains advantage everywhere."[60] Mengzi says, "What one knows without having to reflect upon is pure knowing. What one is able to do without having to study is pure ability."[61] "These are what Heaven has given me."[62] "I have them inherently; they are not welded onto me from outside."[63] This is why he said, "The myriad things are all here within me. To look within oneself and find integrity, there is no greater joy than this!"[64] This is our "original heart-mind."[65] This is what he calls our "peaceful abode" and "proper path."[66] This is what he calls our "spacious residence," "proper place," and "great path."[67] The ancients personally attained this [heart-mind and principle] and so possessed the real thing itself.[68] When they spoke about principle it was principle in itself. When they talked about affairs it was actual affairs. Their Virtue was substantial virtue; their actions were concrete acts [. . . .]

---

59   The references to "reverence," "righteousness," "what is inside," and "what is outside" in the previous lines draw upon and point toward a passage in the *Book of Changes*, which Lu goes on to quote. The earlier part of this passage reads: " 'Straight' refers to being correct [on the inside]; 'square' refers to being righteous [on the outside]. Cultivated people are reverently attentive to keep themselves straight on the inside and righteous to keep themselves square on the outside. When they have established themselves as reverently attentive and righteous, their Virtue shall not dwell in isolation." See the "Elegant Words" commentary for the hexagram *Kun*.

60   Ibid.

61   *Mengzi* 7A15.

62   *Mengzi* 6A15

63   *Mengzi* 6A6. Lu reverses the order of the original lines.

64   *Mengzi* 7A4.

65   *Mengzi* 6A10.

66   *Mengzi* 2A7 and 4A11, respectively.

67   All three terms are found in *Mengzi* 3B2.

68   Literally, they had its substance (*shi* 實). In the following lines, I translate *shi* as "the real thing itself," "[the thing] in itself," "actual," "substantial," and "concrete." The idea is that the ancients were not dealing with speculative theories, hypothetical accounts, or semblances of principles. They dealt exclusively in real events and robust virtues.

Letter to Supervisor Zhao[69]

[. . .] The Dao fills up the universe; there is no way it can be concealed or hidden. In regard to Heaven it is called *yin* 陰 and *yang* 陽.[70] In regard to earth it is called *rou* 柔 and *gang* 剛.[71] In regard to human beings it is called benevolence and righteousness. And so, benevolence and righteousness are the original heart-minds of human beings. Mengzi said, "As for what is preserved in human beings—how could they be without benevolence and righteousness!"[72] He also said, "I have them inherently; they are not welded onto me from outside."[73] When the ignorant and unworthy fall short of them, this is because they are beclouded by desires for material things and lose their original heart-minds.[74] When the worthy and the wise exceed them, this is because they are beclouded by personal opinions and lose their original heart-minds. And so, the *Great Appendix to the Book of Changes* says, "When the benevolent see it, they call it benevolence. When the wise see it, they call it wisdom. The common people use it every day but without understanding what it is. This is why the Dao of the cultivated person rarely is [realized in the world]."[75]

Those in the thrall of desires for material things gallop after such things and don't know where to abide.[76] Those in the thrall of personal

---

69   The addressee is Zhao Ruqian 趙如謙, who held the post of granary supervisor. This is the first of two letters, written when Lu was fifty years old.

70   *Yin* and *yang* are the two primary types of energies (*qi* 氣) that constitute the physical world.

71   *Rou* and *gang* are the two primary forces associated with *yin* and *yang*, respectively.

72   *Mengzi* 6A8.

73   *Mengzi* 6A6. Lu reverses the order of the original lines.

74   See *Doctrine of the Mean* (*Zhongyong* 中庸), chap. 4. They "lose" them in the sense of having lost sight of or touch with them, but the heart-mind remains within them, heavily and increasingly obscured by selfish concerns and impure vital energy.

75   See the fifth section of the first part of the *Great Appendix*.

76   The reference to the proper place "to abide" is from the first section of the old text of the *Great Learning* (*Daxue* 大學); see James Legge, trans., *Li Chi: Book of Rites*, reprint (New York: University Books, 1967), vol. 2, p. 411. Building upon the work of Cheng Yi, Zhu Xi rearranged and augmented the *Great Learning*, splitting the text into a classic (*jing* 經) of seven short sections (which he attributed to Kongzi) and a

opinions gallop after such opinions and don't know where to abide. And so [Mengzi said], "The Dao is nearby but is sought in things far away; one's task lies in what is simple but is sought in what is difficult."[77] Can the Dao be far away? Can affairs be difficult? Because peoples' opinions are insubstantial, they create difficulties for themselves. If they truly grasped their error, their beclouding would dissipate, their confusion would dissolve, and they would find the proper place to abide. The Dao remains fundamentally unchanged [within you]. How could [attaining the Dao] be like reaching for something with your hand? In such a case, you must reach for something that is outside in order to attain it [. . . .]

Letter to Wang Shunbo[78]

[. . .] Generally speaking, within schools of learning there are teachings and there are the actual forms of life.[79] Confucians have Confucian teachings; Daoists have Daoist teachings; Buddhists have Buddhist teachings. There are many schools of learning in the world, but these are the three major schools.

In the past, those who had a teaching were grounded in the corresponding form of life. In later times, those who sought the form of life had to depend on the corresponding teaching. And so, whenever

---

commentary (*zhuan* 傳) of ten sections (which he claimed was the work of Kongzi's disciple Zengzi). The original text, in thirty-nine sections, appears as the thirty-ninth chapter of the *Book of Rites* (*Liji* 禮記). In cases where the reference explicitly concerns Zhu's reading of the text, I will cite his revised version. In all other cases, I will cite the original "old version" of the text. James Legge has translated both versions, and I will provide the page numbers in the appropriate translation by Legge. For the complete translations, see Legge, *Li Chi*, vol. 2, pp. 411–24 and James Legge, trans., *Confucian Analects, the Great Learning, and the Doctrine of the Mean*, vol. 1 of *The Chinese Classics*, reprint (Hong Kong: University of Hong Kong Press, 1970), pp. 355–81.

77   *Mengzi* 4A12.

78   Wang Shunbo's 王順伯 given name was Houzhi 厚之 (n.d.). He was the great-grandson of Wang Anshi's 王安石 (1021–1086) younger brother Wang Anli 安禮, and an accomplished scholar of bronze and stone inscriptions.

79   The distinction between teaching (*shuo* 說) and form of life (*shi* 實) connotes the difference between *an account* of some form of ethical life and *the reality* or *experience* that forms the basis of that account.

students seek some form of life, they must first practice the corresponding teaching. But even once people have begun to practice a teaching, there are some who succeed and some who do not. Some succeed in living the actual form of life, and some succeed only in getting the teaching and fail to live the actual form of life. Within a given teaching, there are distinctions between what is shallow and profound, subtle and crude, partial and complete, and pure and adulterated. Such distinctions also are found within the actual practice of a form of life. All of the differences described above are found within every school and noted by those within the schools themselves. If we consider the mutual criticisms that members of the three schools level at one another concerning their differences and similarities—what they grasp and what they miss, what they are right about and what they are wrong about—and if we explore the distinctions between what is shallow and profound, subtle and crude, partial and complete, and pure and adulterated in regard to what each school succeeds in or fails at in terms of both their teaching and actual form of life, we cannot determine whether every school does equally well or if any one is the best.

In your last two letters to my elder brother [Jiushao], your overall point was that Confucianism and Buddhism were the same, and that if we compare them point by point, we will find that they are, as they say, "equal in every regard." But I have used the two words "righteousness" (*yi* 義) and "profit" (*li* 利) to differentiate Confucianism from Buddhism.[80] I have also used the words "public" (*gong* 公) and "private" (*si* 私),[81] but really what I have in mind is righteousness and profit.

When Confucians consider the life that human beings live between Heaven and earth, they say that we are the most intelligent and valuable

---

80   Compare *Analects* 4.16, "The cultivated person understands righteousness; the petty person understands profit," and 14.12, "Those who in view of profit think of righteousness, in view of danger are willing to risk their lives, and under duress do not forget what they said in the past—these may be regarded as complete human beings."

81   The word *si* describes things that are personal or private. When opposed to *gong*, *si* connotes inappropriate or excessive concern for such interests and so can be understood as strongly implying a sense of selfishness. For an excellent historical survey of these concepts in the context of East Asian Confucianism, see Huang Chun-chieh, "East Asian Conceptions of the Public and Private Realms," in Yu Kam-por, Julia Tao, and Philip J. Ivanhoe, eds., *Taking Confucian Ethics Seriously: Contemporary Theories and Applications.*

of all the myriad creatures and along with Heaven and earth are one of the "three acmes."[82] For Heaven, there is the Dao of Heaven; for earth, there is the Dao of earth; for human beings, there is the Dao of humanity.[83] If humans fail to fully instantiate the Dao of humanity, then they cannot stand together alongside Heaven and earth. Humans have five senses and each has its particular function or task.[84] From these arise the distinctions between right and wrong, success and failure. From these arise teaching and learning. This is the foundation upon which Confucian teachings have been established, and why I say they concern what is righteous and public.

When Buddhists consider the life human beings live between Heaven and earth, they say that there is [a cycle of] birth and death, transmigration and rebirth, and suffering and affliction. They regard life as extremely painful and seek a way to avoid it. According to them, those who have attained the Dao and achieved enlightenment realize that originally there is no birth and death, transmigration and rebirth, or suffering and affliction. This is why their teachings claim [the cycle of] "birth and death is a great affair."[85] The so-called resolution to become a bodhisattva, to which you refer, only concerns this one great affair. This is the foundation upon which Buddhist teachings have been established, and why I say they concern what is profitable and personal.

Because [Confucians] are concerned only with righteousness and the public [good], they seek to put the world into good order. Because [Buddhists] are concerned only with profit and personal [good], they seek to flee

---

82   The ideas expressed in this last sentence can be found throughout the Confucian corpus. The specific reference to the "three acmes" is from the second section of the first part of the *Great Appendix*.

83   For this idea, see the tenth section of the second part of the *Great Appendix*.

84   For the five senses, see the "Record of Learning" ("Xueji 學記") chapter of the *Book of Rites*. For a translation, see James Legge, *Li Chi*, vol. 2, p. 90. For the idea that each sense has its proper function or task, see the "Great Plan" chapter of the *Book of History*. For a translation, see James Legge, trans., *The Shoo King*, vol. 3 of *The Chinese Classics*, reprint (Hong Kong: University of Hong Kong Press, 1970), pp. 326–27.

85   Chapter 5 of the *Transmission of the Lamp* (*Jingde chuandenglu* 景德傳燈錄) says, "[The cycle of] birth and death is a great affair, impermanent and fleeting." Compare the *Platform Sutra*, Section 4.

ne world [completely].[86] Although Confucian [teachings] talk about "what is without sound or scent" and "what is beyond method and embodiment," their guiding aim always is to put the world into good order.[87] Although Buddhist [teachings] talk about saving all sentient creatures, even those yet to be born, their guiding aim always is to flee the world [completely].

Now, those who practice the Way of the Buddha all are human beings. Since they are human beings, how can they completely cast off the benevolence and righteousness that we Confucians [advocate]? Even though they leave their families, they still advocate practicing the four kindnesses.[88] In their everyday lives, the principles [that we teach] remain rooted in their heart-minds and cannot be eradicated or erased. They clearly preserve them, at least in certain respects. Nevertheless, their teachings were not developed with the aim of preserving these principles. And so, whether or not they are preserved is of no importance to those who are far advanced in the earnest practice of their Way.

As for us Confucians, we say, "That whereby human beings are distinguished from [other] animals is subtle and minute. The common people abandon it, while the cultivated person preserves it."[89] Buddhists are concerned with not yet being free from transmigration and rebirth and the endless cycle of birth of death, which they call "floating and sinking in the sea of birth and death." But how could our sages and worthies remain "floating and sinking in the sea of birth and death?"[90]

---

86   That is to say, they seek a path that leads out of cyclic existence altogether.

87   For the first quotation, see the *Book of Songs*, Mao # 235. For a translation, see James Legge, trans., *The She King*, vol. 4 of *The Chinese Classics*, reprint (Hong Kong: University of Hong Kong Press, 1970), p. 431. It is also quoted in the concluding section of *Doctrine of the Mean*, chap. 33. For the second quotation, see the fourth section of the first part of the "Great Appendix".

88   "To leave one's family" is to take up the religious life as a monk or nun. The four kindnesses are good acts that all laymen should practice toward their fathers and mothers, their rulers, all sentient creatures, and the "three treasures"—the Buddha, the *dharma*, and the *sangha* (the community of monks and nuns).

89   *Mengzi* 4B19.

90   Lu's point is that since Confucian sages and worthies were such eminently good people, they could not possibly be trapped in the endless cycle of transmigration and rebirth. Buddhists, though, would respond that escaping the cycle of birth and death requires an understanding of the ultimate emptiness of all things, not just the performance of good acts. The latter, when performed in the absence of the insight regarding emptiness, is still a source of karma and hence works to keep one within cyclic existence.

Our sages and worthies do not suffer from what the Buddhists are concerned about. As a result, their teachings were not developed with the goal of avoiding such things, and these topics are not the guiding aim of what they say.

And so, our sages and worthies do not suffer from what the Buddhists are concerned about, but the sages and worthies of Buddhism do suffer from what we Confucians are worried about [i.e., not working to put the world into good order]. If one were to hold Buddhist sages and worthies to the standard one finds in the *Spring and Autumn Annals*, even children know they could not avoid blame.[91] If one looks at them in terms of what their teachings were developed to address, then the difference between Confucianism and Buddhism is the difference between the public and private and between righteousness and profit, respectively. They are distinct from each other and mutually exclusive; one cannot say they are the same [. . . .]

Letter to Zhu Yuanhui (Zhu Xi)[92]

[. . .] The sages and worthies of ancient times only looked to principle to determine what is right. Yao and Shun were sages but they "consulted the hay bearers and firewood carriers."[93] Zengzi had his sons change the mat beneath him, but this [inappropriate mat] was noticed by a young

---

91   The *Spring and Autumn Annals* (*Chunqiu* 春秋) is a terse record of the reigns of twelve dukes from the state of Lu, spanning the years 722 to 481 B.C.E. According to a view that was brought forth by Mengzi and that became widely influential in the later tradition, the text, along with its commentaries, presents a "praise and blame" account of the actions of the rulers it covers. Lu is saying here that Buddhist sages and worthies would come in for considerable blame and little praise if held to the text's standard of benevolent rule. For a translation, see James Legge, trans., *The Ch'un Ts'ew with the Tso Chuen*, vol. 5 of *The Chinese Classics*, reprint (Hong Kong: University of Hong Kong Press, 1970).

92   Zhu Yuanhui 朱元晦 (1130–1200) is better known as Zhu Xi 朱熹. This is the first of a set of three letters written to Zhu commenting upon an exchange of letters that Zhu had with Lu Xiangshan's elder brother Suoshan. Compare note 118 in this part of the volume. This letter was written when Xiangshan was fifty years old.

93   This is a line from the *Book of Songs* (see *Mao* # 254). For a translation, see Legge, *The She King*, p. 501.

servant boy who was holding a candle.[94] The commentary on the hexagram *Meng* 蒙 in the *Book of Changes* says, "Accepting the advice of a woman will lead to good fortune."[95] So, even the words of women and young boys should not be disregarded. Mengzi said, "It would be better to be without books than to trust in them completely. In the 'Completion of War' chapter of the *Book of History*, I accept only two or three strips [of characters]."[96] If words do not accord with principle, even though they come from some ancient text, one must not presume to trust them completely. Even the wise can make one mistake in a thousand; even the ignorant can have one insight in a thousand. How can one be lax in one's view of what people say?

[In a letter,] my elder brother, Suoshan, said, "The *Explanation of the Diagram of the Supreme Ultimate* is different in kind from *Comprehending the Book of Changes*, and I doubt that the former is really the work of Zhou Dunyi. If this is wrong [and it really is Zhou's work], then perhaps it was written at a time when his learning had not matured. Or perhaps it represents the work of some other thinker, and people in later ages have failed to see [that Zhou is not the author]. The 'Principle, Human Nature, and the Decree' chapter of *Comprehending the Book of Changes* says, 'Abide in the mean. The two vital energies (*qi* 氣) and five forces[97] transform and generate the myriad things. The five produce their diverse forms, while the two vital energies provide their substance or material. The two vital energies at their root are one.'[98] When this

---

94   The reference is to a story in the "Tan Gong 檀弓" chapter of the *Book of Rites*. Zengzi's sons had used a more lavish mat for their ill father to lie upon. When its quality was noted by a young lad bearing a candle, Zengzi insisted that it be replaced with a mat appropriate to his station. He died soon after the replacement was made. For a translation, see Legge, *Li Chi*, vol. 1, p. 128. Compare *Analects* 9.12.

95   The line commentary in the *Book of Changes* on the second (undivided) line says, "Showing forbearance toward the ignorant will lead to good fortune. Accepting the advice of a woman will lead to good fortune. . . ."

96   *Mengzi* 7B3. "Strips" refers to the strips of bamboo upon which the text was written. Compare Wang's reference to the same passage in Part Three, note 172.

97   Quoting *Comprehending the Book of Changes*, chap. 22. For a complete English translation, see Wing-tsit Chan, trans., *A Source Book in Chinese Philosophy*, reprint (Princeton, NJ: Princeton University Press, 1973), pp. 465–80. The two vital energies are the *yin* and the *yang*. The five forces or five agents (*wuxing* 五行) are earth, metal, water, wood, and fire.

98   Ibid.

text talks about 'one' or the 'mean,' this is the supreme ultimate. It never adds ultimate-less on top of the supreme ultimate. In the 'Activity and Tranquility' chapter, it talks about the five forces, *yin* and *yang*, and the supreme ultimate, but again, there is no use of the term 'ultimate-less.' Regardless of whether the *Explanation of the Diagram of the Supreme Ultimate* is really someone else's work, [which Zhou Dunyi] passed on, or a work that he himself composed when he was young, we know that by the time he wrote *Comprehending the Book of Changes* he never mentioned 'ultimate-less.' From this we can surmise that by this time he realized that this idea was wrong." We must carefully and seriously consider Suoshan's view on this topic.

You say that "Suoshan reads other people's work in a forced manner, that he is unable to fully grasp their underlying sensibilities and impetuously imposes his own ideas [upon their texts]. As a result, he takes too lightly the task of establishing his own theory; he just focuses on talking at length and therefore is not always in accord with principle."

The *Great Learning* (*Daxue*) says, "Having eliminated [bad qualities] in oneself, only then should one condemn them in other people."[99] In terms of their being human beings, there is no distinction here between the ancients and contemporary people, between the wise and the ignorant, the worthy and unworthy; they all have things to say; they all have writings to share. When one looks at the letters that you have sent to Suoshan, it is clear that you have not yet fulfilled this maxim [from the *Great Learning*]. And so how can you take Suoshan to task!

In your letter to Suoshan, you say, "If one does not talk about the ultimate-less, then the supreme ultimate will be equated with some thing and prove inadequate as the source and basis for the myriad transformations. If one does not talk about the supreme ultimate, then the ultimate-less will fade into emptiness and stillness and prove inadequate as the source and basis for the myriad transformations."

Without a doubt, the supreme ultimate is how things are in principle and this is why Kongzi explained this idea clearly. He did not rely upon unsubstantiated theories to establish his view, which simply would have encouraged later people to spread idle and misleading gossip through

---

99   The quotation is from the twentieth section of the old text of the *Great Learning*; see Legge, *Li Chi*, vol. 2, p. 418.

speech and writing.[100] That the supreme ultimate is the source and basis of the myriad transformations is simply what it always has been. How could the questions of whether or not it can prove adequate to this task or capable of fulfilling this role be settled by whether or not people *talk* about it?

The *Great Appendix to the Book of Changes* says, "Within the changes is the supreme ultimate."[101] Kongzi talked about what is or what exists; now you talk about what is not or what does not exist. Why? When Kongzi composed the *Great Appendix*, he did not talk about the ultimate-less. As a result, has the supreme ultimate been equated with some thing and proven inadequate as the source and basis for the myriad transformations? In the "Great Plan" chapter of the *Book of History*, it says that the ultimate of royalty (*huang ji* 皇極) is the fifth of the nine divisions [within the great plan].[102] It doesn't talk about the ultimate-less. In this case, too, has the supreme ultimate been equated with some thing and proven inadequate as the source and basis for the myriad transformations?

The supreme ultimate simply is what it always has been. You, though, just talk on and on and end up piling up nonsense. This is precisely the problem you described as "taking too lightly the task of establishing one's own theory, just focusing on talking at length, and therefore not always being in accord with principle."[103] You are renowned as a scholar who carefully examines each sentence and explores the meaning of every word. It is only fitting for you to exert even more effort and care so that you can establish your own theory precisely and accurately. Such endeavor

---

100   "Unsubstantiated theories" is the translation for *kong yan* 空言 (lit. "empty talk"). Lu is here referring to the well-known idea that when Kongzi wrote the *Spring and Autumn Annals* he realized, "The unsubstantiated theories I wanted to write down would not be as penetrating and clear as showing how these are manifested in the conduct of actual affairs." See Sima Qian's *Records of the Historian* (*Shiji* 史記), chap. 130. Lu is taking Zhu to task for failing to ground his theory in classical sources. This shows that Lu by no means relied only on appeals to "intuition" to argue for his view.

101   See Book 1, Section 11. This passage goes on to say, "This generates the two principles. The two principles generate the four images. The four images generate the eight trigrams." In other words, the passage shows how the supreme ultimate is the source and basis for the myriad things.

102   For a translation, see Legge, *The Shoo King*, pp. 323–24.

103   These are the very faults that Zhu previously accused Lu Suoshan of having.

will dispel any doubts and resolve any confusions and work to overturn these hasty and careless views. It is only fitting that you reflect upon these matters for yourself.

In your second letter [to my brother Suoshan] you went on to say, "the ultimate-less is what is without form and the supreme ultimate is what has principle" and "Zhou Dunyi feared that students would mistakenly think that the supreme ultimate was a distinct material thing and so he employed the two characters *wuji* 無極 ["ultimate-less"; lit. "lacking an ultimate"] in order to make this clear."[104] But the *Great Appendix to the Book of Changes* says, "What is above form is called the Dao."[105] It also says, "The alternation of *yin* and *yang*—this is called the Dao"[106] If the alternation of *yin* and *yang* already marks the state of being above form, how much more clear is it that this must be true of the supreme ultimate! Everyone who understands the meaning of the text knows that this is true. I have never heard of anyone, since the *Great Appendix* first came into being down to contemporary times, who mistakenly thought that the supreme ultimate was a distinct material thing. If there are some who are so dull that they make this kind of mistake, why shouldn't we just treat them as people who lack the ability to "come back with the other three corners" [when given the first]?[107] Why would such a possibility worry old Zhou Dunyi to the point where he would make the special effort of adding the two characters *wuji* on top of the supreme ultimate in order to explain what it means?

104   See *Da Lu Zijing* 答陸子靜 in *Zhuzi wenji* 朱子文集 (Taipei: Defu wenjiao jijinhui, 2000), vol. 4, pp. 1434–35.

105   See the fifth section of the first part of the *Great Appendix*.

106   See the twelfth section of the first part of the *Great Appendix*. Lu presents a valid argument based on an impeccable source. For if the alternation of *yin* and *yang* is the Dao, and the Dao is above form, then the alternation of *yin* and *yang* must be above form. But these two are generated out of the supreme ultimate, and so it must be anterior to them in the realm of what is above form.

107   A reference to *Analects* 7.8: "The master said, 'I do not open up the Way to those who lack ardor; I do not offer explanations to those who are not trying to explain things for themselves. If I hold up one corner [of the square] and they cannot come back with the other three, I do not repeat the lesson.'" Lu's point is that even Kongzi did not worry about or continue to teach people who were so dull or unmotivated that they would make the kind of mistake Zhu thinks *most* students would be likely to make.

Furthermore, one can't use words about things with specific forms to explain what the word "ultimate" (*ji* 極) means. Now, in general, the supreme is the middle or mean.[108] So, to say *wuji* [lit. "lacking an ultimate"] would be like saying "lacking a middle." How could this ever do? If one is worried that students will get mired in [an excessive concern with] material things and wants to offer further explanation, then it would be appropriate to say something like what one finds in the *Book of Songs* where it talks about "the workings of high Heaven" and elaborates on this by saying, [they] "are without sound or scent."[109] How could one ever see fit to add *wuji* on top of the supreme ultimate?

Zhu Zifa[110] says that Zhou Dunyi obtained the *Diagram of the Supreme Ultimate*[111] from Mu Bozhang and that the tradition that led to Mu Bozhang finds its source in Chen Xiyi.[112] This claim must be evaluated, because Chen Xiyi's system of philosophy is an expression of the philosophy of Laozi.[113]

The two characters *wuji* are from the chapter that begins with the line "know the male" in the *Laozi*;[114] it does not appear anywhere in the writings of our sage [Kongzi]. The opening chapter of the *Laozi* says, "The nameless (*wu ming* 無名) is the beginning of Heaven and earth; the named (*you ming* 有名) is the mother of the myriad creatures."[115]

---

108   The idea is that this balanced state, in which there are no distinct, separate forms, is the source of all particular things.

109   See *Book of Songs, Mao* # 235. For a complete translation, see Legge, *The She King*, p. 431.

110   Zhu Zifa 朱子發 (d. 1138), whose personal name was Zhen 震, was a Northern Song dynasty native of Hubei Province.

111   For a discussion of the diagram and its importance for Neo-Confucian philosophy, see Fung Yulan, *A History of Chinese Philosophy*, reprint (Princeton, NJ: Princeton University Press, 1973), pp. 434–51.

112   Mu Bozhang 穆伯長 or Mu Xiu 穆修 (980–1048) was a native of Yuncheng 鄆城 County in Shandong Province. Chen Xiyi 陳希夷 or Chen Tuan 陳摶 (906–989) was an important Daoist philosopher of the Song dynasty. He was a native of Zhen Yuan 真源, now located east of the Luyi 鹿邑 County of Henan Province.

113   Laozi is one of the mythical founders of Daoism and the purported author of the *Laozi*.

114   Chapter 28 in the standard text of Wang Bi 王弼 (226–249 B.C.E.).

115   Lu is reading these two terms in a particular way, a way that suits his larger aims. For a different reading, see my translation: Philip J. Ivanhoe, trans., *The Daodejing of Laozi* (Indianapolis: Hackett, 2002), p. 1. The language appendix of this work offers a detailed analysis of the grammar and interpretive possibilities of the first chapter of the *Laozi*.

And yet, at the end [of the chapter], he [Laozi] equates them [i.e., the nameless and named] with each other. This is Laozi's guiding doctrine, and yet [the opening lines of the *Explanation of the Diagram of the Supreme Ultimate*]—"the ultimate-less and yet the supreme ultimate"— expresses the very same idea!

Laozi's philosophy is incorrect because he did not clearly comprehend principle. This is what beclouded his understanding. You have exerted great effort in following this teaching [regarding the ultimate-less and supreme ultimate] and practiced it for a long time; why have you never been able to discern what is wrong with it? It is absolutely clear that the teaching about "residing in the mean"[116] found in *Comprehending the Book of Changes* is not the same in kind; why have you not distinguished between them?

The two characters *wuji* appear in the opening line of the *Explanation of the Diagram of the Supreme Ultimate* and yet are not found anywhere in *Comprehending the Book of Changes*. The sayings and writings of the two Cheng brothers are quite extensive, but they, too, never once mention the expression *wuji*.[117] Even if we grant that Zhou Dunyi really did have the diagram [of the supreme ultimate] from the start, when we consider that he never mentions the term "ultimate-less" in his later works, we can see that his philosophy had advanced and that he no longer endorsed such a view [. . . .]

Second Letter (to Zhu Xi)[118]

[. . .] "Human beings can fill out the Dao; the Dao does not fill out human beings."[119] This principle (*li* 理) exists throughout the universe.

---

116   See the quotation from *Comprehending the Book of Changes*, chap. 22, given previously.

117   The Cheng brothers are Cheng Mingdao 程明道 or Cheng Hao 程顥 (1032–1085) and Cheng Yichuan 程伊川 or Cheng Yi 程頤 (1033–1107). For a study of their work, see Angus C. Graham, *Two Chinese Philosophers: The Metaphysics of the Brothers Ch'eng*, reprint (La Salle, IL: Open Court, 1992).

118   This is the second of three letters written to Zhu commenting upon an exchange of letters that Zhu had with Lu Xiangshan's elder brother Suoshan.

119   *Analects* 15.28. Compare *Analects* 19.2 The idea is that merely knowing or avowing allegiance to the Dao does not make one ethically better; the task lies in living according to and fulfilling the Dao.

Whether or not human beings understand or follow it never has added to or diminished it in any way. Nevertheless, given what they are, human beings have a particular task [to complete]. Granting the images of [the myriad] things and sheltering them is the task of Heaven.[120] Completing the physical forms of [the myriad] things and supporting them is the task of earth. Regulating and completing the Way of Heaven and earth and "helping to carry out the proper operations of Heaven and earth in order to assist and support the people is the task of rulers."[121]

Mengzi said, "When young, [they] study [what is proper]; when in their prime, they desire to implement it."[122] What he refers to here as the "desire to implement it" is [the desire] to implement what they have studied in order "to rectify the ruler's heart-mind" and to draw their ruler to the Dao.[123] With their ruler, they "discuss the Dao, order the state, and harmonize the *yin* and the *yang*" in order to spread the Dao throughout the world.[124] What Mengzi refers to as "studying [what is proper]" is to follow one's teachers, parents, and friends; read books and explore the past; learn, question, reflect, and discriminate—all in order to understand this Dao. And so, to study the Dao when young and to implement it when in one's prime is the task of any cultivated person.

---

120   Literally, the "images" refer to the sun, moon, stars, and planets in the heavens, but metaphorically the line describes how Heaven produces the images (*xiang* 象) of things, which later become physical forms (*xing* 形) and then distinct material things (*qi* 器). This idea is picked up and continued in the next line. Compare the opening section of the first part of the *Great Appendix:* "The images are completed in Heaven; the forms are completed on earth." According to such a scheme, the things of the world coalesce out of and in time dissolve back into an amorphous state; the whole process is guided by the principles mentioned in the opening line, which follows the quotation.

121   Quoting lines from the line commentary on the hexagram *Tai* 泰 in the *Book of Changes.*

122   *Mengzi* 1B9.

123   The quotation is from *Mengzi* 4A20. The word "rectify" (*ge* 格) came to be of central importance in the debate between Zhu Xi and Wang Yangming over how to interpret the term *gewu* 格物. Zhu insisted that it meant "to investigate things," while Wang, influenced by the line of thought seen here, argued that it meant "to rectify [one's thoughts in relation to] things." See the part on Wang in this volume and especially Section 7 of *A Record for Practice.*

124   The quotation is from the "Zhou Officials" ("Zhouguan 周公") chapter of the *Book of History.* For a complete translation, see Legge, *The Shoo King,* p. 527.

We all "lack a regular teacher."[125] Wandering through the muddled mass of teachings, we search and look, both high and low. Although one may claim one understands principle, how can one be sure that this is not just a private opinion or deluded view? One clap of thunder follows another; one person sings and hundreds join in harmony—we cannot know if we are right or wrong. We must exercise extreme caution in this regard!

It is fortunate that people doubt one another and do not agree. In the midst of those who share a common aspiration, it is naturally appropriate that all fully express their sincere thoughts and apply themselves to "cutting and polishing" one another in an effort to reach agreement about what is right and true.[126] The respect in which "great Shun was greater [than even Zilu or Yu] was in agreeing with others. He delighted in adopting the ideas of others in order to help him do what is good."[127] [When he was living in rustic conditions and among crude people,] "whenever he heard a single good word or saw a single good act, he was like a mighty river overflowing its banks. Flooding forth, none could stand in his way."[128]

What is our aspiration? What should we seek? Only what is right and true. "To hold tightly—as if it were emblazoned on one's chest—and never lose" any enlightened teaching or fine opinion that one has heard in the past and to delight in sharing these with others is how one works toward the right and true.[129] If this morning, in the course of cutting and polishing, we discover that something is false and wrong, we will abandon the practices of former days—regarding such a change as if we were escaping after having fallen into a pit or avoiding thistles and thorns. Our resolve to renew ourselves will become "like a mighty river overflowing its banks." If we can do this, we can realize our aspiration. How could those who possess only petty knowledge, who are accustomed to lowly and crude practices, and who glory in victory but are ashamed

---

125   Compare *Analects* 19.22, which describes how Kongzi "lacked a regular teacher" but endeavored to study the ancients and learn from whomever he could.

126   The reference is to a line from the *Book of Songs* or, more precisely, to Kongzi's interpretation of it. See *Analects* 1.15.

127   See *Mengzi* 2A8.

128   *Mengzi* 7A16.

129   The quoted material is from *Doctrine of the Mean*, chap. 8.

of defeat possibly understand this? An ancient and enlightened teaching tells us, "[If cultivated people] are unclear on any points, they will not set the problem aside."[130] I have dared to present these issues [to you] in all their minute detail [. . . .]

The primary focus of your last letter is the term "ultimate-less" (*wuji* 無極), but your account relies upon an explication of "principle" (*li* 理). Your most important point is, "Through this [i.e., the *wuji*] we are able to have a luminous and veridical apprehension of what the supreme ultimate really is in itself."[131] But in my humble opinion, you, my dear friend, have not experienced a veridical apprehension of the supreme ultimate. If you had really, accurately apprehended the supreme ultimate, you would not have preceded [your discussion of the supreme ultimate] with talk about the ultimate-less or followed it by appending the expression "[what the supreme ultimate] really is in itself" (*zhen ti* 真體). To begin your discussion with talk about the "ultimate-less" is precisely [as you yourself have said] "to stack a bed on top of one's bed." To follow the discussion by adding the expression "[what the supreme ultimate] really is in itself" is precisely [as you yourself have said] "to build a house underneath one's house."[132] The claims made by an insubstantial view certainly are inherently unlike those made by a substantial view.

Concerning the supreme ultimate, you have said, "It is precisely because it is the absolute and extreme ultimate for which no name can be named that we distinguish it by calling it 'the supreme ultimate' [. . . .] We refer to it as we do because it is the most extreme ultimate in all the world and nothing more can be said about it than this."[133] Why, then, is there any need to add the term "ultimate-less"? If you want to talk about the fact that it [i.e., the supreme ultimate] exists in no definite place and has no distinctive form,[134] then, as I urged you to do in my earlier letter, it would be appropriate to say something like what one finds in the *Book of Songs* where it talks about "the workings of high

---

130   The quotation is from *Doctrine of the Mean*, chap. 20.

131   Quoting an earlier letter, the fifth Zhu wrote to Lu, in which Zhu responds to a prior letter from Lu. See *Da Lu Zijing Wu* 答陸子靜五 in *Zhuzi wenji*, p. 1440.

132   Ibid., p. 1441.

133   Ibid., p. 1441.

134   Zhu raises such issues throughout his writings.

Heaven" and elaborates on this by saying, [they] "are without sound or scent."¹³⁵ Why do you think it is best to add the term "ultimate-less" on top of the supreme ultimate? The *Great Appendix to the Book of Changes* says, "The spiritual [efficacy of the sage] has no definite place." How can you talk about the spiritual not existing at all? It goes on to say, "The changes [the sage produces] have no definitive form."¹³⁶ How can you talk about the changes not existing at all? Laozi taught that "what does not exist (*wu* 無) is the beginning of Heaven and earth; what exists (*you* 有) is the mother of the myriad creatures."¹³⁷ He also said that "by cleaving always to what does not exist, one can contemplate their mystery; by cleaving always to what exists, one can contemplate their manifestations."¹³⁸ Simply by placing the word for "not existing" or "lacking" (*wu* 無) before "ultimate" (*ji* 極), you have the philosophy of Laozi. How can you deny this? It is only because Daoists are beclouded in this way [i.e., in believing in the primacy of what does not exist] that they have drifted into relying upon prognostication and magic in an attempt to ward off fear and superstition.

This principle, though, has always existed in the universe. How can one say that it does not? If there were no principle, then "rulers would not be rulers, ministers would not be ministers, fathers would not be fathers, and sons would not be sons."¹³⁹ Yang Zhu never espoused doing without a ruler, but Mengzi understood him as supporting this idea. Mo Di never espoused doing without a father, but Mengzi understood him as supporting this idea.¹⁴⁰ This shows why Mengzi was one who

---

135   See note 109 in Lu's "Letter to Zhu Yuanhui (Zhu Xi)."

136   See the fourth section of the first part of the *Great Appendix*.

137   These claims are based on a particular reading of lines from the opening chapter of the *Laozi*. Compare the discussion of these issues in Lu's "Letter to Zhu Yuanhui (Zhu Xi)."

138   See *Laozi*, chap. 1.

139   The quotation is from *Analects* 12.11. Lu's point is that without principle to serve as the ultimate moral standard, there can be no firm basis for such normative distinctions. The implication is that Zhu's view sides with the Daoists (and Buddhists) in seeing some conception of nothingness or emptiness as the ultimate ground of the phenomenal world. Lu correctly sees this view as a dire threat to the foundations of Confucian ethics, as understood in his time.

140   For these thinkers and Mengzi's opposition to them, see *Mengzi* 3B9, 7A26, and 7B26.

"understands words."[141] The ultimate is none other than this principle. The middle or mean (*zhong* 中) is none other than this principle. The fifth of the nine divisions [within the great plan] is called the "ultimate of royalty" (*huang ji* 皇極).[142] Is it not so named because it represents the middle or mean among [the nine divisions]?[143] Human beings are born endowed with the mean of Heaven and earth;[144] the *Book of Songs* says, "[You] established us, your teeming multitudes, and ensured that each received the mean."[145] Is it not that [Heaven] endowed them with the mean [as their nature]? The *Doctrine of the Mean* says, "The mean is the great root of all under Heaven. Harmony is the all-pervading Way of all under Heaven. To extend the mean and harmony is how Heaven and earth take their proper places and the myriad creatures are nourished."[146] This principle is indeed the utmost (*zhi* 至); how could there be some supreme ultimate existing beyond [and apart] from this? [You believe that] if one takes the ultimate (*ji* 極) as the mean (*zhong* 中), one does not understand principle. But do you think that if you take the ultimate as having form, then you *do* understand principle?[147] In terms of meaning or sense, there certainly are individual words that possess a range of different meanings. In terms of use, some words can be used with a single meaning or with a number of equally valid yet different meanings. And yet, the reference of a word can also be

---

141   This is something Mengzi said of himself. See *Mengzi* 2A2.

142   This is a reference to the "Great Plan" chapter of the *Book of History*. See the discussion and note 102 in the "Letter to Zhu Yuanhui (Zhu Xi)."

143   Lu's point is that in this case an "ultimate" is located in the precise middle of a range of different phenomena and not in some abstract realm where nothing at all exists. The "ultimate of royalty" is the name of the central square in a larger square composed of nine equal squares.

144   See the *Zuozhuan* for the thirteenth year of Duke Cheng. For a translation, see Legge, *The Ch'un Ts'ew*, p. 379.

145   See *Book of Songs*, Mao # 275. For a complete translation, see Legge, *The She King*, p. 581. Lu reads these lines according to the commentarial tradition that interprets the character for "supreme" (*ji* 極) as "mean" (*zhong* 中). This, of course, can be seen as supporting his general equation of these two characters.

146   The quotation is from *Doctrine of the Mean*, chap. 1.

147   The first option is the interpretation advocated by Lu; the second the one that he is ascribing to Zhu. The latter view clearly is not a charitable representation of Zhu's view, though Lu would argue that since Zhu insists that there is the ultimate-less, he must then think that the supreme ultimate belongs to the realm of forms.

distinguished by whether it is a substantive (*shi* 實) or an amorphous (*xu* 虛) word.[148] In the case of amorphous words, one should simply talk about the senses or meanings of the word. In the case of substantive words, one should talk about what the word refers to. When one is interested in what a word refers to, appealing to the senses or meanings of the word sometimes will not provide an adequate account. Take, for example, the character *yuan* 元. It can mean the "beginning," "leader," or "great." In describing the great good fortune (*yuanji* 元吉) of the fifth line of the hexagram *Kun* 坤 or the great accomplishment (*yuanheng* 元亨) of the hexagram *Tun* 屯, it serves as an amorphous word. [In these cases, though,] it means only "great," and one cannot substitute any of its other meanings.[149] In the line, "[How great] is the origin (*yuan* 元) of *Qian*,"[150] *yuan* is used as a substantive word. If we want to describe what this refers to, it is what the "Commentary of King Wen" talks about as the "good" and "benevolent."[151] In this case, how could it be adequate merely to appeal to the senses or meanings of the word? The word "ultimate" (*ji* 極) offers another example. [When used in] the terms "supreme ultimate" (*taiji* 太極) and the "ultimate of royalty" (*huangji* 皇極), it is a substantive word. The object to which it points does not admit multiple references. What fills up this entire universe is only this principle. [In this case, too,] how could it be adequate merely to appeal to the senses or meanings of the word? The mean is none other than the utmost principle (*zhi li* 至理). When has it ever failed simultaneously to have the sense of "utmost?" The *Great Learning* and the "Elegant Words" commentary by Kongzi all talk about knowledge of the utmost (*zhi zhi* 知至).[152] The utmost referred to here is none other than this principle.

---

148   The former are roughly nouns and pronouns: words that designate some fixed, substantial thing. The latter are words that function as verbs, adjectives, adverbs, etc.

149   See the "symbolism" commentary on the fifth (divided) line of the hexagram *Kun* and the line comment on the hexagram *Dun*.

150   The quotation is from the "Hexagram Statements" ("Tuanci 彖辭") commentary for the hexagram *Qian* 乾, which symbolizes Heaven.

151   This refers to the "Elegant Words" commentary on the hexagram.

152   Lu reads the expression *zhi zhi* 知至 consistently as "knowledge of the utmost" in both of these texts. In his terms, the second character is a substantive word. Zhu reads it this way only in the latter case. In the case of the *Great Learning*, he reads the expression as a noun plus a predicate adjective, with the meaning: "Knowledge is completed." On this interpretation, the second character is what Lu calls an amorphous word.

To those who read the *Book of Changes*, I say, "To understand the
supreme ultimate is to understand the utmost." To those who read
the "Great Plan" chapter of the *Book of History*, I say, "To understand
the ultimate of royalty is to understand the utmost." How can this be
denied? Whenever [these words] refer to this principle, one can call it
the ultimate, the proper mean, or the utmost; the referent in each case
is one and the same. In the lines, "If any one is abundant in the extreme
(*ji* 極), this is ominous. If any one is lacking in the extreme, this is
ominous,"[153] the character *ji* 極 is used twice as an amorphous word, but
it only has the sense or meaning of "to the utmost" (*zhi* 至).[154] Contrary
to what I had expected, you quite correctly say that "[the character] *ji*
極 means the utmost ultimate (*zhi ji* 至極) *and nothing else*." Your use
of the final particles meaning "and nothing else" (*eryi* 而已) is perfectly
appropriate![155] You, my friend, are renowned as a sophisticated and
erudite philologist and master of commentaries. What has led you to
become so confused that you remain unclear about the meaning of
principle and as a result of your profoundly idiosyncratic views miss it
altogether?

As for your explicit claim that *yin* and *yang* are forms (*xing* 形) and
material things (*qi* 器) and cannot be regarded as the Dao—this is even
more difficult to accept![156] The *Book of Changes* teaches that the Dao is
"the alternation of *yin* and *yang*" and that is all.[157] As for preceding and

---

153   For a translation, see Legge, *The Shoo King*, pp. 339–40.

154   Lu's point is that in this case, the word refers to a relative extreme and not the
supreme ultimate, which is the absolute standard for all phenomena.

155   The quotation is from *Zhuzi wenji*, p. 1440. Lu focuses on Zhu's use of the
intensifying particles *eryi* and reads him as saying something stronger than he intended.
For Zhu, the supreme ultimate or principle is the ultimate standard for all phenomena,
but he thought that above this there was also the "ultimate-less." Twisting Zhu's words
slightly, Lu takes this sentence to be saying that there is nothing beyond the supreme
ultimate.

156   Lu offers the gist of what Zhu says in the letter that he has referred to throughout.
See *Zhuzi wenji*, p. 1441. Zhu claims that the *yin* and the *yang* are forms and material
things, which are within form (*xing er xia* 形而下), while the supreme ultimate is the
Dao, which is above form (*xing er shang* 形而上).

157   See the fifth section of the first part of the *Great Appendix*.

following, beginning and ending, movement and stillness, darkness and light, above and below, advancing and retreating, going and coming, closing and opening, filling and emptying, waxing and waning, honor and lowliness, nobility and baseness, exterior and interior, hidden and manifest, attracting and repelling, agreeing and opposing, preservation and annihilation, gaining and losing, going out and coming in, carrying things out and storing them away—how could these be anything other than the alternation of *yin* and *yang*? Odd and even seek out each other and transform without end.[158] This is why the text says:

> The Way of the *Book of Changes* is ceaseless shifting and shuffling. [Its lines] transform and change without residing in any fixed abode. They flow throughout the six positions,[159] ascending and descending without a constant pattern. Hard and soft [lines][160] trade places; [their movement] cannot be captured by any set formula; they transform according to what is appropriate.[161]

The "Explanations of the Trigrams" says:

> Contemplating the changes in the *yin* and *yang* lines; they [i.e., the sages] formed the trigrams. Explicating the strong (*gang* 剛) and weak (*rou* 柔) lines, they produced the line statements.[162] These harmonized with and conformed to the Way and Virtue and were perfectly ordered in regard to righteousness. They made a thorough study of principle and an exhaustive exploration of human nature in order to understand their proper destiny.[163]

---

158   "Odd" refers to the unbroken *yang* lines in hexagrams and hence the *yang*; "even" refers to the broken *yin* lines and hence the *yin*.

159   The six line positions composing each hexagram.

160   *Yang* and *yin* lines, respectively.

161   See the eighth section of the second part of the *Great Appendix*.

162   The "strong," or solid, lines are *yang*; the "weak," or broken, lines are *yin*. The line statements (*yao* 爻) are comments on each line of a trigram.

163   See the first section of the "Explanations of the Trigrams" (Shuogua 說卦) commentary to the *Book of Changes*.

It also says:

> Long ago, the sages composed the *Book of Changes* so that
> it would conform with the principles underlying nature
> and destiny. They established the Way of Heaven by
> talking about *yin* and *yang*. They established the Way of
> earth by talking about weak and strong. They established
> the Way of human beings by talking about benevolence
> and righteousness.[164]

The second section of the *Great Appendix* elaborates further, saying:

> The *Book of Changes* is broad, great, detailed, and
> comprehensive. In it, one finds the Way of Heaven. In it,
> one finds the Way of human beings. In it, one finds the
> Way of earth. It embraces these three powers and doubles
> them, yielding six [lines in each hexagram]. The six lines
> are nothing other than the Way of the three powers.[165]

But your view is that the *yin* and the *yang* are not the Dao, and you
explicitly refer to them as "forms" and "material things." How can you
lack such insight regarding the difference between the Dao and material
things? [. . .]

Second Letter to Senior Official Li[166]

In your most recent correspondence, you said, "Rather than apply the
heart-mind (*rongxin* 容心) and establish something novel, better to settle
the heart-mind (*pingxin* 平心) and rely on principle."[167] This is beauti-
fully put! Nevertheless, the characters for "apply the heart-mind" are not

---

164   The second section of the "Explanations of the Trigrams" commentary to the
Book of Changes.

165   See the tenth section of the second part of the *Great Appendix*.

166   We know only that Li 李 was a senior official in Jin Qi 金谿, an area in the
eastern part of Linchuan 臨川 District of Jiangxi Province at the time this letter was
written.

167   The original is a rhymed couplet: *rongxin liyi buruo pingxin renli* 容心立異不
若平心任理.

found in the classics. The *Liezi* (列子) offers the only reference to this expression in the line, "Why should I be concerned (*rongxin* 容心)?"[168] The two characters for "settle the heart-mind" are not found in the classics either. Their source can be traced to the *Zhuangzi*: "Of things that are 'settled' or 'level' (*ping* 平), still water is the most perfect and can serve as the standard. It guards what is within and shows no disturbance on the outside."[169] Although Zhuangzi attributes these lines to Kongzi, they are not the master's words.[170] Zhuangzi himself admits that "nine out of ten of the things in my book are borrowed."[171] Zhuangzi often uses words and actions attributed to the master to ridicule or poke fun at Kongzi. If [they are] not used in this way, then he "borrows" [them] to express respect for his own teacher [i.e., Laozi] or to spread his own views. But in every case, these are fictions. Later people who take these as authentic are simply displaying their ignorance. In his letter to Li Yi discussing literature, Han Changli used the expression, "Examine into it with a settled heart-mind (*pingxin* 平心)."[172] After his essay became popular, the expression "settled heart-mind" became increasingly

---

168   An eclectic text probably composed in the third to fourth century C.E. but containing material from much earlier. For the most part, it is Daoist in character. For a translation and study, see A. C. Graham, *The Book of Lieh-tzu*, reprint (London: John Murray, 1973). [lines are from the first chapter of the *Liezi*.]

169   See chapter five of the *Zhuangzi*.

170   The passage in the *Zhuangzi* presents Kongzi as the spokesman for the Daoist point of view. This is one of the many distinctive uses of humor found in the *Zhuangzi*. For a discussion of this point, see Karen L. Carr and Philip J. Ivanhoe, *The Sense of Antirationalism: The Religious Thought of Zhuangzi and Kierkegaard* (New York: Seven Bridges, 2000), pp. 92–102.

171   This line is from the "Borrowed Words" ("Yu yan 寓言"), the twenty-seventh chapter of the *Zhuangzi*.

172   Han Changli's 韓唱黎 (768–824) courtesy name was Tuizhi 退之, but he is better known by his given name, Yu 愈. He was one of the most famous literati of the Tang dynasty and a major figure in the revival of Confucianism. His letter to Li Yi 李翊, which was written in August of 801, is a classic discussion of how the development and exercise of literary skill can serve as a form of moral self-cultivation. For my own translation of the letter, see Philip J. Ivanhoe, *The Essays and Letters of Zhang Xuecheng* (Stanford, CA: Stanford University Press, forthcoming, 2009), appendix. For a different translation and discussion of the letter, see Charles Hartman, *Han Yü and the T'ang Search for Unity* (Princeton, NJ: Princeton University Press, 1986), pp. 241–47. Han Yu was criticized by Wang Yangming; see Part Three, note 157.

widespread in the speech and writings of students and officials. But if we thoroughly examine the principles underlying both of these expressions, we discover that neither qualifies as the most elevated kind of teaching.

To ask "Why should I be concerned?" is an expression of being without the heart-mind (*wu xin* 無心). And the fact that the latter two characters are not found anywhere in the classics lends credence to this claim. Human beings are not pieces of wood or stone. How can they be without the heart-mind? The heart-mind is the most honorable of the five senses.[173] The "Great Plan" chapter of the *Book of History* says, "[Excellence] in reflection is called astuteness . . . and astuteness becomes sageliness."[174] Mengzi said, "The function of the heart-mind is to reflect. If one reflects, one gets things right. If one does not reflect, one will not get things right."[175] He also said, "What is preserved in human beings, how could it be other than benevolence and righteousness!"[176] He further said, "Could it only be in relation to the heart-mind that we find nothing in common [among human beings]?"[177] He also said, "The way in which cultivated people differ from others concerns preserving the heart-mind,"[178] and, "It is not only the worthy who possess this heart-mind; all people have it. The worthy simply are successful in ensuring that they do not lose it."[179] Mengzi also said, "The respects in which human beings differ from [other] animals are exceedingly minute and subtle. Most people abandon these differences, while cultivated people preserve them."[180] When he talks about how "[most people] abandon these differences," he is talking about abandoning this heart-mind. That is why

---

173   The other senses are touch, taste, sight, and hearing. Each is associated with an "organ": the body, mouth, eyes, ears, and heart-mind, respectively. Compare note 84 in this part of the volume.

174   For a translation of the context of these remarks, which describes various excellences or virtues associated with different senses or capacities, see Legge, *The Shoo King*, pp. 326–27.

175   *Mengzi* 6A15.

176   *Mengzi* 6A8.

177   *Mengzi* 6A7.

178   *Mengzi* 4B28.

179   *Mengzi* 6A10.

180   *Mengzi* 4B19.

he says, "This is called losing one's fundamental heart-mind."[181] When he talks about how "[cultivated people] preserve them," he is talking about preserving this heart-mind. That is why he says, "Great human beings do not lose their childlike heart-mind."[182] The "four sprouts" are none other than this heart-mind.[183] "What Heaven has endowed me with" is none other than this heart-mind.[184] People all have this heart-mind. Every heart-mind possesses this principle. The heart-mind is principle. That is why [Mengzi] says, "Principle and righteousness please my heart-mind as grain- and grass-[fed meat] pleases my palate."[185]

What should be valued in students [of the Way] is their desire to thoroughly examine and understand this principle and develop this heart-mind. If they show any ignorance or obscuration, if they waver in their commitment or fall into vice, then it means this heart-mind is not clear and this principle is not bright. Such a state is called "Not attaining what is correct."[186] The views and speech of such people will, as a matter of course, be depraved. Once one falls into such a state, the only way out is to engage in concerted discussion and study. And so, the heart-mind *must* decide what is depraved and what is correct. To believe that one should be without the heart-mind (*wu xin* 無心)—this indeed is a depraved thing to say! As for "the stupid and unworthy who fall short" and do not attain what is correct or "the worthy and wise who overshoot"[187] and also fail to attain what is correct, they indulge themselves in music, sex, possessions, and profit, are gripped by deceit and guile, hemmed in by the petty details and trifling aspects of conduct, and drift into high-flown speculation and frivolous conversation. While they surely do differ in being wise or foolish, worthy or unworthy, they all suffer from the common malady of this heart-mind's not attaining what is correct and being obscured by partiality so that this Dao is not made bright and implemented [in the world]. [. . .]

---

181 *Mengzi* 6A10.

182 *Mengzi* 4B12.

183 The four sprouts (*siduan* 四端) are the four nascent moral sensibilities that Mengzi believes all humans possess as part of their nature. See *Mengzi* 2A6.

184 For the quotation, see *Mengzi* 6A15.

185 *Mengzi* 6A7.

186 The quoted material is from the fifteenth section of the old text of the *Great Learning*; see Legge, *Li Chi*, vol. 2, p. 416.

187 Lu here is paraphrasing *Doctrine of the Mean*, chap. 4.

(First) Letter to Zhu Jidao[188]

This "principle" exists throughout the universe and has never been hidden or absent. Heaven and earth are what they are simply because they accord with this principle without allowing any prejudice to intervene. Along with Heaven and earth, human beings have been established as one of the three acmes.[189] How can they allow personal prejudice to lead them to not accord with this principle? Mengzi said, "First, firmly establish what is great [within you]; then, what is petty cannot steal it away."[190] It is only because people do not firmly establish what is great within them that it is stolen by what is petty, which leads them to differ from Heaven and earth. If you truly are able to firmly establish what is great within you, how could practicing the various poetic and prose styles that one must master in preparation for the examinations possibly overwhelm you, my friend?[191] Your son should set his heart on excelling at what is most admirable and consider the upcoming examination process as a great blessing. This will not fail! It would be most fortunate if you encourage him to nourish this [admirable] aim by reading classical texts.

(Eighth) Letter to Wu Zisi[192]

This "principle" fills up and extends throughout the universe! Not even Heaven, earth, ghosts, or spirits can fail to follow this principle—how much less can human beings afford to do so? If one truly understands this principle, then there is no longer any prejudice separating oneself

---

188   Zhu Jidao's 朱濟道 (n.d.) given name was Fu 桴, and he was a native of Zhejiang Province. His younger brother Xiangdao 享道 was an avid follower of Lu Xiangshan.

189   The reference to the "three acmes" is from the second section of the first part of the *Great Appendix*. Compare note 82 of "Letter to Wang Shunbo."

190   *Mengzi* 6A15. The great within us is our heart-mind; the petty is our physical nature.

191   One needed to practice various styles of poetry and write in the highly stylized "eight-legged essay" style of prose to pass the imperial examinations. Both these styles contrast with the ancient classical style.

192   I do not know any details about Wu Zisi 吳子嗣.

from others. [Then, one will "see] the good that is in others as if it were in oneself."[193] And so, when others do what is good, it is like oneself doing what is good. "Seeing others who are accomplished and sagely, one will delight in them in the depths of one's heart-mind—not just in one's speech."[194] "One will offer them opinions and advice, protect and care for them, teach and instruct them."[195] This is true human feeling and being fully in accord with principle. How could there be any jealousy or suspicion between such people? "Complete integrity . . . is not simply the perfection of the self but the way to perfect other creatures as well. Perfecting the self is benevolence; perfecting other creatures is wisdom. This is the Virtue of human nature and the Way to unite the inner and outer [aspects of life]. The only concern [of those who possess complete integrity] is that they have not managed to perfect themselves." [. . .][196]

---

193   The quotation is from the *Sayings from Kongzi's School* (*Kongzi jiayu* 孔子家語) 15.14. The line in the original text continues by concluding, "this is why the master did not contend with others" and describes one of three respects in which Zengzi claims he has not fulfilled the master's teachings. The point is that if we can regard the good in others as if it were our own, we will not waste time comparing ourselves to and competing with them and there will be no possibility of jealousy or envy. Thanks to Justin Tiwald for pointing out this reference.

194   See "Declaration of the Duke of Qin" in the *Book of History*; see Legge, *The Shoo King*, p. 629. This passage is quoted in the thirtieth section of the old text of the *Great Learning*; see Legge, *Li Chi*, vol. 2, p. 420. The larger context of this passage includes the idea, evident in the previous quotation, that the best people see the good in others as if it were their own. Compare Wang Yangming's appeal to the same passage in his letter "To Huang Zongxian."

195   See "Without Leisure" in the *Book of History*; see Legge, *The Shoo King*, p. 471.

196   The quotation is from *Doctrine of the Mean*, chap. 25.

RECORDED SAYINGS[197]

1. "There is no affair outside the Dao; there is no Dao outside affairs."
The master often spoke these lines.

2. "The Dao lies within the universe. When has it ever suffered any
affliction? Human beings bring afflictions upon themselves. The ancient
sages and worthies simply eliminated human afflictions. How could they
add to or diminish the Dao?"

3. "The principles of the Dao simply are right in front of your eyes. Even
those who perceive the principles of the Dao and dwell in the realm of the
sages see only the principles of the Dao that are right in front of your eyes."

4. "In the transition between the reigns of Yao and Shun, the Dao rested
in Gao Yao's [hands].[198] In the transition between the Shang and Zhou
dynasties, the Dao rested in Jizi's [hands].[199] Heaven, in producing human
beings, certainly ensures that there will be some who take up the responsibility of making clear the Dao. Gao Yao and Jizi were such men. The reason
Jizi feigned madness was precisely so that he could transmit the Dao.[200] Once
he had presented the "Great Plan" to King Wu, he lived among the barbarians so that he would not have to eat the grain of the Zhou dynasty."[201]

---

197 Presented here are six examples of sayings or brief, focused teachings attributed to Lu.

198 Gao Yao 皋陶 was Emperor Shun's minister of crime and was appointed chief
minister when Emperor Yu succeeded Shun.

199 Jizi 箕子 is commonly known as the "Viscount of Ji." When the Zhou conquered
the Shang, he refused to serve the new ruler, King Wu, who had in fact delivered him from
prison. Instead, Jizi fled or perhaps only threatened to flee to live among the barbarians (some
say to Korea). His devotion to his fallen, though unworthy, former sovereign so moved King
Wu that the king enfeoffed him in this territory. The Viscount of Ji then felt obliged to attend
King Wu's court. The king regularly consulted him on matters of state policy, which eventually
led Jizi to bestow upon the king the "Great Plan." See Legge, *The Shoo King*, pp. 320–24.

200 Jizi feigned madness because he no longer wanted to serve the wicked tyrant
Zhou 紂, who refused to heed his wise counsel.

201 Although Jizi served in the Zhou court, he still preserved his loyalty to the fallen
Shang and refused to be supported by the Zhou dynasty.

5. "The *Analects* contains many passages for which we lack the full context, so it is hard to get a handle on them. For example, there are passages such as "If one's wisdom is sufficient to attain it, but one's benevolence is insufficient to maintain it . . ."[202] We don't know what it is that wisdom [is supposed to] attain and benevolence [is supposed to] maintain. Or, for example, in the passage, "To study and on occasion practice it," we don't know what it is that we are supposed to on occasion practice.[203] If one's study lacks a fundamental root or basis, then such passages are not easy to read. If one's study has a fundamental root or basis, then one will know that what "knowledge attains" is *this*, what "benevolence maintains" is *this*, what one is to "on occasion practice" is *this*, what one delights in is *this*, and what one takes joy in is *this* [fundamental root or basis]. Like water pouring off a high roof: if one understands the fundamental root or basis, the six classics are all one's footnotes!"[204]

6. "The teaching about 'Heavenly principles' and 'human desires' obviously is not the most elevated of views. If principle is the Heavenly and desires are the human, then this denies the identity of the Heavenly and the human. For the most part, this teaching can be traced to Laozi. The 'Record of Music' chapter of the *Book of Rites* (*Liji* 禮記) says:

> Human beings are still and quiet at birth; this is their Heavenly nature. When influenced by things, they begin to stir; these movements are the desires of [our] nature. When we come into contact with things, our consciousness becomes aware of them; as a result, likes and dislikes take shape. . . . When [this process reaches the point where] one is unable to reflect upon oneself, Heavenly nature is obliterated.[205]

202　See *Analects* 15.33. Wang Yangming's given name, Shouren, is composed of two words taken from this passage: maintain (*shou* 守) benevolence (*ren* 仁).

203　See *Analects* 1.1.

204　The line about water off a high roof is taken from the *Book of History*. See the entry on Emperor Gaozu in its "Basic Annals." Traditionally, the six classics are the *Book of Changes*, the *Book of Songs*, the *Book of History*, the *Book of Rites*, the *Book of Music*, and the *Spring and Autumn Annals*. When the *Book of Music* was lost, the *Rites of Zhou* was added to replace it.

205　For a translation of the entire passage, see Legge, *Li Chi*, vol. 2, p. 96.

For the most part, the teaching about 'Heavenly principles' and 'human desires' is derived from this passage, and these words in the 'Record of Music' are rooted in Laozi's teachings.

"Furthermore, to claim that stillness alone is Heavenly nature—does this imply that movement is *not* an expression of Heavenly nature? The *Book of History* says, 'The human heart-mind is precarious. The heart-mind of the Dao is subtle.'[206] Many commentators understand the 'human heart-mind' to mean human desires and the 'heart-mind of the Dao' to mean Heavenly principle.[207] But this is wrong. There is only one heart-mind. How could human beings have two heart-minds? If one speaks from the perspective of human beings, then one says that it is 'precarious.' If one speaks from the perspective of the Dao, then one says that it is 'subtle.' A lack of reflection leads to wildness; an ability for careful reflection leads to sagehood.[208] Is this not precarious! [It is] without sound or scent, without form or embodiment.[209] Is this not subtle! If we draw upon the *Zhuangzi*, we find, 'Minute and insignificant, they join in with human beings! Immense and great, alone they roam within Heaven!'[210] The *Zhuangzi* also says, 'The Way of Heaven and the Way of human beings are far apart from one another!'[211] This clearly is to split and divide the Heavenly and the human into two separate things."

---

206   The quotation is from the "Counsels of the Great Yu" chapter of the *Book of History*. For an alternative translation and more context, see Legge, *The Shoo King*, p. 61.

207   Lu is pointing to those who follow the interpretation of what contemporary scholars call the Cheng-Zhu School.

208   In numerous places, the *Book of History* encourages careful and repeated reflection or thought (*nian* 念). See, for example, Legge, *The Shoo King*, pp. 55, 58, 324, 329, 390, and others.

209   The first line is from *Mao* # 235 in the "Greater Odes" ("Daya 大雅") section of the *Book of Songs*. For a translation of the entire ode, see Legge, *The She King*, pp. 427–31. This line is quoted in *Doctrine of the Mean*, chap. 33. The second line is reminiscent of ideas found in the *Book of Changes*.

210   These lines are close to lines from "The Sign of Complete Virtue," the fifth chapter in the *Zhuangzi*. The original, though, has something different for the final line: "alone, they perfect the Heavenly [within them]."

211   This is a close paraphrase of lines from "Keeping Things in Place," the eleventh chapter in the *Zhuangzi*.

EXPOSITORY ESSAYS[212]

Explaining the *Book of Changes*

This "principle" fills up the universe; who can escape from it? If one accords with this principle, there will be good fortune. If one opposes this principle, there will be misfortune. Those who are ignorant and prejudiced [in regard to this principle] become deluded and stupid. Those who are penetrating and discerning [in regard to this principle] become enlightened and intelligent. The deluded and stupid do not perceive this principle; and so, they oppose it and encounter misfortune. The enlightened and intelligent perceive this principle; and so they are able to accord with it and attain good fortune. Commentators on the *Book of Changes* say that *yang* is eminent while *yin* is humble; strong lines are enlightened while weak lines are benighted. This truly is the case. For example, take the hexagram *Jin* 晉.[213] In its upper trigram ☲ *Li* 離, a single *yin* line lies between two *yang* lines and serves as the enlightened ruler. The three *yin* lines of the lower trigram ☷ *Kun* 昆 follow the enlightenment [manifested in] the upper trigram and so good fortune is attained.[214] Anything that opposes the double *yang* lines [in the upper trigram] would encounter misfortune. What makes *Li* enlightened is that it is enlightened about this principle. Since the three *yin* lines of *Kun* are able to follow this enlightenment, it is fitting that they should attain good fortune as well as every benefit. This is how being enlightened about and following principle leads to goodness. It is equally proper that those who do not thoroughly follow this course do not enjoy the full

---

212 Presented here are four short expository essays Lu wrote on various classical texts or themes.

213 This is hexagram 35.

214 One of the chief lessons of the hexagram is that an enlightened lord and compliant subordinate need each other, and both are required for a successful and harmonious state.

benefits of goodness. How can one talk about the *Book of Changes* with those who are unenlightened about this principle and instead become muddled discussing extraneous matters concerning the names or composition of the hexagram lines? Is there ever a time when one can afford to be muddled about the view that *yang* is eminent while *yin* is humble, strong lines are enlightened while weak lines are benighted?

Explaining Learning

The ancients entered [the path of] greater learning at age fifteen.[215] The *Great Learning* says, "The Way of greater learning lies in making bright one's bright Virtue, renovating the people, and coming to rest in the highest good."[216] This [line] talks about the purposes of greater learning. The desire to make bright one's bright Virtue throughout all under Heaven is the goal of entering [the path of] greater learning. "Rectifying one's thoughts in relation to things" and "extending knowledge" are how one takes up the task.[217] The *Doctrine of the Mean* talks about "broad learning," "critical inquiry," "careful reflection," and "illuminating discrimination"—these describe the method for "rectifying one's thoughts in relation to things."[218] Reading books and having close relationships with teachers and friends are both aspects of learning. "Reflection" is something that one must do on one's own, but "questioning" and "debating" both are things that one needs others in order to do. Even the ancient sages relied upon earlier insights and the views of friends and teachers in order to enable them to advance [in their learning]. How much more must those who are *not* sages avail themselves of such help! How could anyone be capable of advancing in their learning by relying exclusively on their personal understanding?

---

215   The "greater learning" roughly is the higher forms of learning appropriate for adults. See the "Preserving Tradition" ("Baochuan 保傅") chapter of the *Rites of the Elder Dai* (*Da Dai liji* 大戴禮記). Compare *Analects* 2.4.

216   The quoted material is the opening lines of the first section of the old text of the *Great Learning*; see Legge, *Li Chi*, vol. 2, p. 411.

217   These are steps in learning found in the second and third chapters of the old text of the *Great Learning*; see Legge, *Li Chi*, vol. 2, pp. 411–12.

218   These aspects of learning are found in *Doctrine of the Mean*, chap. 20.

However, earlier insights expressed principles in response to particular times and so what they recommend does not always agree. The records of such insights also can be genuine or false, perfect or flawed. If one is not able to pick out [what is correct], then one's regard for these insights will end up being rather tepid. If one looks to teachers or friends in order to resolve such issues, one will find that the views of teachers and friends also do not always agree. Among them, one will find what is right and what is wrong, what is proper and what is not. If one is not able to pick out [what is correct], then one's allegiance to these views will end up being rather tepid. If one's regard for and allegiance to these views is rather tepid, where will one ultimately come to rest? One will be like the person who tried to build his house [according to advice he received from people passing by] on the road; the task will never be completed.[219] If you want to choose just one [piece of advice] and follow it, then how will you ever know if this is nothing more than your personal opinion or prejudiced point of view? Zimo held to the middle position, but Mengzi still thought that he "grasped one thing while forsaking one hundred others."[220] How can grasping one thing while forsaking one hundred others be the proper way to learn? How can students of later ages possibly follow such a course?

Explaining the Analects

"Those committed to benevolence are free of wickedness."[221] "Wickedness" is not the same as "having faults."[222] One can immediately resolve to avoid wickedness; one cannot immediately resolve to avoid having any faults. A worthy, such as Ju Boyu 蘧伯玉, will seek "to reduce his faults but still not be able to do so."[223] A sage, such as Kongzi, will still say, "If I could be granted a number of years more and study the *Book of Changes*

---

219   These are a paraphrase of lines from the *Book of Songs* (*Mao #* 195). For a complete translation, see Legge, *The She King*, p. 332.

220   For Zimo and for Mengzi's criticism of him, see *Mengzi* 7A26. Zimo is said to have held a view halfway between the purported selfishness of Yang Zhu and the excessive altruism of Mozi.

221   See *Analects* 4.4.

222   For the notion of faults (*guo* 過), or more literally "transgression" or "going too far," see *Analects* 11.16 and *Doctrine of the Mean*, chap. 4.

223   See *Analects* 14.26. Compare *Analects* 15.6.

in my fifties, I could be free of major faults."[224] Is this not even more so in the case of students? How could they immediately be responsible for being without faults? Cultivated people will be greatly concerned about any depravity or wickedness; they will not allow even a hair's breadth [of such inclinations] to remain and will attack them in an instant. If one day they can commit themselves to benevolence, such [depravity and wickedness] will be no more.

"Be committed to the Dao, find support in Virtue, rely upon benevolence, and broadly partake of and enjoy the arts."[225] The Dao is the publicly shared principles that have existed throughout the world for tens of thousands of generations and what human beings together rely and draw upon. For rulers, there is the Way of rulers. For ministers, there is the Way of ministers. For fathers, there is the Way of fathers. For sons, there is the Way of sons.[226] None is without the Dao, but only sages are able to complete and perfect the Dao. And so, when they serve as rulers, they completely fulfill the Way of rulers. When they serve as ministers, they completely fulfill the Way of ministers. When they serve as fathers, they completely fulfill the Way of fathers. When they serve as sons, they completely fulfill the Way of sons. In whatever capacity they serve, they completely fulfill the Way of that station and role.

Ordinary people are not able to complete and perfect the Dao; on the other hand, how could they be completely without the Way? The Master said, "Who can leave [a room] without going out the door? Who can fail to rely and draw upon the Dao?"[227] Those who labor in the fields have never been without respect for their rulers and love for their parents, nor have they ever failed to carry out the work of respecting their rulers and loving their parents. The beginning sprouts of the Way of the minister lie precisely in such things! Nevertheless, if those above fail to teach and those below fail to study, not only will they fail to extend what they do to complete and perfect [the Way], but, obscured by material things and confused by desires, they will drift far [from the Way]—to the point where those who [merely] retain some vestige of the Way may at times

---

224   See *Analects* 7.16.
225   See *Analects* 7.6.
226   The idea Lu is developing here can be found in *Analects* 12.11.
227   See *Analects* 6.17.

lose it completely. Acts of regicide and parricide are done in those moments when such people lose the Dao completely. The common people depend upon the teachings of those above in order to follow the Dao, while scholars rely and draw upon their studies to follow the Dao. Nevertheless, if they lack a commitment, they will not be able to carry out their studies, and if they do not study, they will not understand the Way. And so, the way to attain the Dao is through study, and the way to carry out study is through commitment. The Master said, "When I was fifteen years old, I established a commitment to study."[228] He also said, "Scholars who are committed to the Dao but are ashamed of shabby clothes or unsavory food are simply not worth discussing."[229] When Mengzi said, "Scholars elevate their commitment," he meant the same thing as when he said, "[Cultivated people] are committed to the Dao."[230] "The smaller powers are seen in the flowing of streams. The greater powers are revealed in mighty transformations."[231] The latter is the perfect and complete Virtue of the sage. In the "Counsels of Gao Yao," it says that those who "strictly and reverently practice six" of the nine virtues can manage a state well and those who "daily display three" of the nine can manage a family well.[232] The virtues are not all distributed in complete and perfect form to every person. Those below [the class of people just described] may not necessarily have three of the virtues. But as long as they have *one*, they still have virtue. If we consider the case of those who possess just a single virtue, some might not have its complete and perfect form. But if we can find within their natures some slight goodness or minor excellence that brings them close to one of the virtues, they still have virtue. If they can support [these good qualities within themselves] and not lose them, with each day these qualities will accumulate and develop, be more evident and flourishing, and more extensive and great. If they fail to support [these good qualities within themselves],

228   See *Analects* 2.4.

229   See *Analects* 4.9.

230   See *Mengzi* 7A33 and 7A24 for the respective quotations.

231   This is a quotation from *Doctrine of the Mean*, chap. 30. The word translated here as "power" and as "Virtue" in the line following the quotation is *de* 德; it connotes the characteristic efficacy or power of a person, creature, or thing.

232   Lu is quoting and paraphrasing a section from the *Book of History*; see Legge, *The Shoo King*, pp. 71–72.

then with each day they will lose and destroy what they have. How could they possibly hope that these good qualities would accumulate and develop, be more evident and flourishing, and more extensive and great? How could scholars who are committed to the Dao be without Virtue? And so, the master taught them to "find support in Virtue."

Benevolence is the human heart-mind. "To follow one's heart-mind and not overstep what is proper"—this is how sages fully realize benevolence.[233] Of the best disciples that studied with him—for example, Zilu and Ran You—Kongzi said, "I do not know whether he is benevolent."[234] Only in regard to those such as Yan Yuan and Zhong Gong did he grant that one could regard them as benevolent.[235] Ordinary people cannot hope to be perfectly benevolent. Nevertheless, is it the case that they all obstinately refuse to be benevolent? Ordinary people certainly are not able to do everything that sages do. Nevertheless, they are able, to some extent, to do such things. Ordinary people certainly are not able to keep themselves from doing all the things that sages do not do. Nevertheless, they are able, to some extent, to keep themselves from doing such things. When we consider how [ordinary people] are able, to some extent, to do what sages do and are able, to some extent, to keep themselves from doing what sages do not do, we see that all people receive the mean between Heaven and earth and find a common root in the intelligence of the heart-mind, which cannot be effaced or obliterated [from their nature].[236] If they can fill out what cannot be effaced or obliterated, can "benevolence be far away?"[237] Benevolence is within human beings and

---

233   The quoted line describes Kongzi's behavior after reaching the age of seventy. See *Analects* 2.4.

234   For Zilu and Ran You, see *Analects* 5.7.

235   For Yan Yuan's benevolence, see *Analects* 6.7. He is also highly praised in 2.9, 6.3, 6.11, etc. Lu's claim regarding Zhong Gong's benevolence is not directly supported by the text. In *Analects* 5.5, someone calls Zhong Gong benevolent, but in his response, Kongzi employs the same line, "I do not know whether he is benevolent," that he used in regard to Zilu and Ran You. Zhong Gong, though, is highly praised in *Analects* 6.1, 11.3, etc.

236   Compare "Reflect and You Shall Get Things Right" in the "Short Meditations" section in this volume and the poem "Written at Goose Lake to Rhyme with My Brother's Verse" in the "Poetry" section.

237   This is an allusion to *Analects* 7.30.

cannot be effaced or completely eradicated. It is only because they are unable to rely upon this [i.e., the good tendencies in their heart-minds] in order to advance toward benevolence and instead distance themselves from this and become mired in a realm devoid of benevolence that they obstinately refuse to be benevolent. How could scholars who are committed to the Dao be without benevolence? And so, the master taught them to "rely upon benevolence." The arts are used by all under Heaven; these are things that human beings cannot but practice. To "broadly partake of and enjoy the arts" certainly in no way will harm one's being "committed to the Dao, finding support in Virtue, and relying upon benevolence," and, moreover, the Dao, Virtue, and benevolence can be manifested in [one's practice of the arts]. That is why [Kongzi] said, "broadly partake of and enjoy the arts."

Explaining the *Mengzi*

There is no need to discuss Mengzi's claim that a unified commitment can affect or move one's vital energy; people harbor doubts only about his claim that unified vital energy can affect or move one's commitment.[238] Mengzi went on to illustrate the latter point with his example of someone whose commitment is affected when he stumbles or moves in haste; this should settle any remaining doubts. To be "unified" is to be concentrated on one thing. Commitment certainly is the leader of one's vital energy. Nevertheless, if one's vital energy is concentrated on one thing, then it can affect and move one's commitment. This is why Mengzi not only mentions the need to maintain one's commitment but also warns about not violating one's vital energy. In regard to one's residence, eating, and drinking, one should observe proper measure and moderation. In regard to what one looks at, listens to, says, and does, one must strictly maintain the distinction between the deviant and the correct.[239] These all are examples of the work of not violating one's vital energy. "Always work at it, but do not correct the heart-mind" is one sentence. "Do not neglect [the work], but do not help the growth [of

---

238 See *Mengzi* 2A2.
239 Compare *Analects* 12.1.

one's moral sprouts]" is another.[240] The second sentence explicates the first. Mengzi uses the word "correct" (*zheng* 正) twice but with the same meaning. The first use is in the line "Always work at it, but do not correct the heart-mind." The second use is in the line "One's words must be trustworthy, but without any desire to correct one's conduct."[241] [When the text of *Mengzi* 2A2 is punctuated so that] the word "heart-mind" (*xin* 心) follows the words "do not correct" (*wu zheng* 勿正), then nothing vital is missing. [When it is punctuated so that] there is no "heart-mind" preceding the words "do not forget" (*wu wang* 勿忘), then nothing extraneous is added. This is something that anyone who works on texts is capable of understanding. The word "work" (*shi* 事) in the phrase "Always work at it . . ." is the same as the word "work" in the lines "With care and reverence, [he] gloriously worked for the Lord on High."[242]

Because later scholars fail to attain a proper grasp of Mengzi's underlying philosophy, they have not been clear about the section in the *Mengzi* that describes him as someone who "understands words."[243] They force an interpretation of [Mengzi's four types of] words—"prejudiced," "licentious," "depraved," and "evasive"—so that they exclusively apply to Yangism, Mohism, Buddhism, or Daoism.[244] They ask: Which of these is an example of prejudiced words? Which of these is an example of licentious words? Which of these is an example of depraved words? Which of these is an example of evasive words? They do not understand that these four categories cannot be divided [up so neatly].[245] The words

---

240   Lu continues to quote from the same section of the *Mengzi* (2A2). Here, he is insisting upon a particular punctuation, placing a full stop and breaking the first sentence after, instead of before, the word "heart-mind."

241   See *Mengzi* 7B33.

242   The lines are from *Mao* # 236. For a complete translation of the ode, see Legge, *The She King*, pp. 432–36.

243   See *Mengzi* 2A2. Lu proceeds to quote liberally from this portion of the *Mengzi* throughout the following discussion.

244   "Yangism" denotes the followers of Yang Zhu, who Mengzi described as a kind of egoist. "Mohism" refers to the followers of Mozi (Mo Di), who espoused "impartial care" for all people.

245   Lu is objecting to the one-to-one correspondence between Mengzi's four types of words and the four schools of Yangism, Mohism, Buddhism, and Daoism. As he will go on to argue, the four types describe failings that one finds throughout different schools of philosophy.

[that Mengzi] used in regard to the various philosophers and hundred schools distinguish different features of the various philosophers and hundred schools. "Beclouded," "sunk," "deviant," and "exhausted" are [different] actual qualities; "prejudiced," "licentious," "depraved," and "evasive" are their respective names.[246] A thinker or school first had some actual quality and then came to have the corresponding name. If one wants to grasp what the names "prejudiced," "licentious," "depraved," and "evasive" mean, one must first gain a clear sense of the actual qualities: "beclouded," "sunk," "deviant," and "exhausted." "Beclouded," "sunk," "deviant," and "exhausted" describe matters of degree and depth, not the four schools of thought. If one is beclouded in some way in one's studies, then one will deny what is correct; and so, Mengzi talks about "prejudiced words." If one is beclouded and does not free oneself, then one cannot avoid sinking deeply into this state, and one's words necessarily will become licentious. This is why Mengzi talks about "licentious words." In the early stages of being beclouded, one's words still will be close to what is correct. In fact, though, they will be incorrect, and so after sinking deeply into such a state, one's words cannot but deviate from what they once were close to. This is why Mengzi talks about "depraved words." Once one deviates [from what is correct, one will become exhausted. If exhausted, then in speaking one necessarily will twist and turn, flee and evade. This is why Mengzi talks about "evasive words." And so, if beclouded and unable to free oneself, one cannot avoid sinking into this state. If one continues to sink, one cannot avoid deviating [from what is correct]. Deviating inevitably leads to exhaustion. If one is exhausted and unable to return to what is correct, then there is no longer any cure that can save one.

When Mengzi refuted the followers of Yangzi and Mozi, he simply talked in general terms about putting an end to "depraved talk," fighting against "prejudiced behavior," and banishing "licentious words."[247] At first, he did not differentiate between Yang and Mo in regard to which

---

246 Mengzi pairs each of the former with the latter. And so, from *prejudiced* words, he can tell in what ways someone is *beclouded*; from *licentious* words, he can tell how the speaker has fallen or *sunk*; from *depraved* words, he can tell how someone has *deviated* from the Dao; and from *evasive* words, he can know that the speaker has *exhausted* his or her ability to respond.

247 See, for example, *Mengzi* 3B9.

was prejudiced, which licentious, and which depraved. This is why in the *Analects* we have the six teachings and six forms of beclouding.[248] If we were to discuss the ways in which later scholars are beclouded, how could we have only six! And so, it is important to understand the various ways in which one can be beclouded. The topic can be summed up completely with the one word "beclouding," but Xunzi wrote the "Freedom from Beclouding" chapter in order to provide a thorough analysis of the meaning of the term.[249] If one looks at the *Analects* discussion of the six teachings and six forms of beclouding and Xunzi's "Freedom from Beclouding" chapter, then one can see how the word is used to distinguish between the various philosophers and hundred schools.

The whitest white is pure white. Though one washes it in the mightiest of rivers and dries and bleaches it in the autumn sun, one cannot make it any more purely white. The same is true when discussing Kongzi's Dao. There is no way it can be defiled or confounded by esoteric insights or trumped-up fictions.

---

248   *Analects* 17.8. Lu's point is that these are not tied to any particular thinkers or schools.

249   See "Freedom from Beclouding" ("Jiebi 解蔽"), the twenty-first chapter of the *Xunzi*.

SHORT MEDITATIONS[250]

Assorted Explanations[251]

[. . .] The four cardinal directions, together with up and down, are called "space." The past to the present is called "time." The universe [i.e., space and time] is my heart-mind; my heart-mind is the universe.[252] Tens of thousands of generations ago, sages appeared within this universe and had this same heart-mind and this same principle. Tens of thousands of generations to come, sages shall appear within this universe and will have this same heart-mind and this same principle. Anywhere within the four seas, whenever sages appear, they will have this same heart-mind and this same principle. [But] the idea of agreeing with one's superior, which we see in contemporary times, is terribly wrong.[253] Of course, whenever one finds principle, how can one fail to agree? The ancient sages and worthies shared the same Dao, and their aspirations harmonized with one another. They "all possessed pure Virtue"; and so, as a matter of course, they worked together.[254] Given this, we know that whenever there is disagreement, it is because one has not been able to explore and understand fully the requisite principle. Even a sage as great as Kongzi said things like, "Hui is no help to me!" "Shang is the one who opens things up for me!"

---

250   Presented here are four short meditations Lu wrote on important lines or passages from the classics or on specific themes or topics.

251   This is one of several meditations Lu wrote on a variety of different topics and themes.

252   The compound "space and time" means "the universe." Many of these lines can be found in a passage from Lu's *Chronological Biography*. See the entry for 1152, when Lu was thirteen years old. See also the discussion in the Introduction to this volume.

253   Mozi originally advocated this idea, but Lu is referring to those in his own age who uncritically agree with their superiors. His view is that one cannot but agree with what is correct and cannot but disagree with whatever is incorrect.

254   See the sixth section of the "Books of Shang" chapter of the *Book of History*. For a translation, see Legge, *The Shoo King*, p. 215.

and "I never grow tired of study."[255] Shun said, "When I err, it is your duty to correct me."[256] He said of [Emperor] Yao, "To forsake one's own opinion and follow others . . . only [Emperor] Yao was capable of such things."[257] And so, we see that one cannot always say, "Oh yes!" Sometimes, one must say, "Oh no!" Truly, cultivated people cannot [always agree with their superiors], but that does not threaten their status as cultivated people. Truly, petty people, though capable of always agreeing, forever remain petty people.[258]

The universe's affairs are one's own affairs. One's own affairs are the universe's affairs.

The human heart-mind is the acme of intelligence. This principle is the acme of illumination. All human beings possess this heart-mind. Every heart-mind possesses this principle [. . . .]

Reflect and You Shall Get Things Right[259]

Righteousness and principle are in the heart-minds of human beings. As a matter of fact, these are what Heaven has endowed us with, and they can never be effaced or eliminated [from our heart-minds].[260] If one becomes obsessed with [desires for] things and reaches the point where one violates principles and transgresses righteousness, usually this is simply because one fails to reflect upon these things [i.e., the

---

255   See *Analects* 11.4, 3.8, and 7.2. In the second quotation, Lu substitutes *qi* 啟 for *qi* 起, which does not change the meaning. The third quotation is a rough paraphrase of Kongzi's original remark.

256   See the "Yi and Ji" section of the "Books of Yu" chapter of the *Book of History*. For a translation, see Legge, *The Shoo King*, p. 81.

257   See the "Counsels of the Great Yu" section of the "Books of Yu" chapter of the *Book of History*. For a translation, see Legge, *The Shoo King*, pp. 53–54.

258   Here and throughout this selection, Lu almost certainly has in mind *Analects* 13.23, where Kongzi says, "Cultivated people harmonize but do not [always] agree. Petty people [always] agree but do not harmonize." This offers a stark contrast to the Mohist idea mentioned earlier.

259   This is a meditation on *Mengzi* 6A15, to which Lu alludes throughout the selection.

260   Compare "Explaining the *Analects*" in the "Expository Essays" section here and the poem "Written at Goose Lake to Rhyme with My Brother's Verse" in the "Poetry" section.

righteousness and principle that lie within one]. If one truly is able to turn back and reflect upon these things, then what is right and wrong and what one should cleave to and what one should subtly reject will begin to stir, separate, become clear, and leave one resolute and without doubts.

Seek and You Shall Get It[261]

Pure knowing lies within human beings;[262] although some people become mired in dissolution, pure knowing still remains undiminished and enduring [within them]. Such [dissolution] is what leads the most foolish and undistinguished people to cut themselves off from contact with the benevolent and cultivated and in extreme cases to "throw themselves away" and fail to seek after it.[263] Truly, if they can turn back and seek after it, then, without needing to make a concerted effort, what is right and wrong, what is fine and foul, will become exceedingly clear, and they will decide for themselves what to like and dislike, what to pursue and what to abandon. They will turn away from the things that the foolish and undistinguished do and turn toward the affairs of the benevolent and cultivated "like a mighty river overflowing its banks and flooding forth to the sea. Who could stand in their way?"[264] This requires nothing more [than to turn back and seek within]; what one seeks is within oneself; there has never been anyone who sought for it but failed to get it. "Seek and you shall get it"—this is Mengzi's teaching.

---

261 This is a meditation on lines that Mengzi quotes in *Mengzi* 6A6 and 7A3: "Seek and you shall get it; neglect it and you shall lose it." What is to be sought and gotten is the heart-mind.

262 Pure knowing (*liangzhi* 良知) is a term of art, taken from the *Mengzi* (see *Mengzi* 7A15). It refers to an innate, fully formed, and perfect moral faculty, an unerring sense of right and wrong, which when sincerely followed comes with sufficient motivation to propel one to action. This is a critical term in Wang Yangming's philosophy as well.

263 "Throwing oneself away" is an expression from the *Mengzi* (see *Mengzi* 4A11). The "it" they fail to seek is the heart-mind, which is the source of pure knowing.

264 *Mengzi* 7A16. In the original, the quotation was used to describe Emperor Shun.

A Village of Benevolence is Beautiful and Fine[265]

To work at it on one's own is not as good as to work at it in the company of others.[266] To work at it with a small group [of companions] is not as good as working at it in a large group. This is an unchanging principle. Benevolence is the human heart-mind. "Does the practice of benevolence depend upon others or upon oneself?"[267] "As soon as I desire benevolence, benevolence has been attained."[268] Now, benevolence certainly is something that one must strive for oneself. Nevertheless, my isolated [practice of] benevolence is not as good as advancing toward benevolence together with others. To advance toward benevolence together with one or two other people is not as good as advancing toward benevolence in a large group. If one advances toward benevolence in a large group, I know that the rich influences and inspiration that one enjoys and the benefits of opportunities to refine, sharpen, and polish oneself that one is afforded are wholly unlike [and superior to] what is available to those who work at benevolence on their own. And so, a single person's benevolence is not as beautiful and fine as the benevolence of a family; the benevolence of a family is not as beautiful and fine as the benevolence of all that family's neighborhood; the benevolence of all that family's neighborhood is not as beautiful and fine as the benevolence of their entire village. "A village of benevolence is beautiful and fine"—this is Kongzi's teaching. How could he have been talking about [what is best for] a single individual?[269]

---

265 This is a reflection on *Analects* 4.1. The line that begins this passage, which Lu takes as the title of his meditation, looks like a common saying. It is attributed to Kongzi in *Mengzi* 2A7. Lu reads the line in a distinctive way; see the following.

266 The "it" referred to here is benevolence.

267 *Analects* 12.1.

268 *Analects* 7.30.

269 The idea is that Kongzi's theme and focus in this passage is how good it is for a whole village to be benevolent, not what an individual needs to do in order to become benevolent. Some commentators advocate the latter reading. For example, Cheng Hao takes the character *li* 里, which Lu reads as "village," to mean "to dwell in" or "to reside." As a result, he interprets the first line as, "To dwell in benevolence is beautiful and fine." See the *Outer Works of the Cheng [Brothers] from Henan* (*Henan Chengshi waishu* 河南 程氏外書), chap. 6.

POETRY

Written in Youth[270]

I have always been brave and broad-minded.
Tigers and leopards by the millions, dragons by the thousands;
I gathered them up, one by one, and swallowed them down in a single gulp!
Sometimes, this unruly herd would not remain quiet;
So, I would roar and chew them up, leaving no trace behind.
In the early morning, I drink up the waters of Bohai;[271]
As evening approaches, I lodge on the peak of Kunlun.[272]
The mountain ranges are my lute;
The long rivers serve as their strings.
Music lost for ten thousand years;
Shall I perform for you? [273]

---

270   This poem was written when Lu was sixteen years old. It not only expresses his
immense self-confidence but also points toward a number of his later philosophical
views.

271   The large bay enclosed by the Shandong peninsula on the east coast of China.

272   A famous mountain range in Tibet. In the course of the poem, Lu travels from
one of the China's farthest points on the eastern coast to one of the highest in the distant
west. Here, we see hints of his later teachings that the universe is identical with his
heart-mind.

273   Lu offers to play the glorious songs of the past, which have been lost to later
ages. In this, we see the idea that the properly attuned mind resonates with and can
reproduce any truth.

Hearing the Orioles

A hundred beaks sing forth spring, without a moment's pause,
But long I doubted that spring had really sprung.
Awakened by yellow orioles chirping in the green trees,
I begin to laugh at my earlier attempts to listen.[274]

Traveling to Arrow Brook in Late Spring
(Two Verses)

(Number One)

Gentle clouds drift across the slanting rays of the sun;
In the quiet of spring, the door of my cottage is only half closed.
Wind comes over the top of the walls, where red apricots are late in
　blooming;
High branches quiver as flowers fly about.

(Number Two)

At a secluded spot along the winding brook, the pure sand is warm;
Green trees intertwine over fine, fragrant grasses.
I do not depart because I have fully savored this place,
But in the bright moonlight, I must bundle up [to stay warm].[275]

---

274   This poem manifests Lu's beliefs in the power and importance of natural intuition and the ability of self-conscious thought to block spontaneous understanding. Spring was unfolding all around him, but he realized this only when he stopped making a concerted effort to *hear* it and was "awakened" by the chirping of the orioles. Compare the selections of poetry by Wang Yangming in this volume, especially the third poem of "Four Verses on Pure Knowing Written for My Students."

275   These two short verses manifest Lu's vivid awareness of every feature of his environment; sight, smell, hearing—every sense—seems to be operating with preternatural sensitivity and precision, putting him in immediate and intimate contact with the universe.

Cicadas

Wind blows and dew forms inside a dried-up body;
The notes "do" and "re" are on the tips of two wings.
Calling out strongly among the evening forest's trees;
They whistle clearly in the flourishing autumn grove.[276]

Presented to a Buddhist Master

Studying Buddhism, living among the mountain groves;
In manner and deportment, you often look like some stout rustic.
[But] when a true follower of the Way happens along;
What proper and refined etiquette you display!
Solemn and serious in discharging your responsibilities;
Your words and comments flow forth freely.
How did you become so accomplished?
Who could say you lack the talents of a high official?[277]

On a Far-off Mountain Road

The village is quiet, the frog's croaking eerie;
From the fragrant forest, a bird calls out a warning.
The mountains are encircled with a myriad of dazzling flowers;
The green, ripe heads of wheat wave in the fields.
Thinking of leaving, I yearn to linger on;
Thinking of returning, my heart is heavy as a mountain.
Having neglected the sorrow of the famine,
I am led to deep reflection.

---

276   This poem focuses on the faculty of hearing and evokes a sense of the cicada's shrill song penetrating and extending to every fiber of Lu's being.

277   As do some of the earlier selections, this poem celebrates the greater authenticity and integrity of the rustic or natural over the refined and artificial. The fact that the central figure of the poem is an eminent monk shows that, like Wang, Lu recognized the achievements and worth of Buddhist practitioners. While adamantly committed to Confucianism, Lu, like the main character of this poem, moved comfortably between these two spiritual perspectives.

Written at Goose Lake to Rhyme with My Brother's Verse[278]

Old graves inspire grief, ancestral temples reverence.
This is the human heart-mind, never effaced throughout the ages.[279]
Water flowing from a brook accumulates into a vast sea;[280]
Fist-sized stones form into the towering peaks of Mount Tai and Hua.[281]
Easy and simple spiritual practice, in the end, proves great and long
   lasting.[282]
Fragmented and disconnected endeavors leave one drifting and
   bobbing aimlessly.[283]
You want to know how to rise from the lower to the higher realms?[284]
First you must—this very moment—distinguish true from false!

---

278   This poem was written when Lu was thirty-six years old to rhyme with a poem
his elder brother had composed. The place of composition was Goose Lake Temple in
Yanshan 鉛山 Prefecture, Jiangxi Province. The occasion was the famous meeting Lu
and his brother had with Zhu Xi. For an account of this event and the relationship
between Lu and Zhu, see Ching, *The Religious Thought of Chu Hsi*, pp. 132–51.

279   Compare "Explaining the *Analects*" in the "Expository Essays" section of this
volume and "Reflect and You Shall Get Things Right" in the "Short Meditations"
section.

280   Compare this and the following line to *Doctrine of the Mean* 26.9.

281   Mount Tai (Taishan 泰山) is located in Shandong Province and Mount Hua
(Huashan 華山) is located in Shenxi Province. Along with Mount Heng (Hengshan 衡
山) in Hunan Province, Mount Heng (Hengshan 恆山) in Hebei Province, and Mount
Song (Songshan 嵩山) in Henan Province, these are the Five Sacred Mountains, repre-
senting the east, west, south, north, and center of China, respectively.

282   This line paraphrases (parts of) the first section of the *Great Appendix*.

283   "Fragmented and disconnected endeavors" alludes to the approach of scholars
such as Zhu Xi who advocated a more gradual method of self-cultivation in which one
studies discrete lessons and builds up a comprehensive and synthetic grasp of the Dao.
This criticism is a major theme in Wang Yangming's teachings.

284   Compare *Analects* 14.35 where Kongzi says, "I study what is below to comprehend what is above."

Written at Wise Illumination Temple

One spring day, I again come to Mount Wise Illumination;
I still have not composed the poem I promised you years ago.
Please check carefully the list of those who have written for you,
Is there anyone as incorrigible as I?[285]

---

285   This selection celebrates a love of nature and the free exchange and mutual
enrichment between Confucianism and Buddhism. The name of the temple suggests
Chan Buddhism; "wise illumination" evokes the ideal of *prajñā* (insight) into the true
nature of reality.

PART THREE

Wang Yangming 王陽明
(1472–1529)

Introduction to Wang Yangming

Wang Shouren 王守仁 (1472–1529), whose courtesy name is Bo'an 伯安 and style Yangming 陽明, was born into a successful and distinguished family in the city of Yue 越 in present-day Zhejiang Province.[1] His father, Wang Hua 王華, was the top graduate (or *optimus; zhuangyuan* 狀元) of his examination cohort in 1481 and enjoyed a successful career as a civil official, rising to the rank of minister of personnel in Nanjing in 1507. Shouren passed the highest civil service exam, obtaining the presented scholar degree in 1499, and went on to lead one of the most extensive, varied, and distinguished careers of any major Chinese philosopher.

After a quite normal and unspectacular beginning as a minor official, Shouren's life took a traumatic and eventful turn in 1506, when he stepped forward to defend fellow officials who had been thrown into prison for opposing the powerful eunuch Liu Jin 劉瑾 (d. 1510). Unfortunately, instead of securing justice for his colleagues, Wang brought calamity upon himself, suffering the humiliating, painful, and life-threatening punishment of publicly being caned forty blows at court. As part of his punishment, he was assigned or, more accurately, banished to an isolated, minor post in the undeveloped hinterland of what is now Guizhou Province, where he was to spend more than two years. Out of

---

1   For more detailed accounts of Wang's life along with translations of his works, see Carsun Chang, *The Development of Neo-Confucian Thought,* vol. 2 (New York: Bookman Associates, 1962), Frederick Goodrich Henke, trans., *The Philosophy of Wang Yang-ming,* reprint (New York: Paragon Book Reprint Corp., 1964), Wing-tsit Chan, trans., *Instructions for Practical Living and Other Neo-Confucian Writings by Wang Yang-ming* (New York: Columbia University Press, 1963), Tu Wei-ming, *Neo-Confucian Thought in Action: Wang Yang-ming's Youth (1472–1509)* (Berkeley: University of California Press, 1976), and Julia Ching, *To Acquire Wisdom: The Way of Wang Yang-ming* (New York: Columbia University Press, 1976).

these ashes, which easily would have meant ruin if not death for most men, Wang rose to remarkable heights. He offered exceptional service as a magistrate in Jiangxi Province and then in a series of posts in both Beijing and Nanjing. As an administrator, Wang significantly improved the economy and security of the areas under his jurisdiction and worked to build schools and encourage education. He originated novel systems of civil defense and pioneered new methods for rehabilitating former criminals, especially those who had taken to banditry and rebellion. Like Lu Jiuyuan before him, Wang had an administrative style that tended to ignore conventional wisdom and looked for practical results. He was very much a hands-on administrator who inspired his subordinates through the power of his personal example. Wang showed exceptional ability as a military commander as well, leading a number of bandit-suppression campaigns and turning back the rebellion of Prince Ning in 1519. This success brought acclaim and with it the criticism of less accomplished but highly ambitious officials, which led him to withdraw into semi-retirement in his native Yue from 1521 to 1527. He was called back to active service again to suppress bandits in 1527 and died while returning from this campaign in 1529. As had Lu, Wang faced death with profound equanimity; his last words purportedly were, "This heart-mind is luminous and bright. What more is there to say?"[2]

Lu and Wang displayed similarities in life as well as at the moment of death: both men were charismatic and influential teachers. Many of the most talented young men of Wang's time became his students. A number of them accompanied him into exile early in his career, and later in life he enjoyed a large and dedicated following.[3] In addition to accounts that directly describe Wang's concern for and obvious delight in the company of his disciples, the records we have of conversations between Wang and his students offer a vivid sense of the affection and concern

---

2   See the entry for the eleventh month of *sui* 57 in Wang's *Chronological Biography*.

3   See *Essential Instructions for Students at Longchang,* included in this volume, for a lucid and concise expression of Wang's goals as a teacher. This text was written during his banishment to Guizhou. See also the letter included here titled "For My Students in Chen Zhou." Wang began to attract disciples as early as 1505. We are told that his lectures in Yue always drew an audience "in excess of several hundred people" and that those who went to study with him "filled up every available house and temple." For a description, see Wing-tsit Chan, *Instructions for Practical Living,* pp. 245–46.

he had for them and the deep impression and profound influence he had upon them.[4] As noted in our discussion of Lu, the role Wang played as a teacher is an important aspect of his philosophy and is reflected in the very genre through which he and Lu communicated their teachings.[5] Both men, but especially Wang, would have found the modern idea that "those who can, do; those who can't, teach" utterly confused and unacceptable. Such a view requires a separation of *knowing* and *acting*, which, as we shall see later, Wang found pernicious as well as implausible, particularly in the case of moral knowledge. In Wang's view, a *really* good person not only necessarily will be motivated to carry out moral action, her care for others will lead her to want to be an effective teacher and to work at developing herself in ways that enable her to convey and move others to the Way. This is surely the path both Lu and Wang traveled, and their lead inspired many disciples to follow them and in time become influential teachers in their own right.[6]

Aspects of Wang's life as well as his philosophy remained subjects of heated controversy immediately after his death, even leading to the revocation of his hereditary honors and privileges. However, by 1567, these fires had burned themselves out and a more fair and accurate assessment of his contributions and worth emerged. Wang then was granted the title "Earl of Xinjian" (Xinjianbo 新建伯) and awarded the posthumous name "Completion of Culture" (Wencheng 文成). Further honors soon followed. In 1584, the imperial court decreed that Wang's memorial

---

4   In addition to the records of conversations, examples such as "Xu Ai's Preface" to *A Record for Practice,* included among our selections here, offer splendid and powerful insights into the interaction between Wang and his disciples.

5   Wang was more self-conscious and explicit about the mode in which his teachings were conveyed than Lu, insisting that it was wrong even to record his conversations with disciples as this tears them out of their required contexts. For a description of this idea and how it could work upon Wang's students, see "Xu Ai's Preface" to *A Record for Practice,* included in this volume.

6   The idea that becoming an effective teacher is part of the goal of self-cultivation is inseparable from the neo-Confucian conception of sagehood. An ethically worthy person might or might not become an influential teacher, but it is part of the very idea of being a sage that one would effectively lead others to the Way. The neo-Confucian view also explains why neo-Confucian scholars placed such emphasis on arts such as calligraphy, painting, and composition. All such pursuits not only helped to develop a more humane sensibility, they also served as vehicles to express the Way and move others to it.

tablet be installed in the official Confucian temple and that sacrifices be offered to him. He is one of only four scholars in the entire Ming dynasty (1368–1644) to receive this high and most distinguished honor.

As we saw is the case with Lu Jiuyuan, Wang's biography contains stories from his youth that purportedly presage his later accomplishments. At the moment of his birth, his grandmother had a dream in which a divine man dressed in purple robes adorned with pearls appeared from out of the clouds and, accompanied by the sounds of drums and flutes, delivered Shouren to her.[7] Taking this as an auspicious sign, his grandfather named him Cloud (Yun 雲). Despite this promising start, the young Shouren did not begin to speak until the age of six,[8] which caused considerable consternation among his family members. But after his name was changed to Shouren, the young Wang showed remarkable abilities for poetry. One example of his talent and skill, a poem he wrote when only ten years old, is included in the present collection.[9] In the same year he composed this poem, we are told that when reading the works of Cheng Hao, Wang came across the lines, "When I practice calligraphy, I maintain an attitude of profound reverential attention— not in order to produce beautiful characters; it is simply a form of study." Wang is said to have commented, "If he didn't want to produce beautiful characters, what was he studying?"[10]

Both Lu and Wang shared a fascination with and focus on military skills and affairs; in Wang's case, this proved to be an important aspect of his life and professional success.[11] Yet another important similarity was their relationship with Zhu Xi. Of course, Wang lived in a later age and unlike Lu had no direct contact with Zhu; however, Wang struggled to work out a relationship with Zhu's legacy throughout his life. Wang's inability to live according to what he took to be the implications of Zhu's

---

7   See the entry for the ninth month in Wang's *Chronological Biography*.

8   See the entry for *sui* 5 in Wang's *Chronological Biography*.

9   See the "Poetry" section in this part.

10   See the entry for *sui* 17 in Wang's *Chronological Biography*. The quotation from Cheng Hao can be found in the *Extant Works of the Cheng [Brothers] from Henan* (*Henan Chengshi yishu* 河南程氏遺書), chap. 3.

11   For a discussion of Wang's military career, see Chang Yü-ch'üan, "Wang Shou-jen as a Statesman," *Chinese Social and Political Science Review* 23:1 (April–June 1939): 473–517.

philosophical views led him to formulate an alternative interpretation of
the Way and to take issue with a number of Zhu's claims. Toward the
end of his life, Wang wrote a controversial work called *Master Zhu's
Definitive Views Arrived at Late in Life* (*Zhuzi wannian dinglun* 朱子晚
年定論), in which he argued that in the final stages of his life Zhu actually endorsed views quite similar to Wang's. While some have interpreted
this simply as a crass attempt to avoid criticism arising from his opposition to Zhu, Wang does point out genuine points of agreement between
his views and those of Zhu.[12] Such an attempt at reconciliation might
well express Wang's desire to find agreement with and perhaps even
imagined favor in the eyes of a thinker he clearly admired and sought to
understand throughout his life.

   Because of Wang's and Lu's historical and intellectual relationship,
my presentation of Wang's philosophy will build upon our earlier discussion of Lu's views. Both Lu and Wang believed that the heart-mind is
principle, and that all human beings share a common fundamental,
or original, heart-mind (*benxin* 本心). All human beings are endowed
with a complete and perfect set of the principles that underlie, inform,
and give meaning to all the objects and events in the phenomenal
world.[13] This is why the traditional association of the views of these two
philosophers as cofounders of the Learning of the Heart-mind is both
warranted and helpful. Wang developed this common idea in his own
distinctive way, regarding this innate moral sense as a faculty, which, as
noted in our discussion of the *Platform Sutra,* he often likened to vision;
drawing upon a term from the *Mengzi,* he called it "pure knowing"
(*liangzhi* 良知).

---

12   There are significant differences between Zhu and Wang, but on a range of core
issues in ethics and metaphysics, there is more similarity between them than much of
the contemporary secondary literature suggests. David W. Tien makes this point, in a
clear and compelling way, in his unpublished essay "Three Common Misconceptions in
Western Studies of Neo-Confucian Metaphysics."

13   In a recent essay, Steve Angle has argued that Wang does not make bold metaphysical assumptions of this kind and instead is much more of a pragmatist about knowledge
in general and moral knowledge in particular. See "Sagely Ease and Moral Perception,"
Dao: A Journal of Comparative Philosophy 5:1 (Winter 2005): 31–56. The majority of
scholars who have specialized on Wang and who have offered comprehensive interpretations of his thought agree very closely with the view that I describe here. For example,
see the works by Chang, Henke, Chan, Tu, and Ching cited in note 1 on p. 101.

Pure knowing can guide us to unerring ethical conduct, but we need to liberate and protect it from the impediments that interfere with its smooth and natural operation. Such impediments include the various grades of impure *qi* 氣 that compose the phenomenal world and lead us to see ourselves as radically separated or alienated from other people, creatures, and things. The influence of *qi* gives rise to and is compounded by our own selfish thoughts and desires (*si yu* 私欲). Selfish desires take root in and consolidate the less-than-pure material aspects of the self—those parts of the self that lead us to see ourselves as separate and isolated from the world—further agitating these impure elements, generating more turbid *qi,* and further obscuring the innate principles of the heart-mind. These aspects of Wang's philosophy can be found in nascent form in the thought of Lu Jiuyuan and are shared in one form or another by all neo-Confucian thinkers, but Wang offered much more detailed and developed ideas than others, especially on the role that "selfish desires" play in the process of separating us from an original unity with the world and the importance of regaining this sense of connection and solidarity.

Once the heart-mind has become beclouded, one will fail to detect and pay attention to the promptings of pure knowing. Instead of seeing the fundamental connection between oneself and the people, creatures, and things of the world, one will view things through a warped and dis-colored lens that distorts and darkens one's perception and presents the world as a largely hostile, objective order that one must control and use for one's own advantage. The only way back to a true sense of the nature of both self and world is by engaging and bringing into play one's pure knowing. Wang referred to this process as the extension of pure knowing (*zhi liang zhi* 致良知).

While both Wang and Zhu drew upon the text of the *Great Learning,* their respective conceptions of how one was to carry out the task of *extending knowledge* offers an encapsulation of some of the central differences between them. Following the text more literally, Zhu taught that one had to extend knowledge (*zhi zhi* 致知) in the sense of enlarging, expanding, or augmenting one's pool of knowledge. The idea is that one must build out, by gaining greater experience and engaging in inference, from those principles one already grasps, to master and incorporate new principles. While Zhu shared Wang's belief that human beings are born with a complete and perfect endowment of principles, unlike Wang he held that the heart-mind *contained* principles, much as a dictionary contains words. All people have access to *some* subset of all the principles of the world much as all people know some of the words in the dictionary, but on Zhu's model we cannot recollect or appreciate many of the words that are stored within our heart-minds without being reminded of their meanings and being guided by lessons we take in from outside. For Zhu, learning consists of augmenting the stock of principles (words) one actively knows and working out their connections to things and events in the world in order to understand the principles (words) one has yet to master, until one's command of the "book of knowledge" is complete. Complete knowledge for Zhu entailed a grasp not only of the discrete phenomena of the world but also their interrelationships within an overarching and sensible universal scheme: the Way. He describes the process of investigating things (*gewu* 格物) and extending knowledge as culminating in a kind of enlightenment.[14]

> Once one has exerted oneself for a long period of time, there will come a day when one attains a comprehensive and unified grasp of the phenomena of the world. Then, one's understanding will reach to the inner as well as the outer, the fine as well as the coarse aspects of all things, and the complete body (*ti* 體) and great function (*yong* 用) of one's heart-mind will be perfectly bright.[15]

In contrast to Zhu, Wang insisted that the heart-mind is principle—the conscious, active, and knowing mode of principle—and that learning occurs only and whenever one properly applies one's heart-mind to the "things" of the world. Wang's teaching of the extension of pure knowing insists that the process of learning is a bringing into play, an unfolding, or an application of knowledge one already possesses. In order to see more clearly how this is supposed to work, we must understand Wang's distinctive interpretation of another phrase from the *Great Learning*:

---

14   For a discussion of *gewu* and the contrast between Zhu's and Wang's interpretations of this important term, see p. 108.

15   This is a portion of Zhu's commentary on the fifth chapter of the *Great Learning*. The notion of "investigating things" is explored later. Compare our earlier discussion of the paired concepts body (*ti* 體) and function (*yong* 用).

gewu 格物—mentioned earlier in our discussion of Zhu's views—and in particular his understanding of what constitutes "things" (*wu* 物).

In keeping with the idea that learning involves the "extension of knowledge," understood as a process of exploration and inference, Zhu interpreted the classical expression *gewu* as the investigation (*ge* 格) of things (*wu* 物), and his interpretation has become so influential that it largely determines the way *gewu* is understood in the contemporary world.[16] Wang, though, resisted such influence; he read the first character, *ge,* as "to rectify," and the second as "heart-mind"; he mustered good classical precedents to support this reading.[17] Thus, in contrast to Zhu's view, according to which we look beyond or *outside* the principles we already grasp to discover and bring under our control new principles we infer or see in the world, Wang urges us to be watchful over our thoughts about and responses to the various phenomena we encounter. We must rectify our thoughts (*gewu*) and in doing so extend pure knowing.

Aside from appealing to classical sources, Wang advanced philosophical arguments for these initially startling interpretations of *gewu* and *zhi zhi.* He began by insisting that things do not exist in any meaningful sense for us until they are perceived by the heart-mind. Objects, events, or ideas only become "things" for us in the act of perception. As we saw in Lu's case, this aspect of Wang's thought has led some people to conclude, hastily and incorrectly, that Wang denied the existence of a mind-independent world. There is *some* similarity between Wang's view and Berkeley's famous claim that to be is to perceive—or to be perceived (*esse est percipi*). But one of the first things one must bring to and keep in mind when seeking to understand Lu's or Wang's views on this issue is that unlike Berkeley they were not seeking to refute various forms of materialism. They were not trying to show that material things did not exist or even that there were things in the world other than material

---

16   For example, modern Chinese dictionaries almost all *define* the term *gewu* by invoking Zhu's *gloss.* The authority of Zhu's interpretation largely has determined how this term gets translated into English, making it more difficult to convey Wang's and other thinkers' very different and distinctive understandings of this classical phrase.

17   For a more complete discussion of some of these issues, see my *Ethics in the Confucian Tradition: The Thought of Mengzi and Wang Yangming,* rev. 2d ed. (Indianapolis: Hackett, 2002), pp. 97–99 and elsewhere. Compare Lu's "Second Letter (to Zhu Xi)" in Part Two of this volume and especially note 123 there.

things. When seen in the context of Wang's overall philosophy, his questions about where "things" are when they are not entertained by the mind take on a very different meaning. Instead of presenting a form of panpsychism, such teachings rightly are seen as efforts to bring people back to the importance of engaging with and reflecting upon the *actual phenomena* they encounter in their day-to-day lives. Rather than assaulting the ontological status of material things, such passages call us to pay attention to how we understand and respond to the various phenomena of the world. For example:

> The master was strolling in the mountains of Nan Zhen 南鎮[18] when a friend pointed to the flowering trees on a nearby cliff and said, "If in all the world, there are no principles outside the heart-mind, what do you say about these flowering trees, which blossom and drop their flowers on their own, deep in the mountains? What have they to do with my heart-mind?"

> The master said, "Before you looked at these flowers, they along with your heart-mind had reverted to a state of stillness. When you came and looked upon these flowers, their colors became clear. This shows these flowers are not outside your heart-mind."[19]

Wang's point here concerns what we would call the nature of secondary qualities, though his primary interests are moral epistemology and the proper way to engage in self-cultivation.[20] He insists that seeking

---

18   This refers to Guiji 會稽 Mountain, located in the southeast of Shaoxing 紹興 District in present-day Zhejiang Province.

19   The quotation (my translation) is from a portion of *A Record for Practice* not included in this volume. Compare Wing-tsit Chan, *Instructions for Practical Living*, p. 222. Frederick Goodrich Henke appends the following note to his translation of this passage: "This would appear to imply that when the mind stops thinking about them [the flowers] they *ipso facto* are no more" (*The Philosophy of Wang Yang-ming*, p. 169, n. 24). This inference strikes me as unwarranted and incorrect.

20   There is genuine similarity, which is evident from the passage quoted above, between Wang's view and the account of moral qualities defended by John McDowell in essays such as "Values and Secondary Qualities," "Projection and Truth in Ethics," and other works collected in his *Mind, Value, and Reality* (Cambridge, MA: Harvard University Press, 1998).

principles by "investigating" or exploring the objects and events of the world, or "inferring" or speculating about imaginary or abstract entities, or studying other people's problems and approaches, only takes us farther and farther from what we most need: a direct and vital sense of our own pure knowing. We gain this only by becoming aware of and attentive to our own responses to the actual phenomena we encounter in the course of each day's activity. We need to deal with the "things" in our own lives. This, though, does not mean we simply turn and gaze inward; Wang explicitly rejects such an approach.

> The principles of things are not outside one's heart-mind. If one looks outside the heart-mind and seeks the principles of things, one will find no principles. [On the other hand], to abandon the principles of things and seek one's heart-mind—what would one [hope to] find?[21]

Confucians often discuss ethics in terms of musical or culinary analogies, and I would like to continue this tradition by offering some illustrations of what I take to be Wang's view. Consider the case of a sad or foreboding piece of music. If we want to understand this piece, how should we proceed? Should we study the music itself in the sense of exploring and analyzing the score? Is this where we hope to find the quality of sadness or foreboding? Clearly, this is not how to proceed. The music *itself*—the score or even a given performance—is neither sad nor foreboding. What about the people *playing* or *listening* to the music; can we find sadness or foreboding *in them?* Perhaps, but if this were the case, it might well be a contingent fact about these performers or listeners; in any event, what we would find is *their* sadness or foreboding, not the sadness or foreboding of the music. Wang would insist that in order to understand the quality that makes a piece of music sad or foreboding, we need to pay attention to our *response to* the music. More precisely, we need to pay attention to how a representative and unbiased listener would respond—someone not already sad or anxious or in any other way affected in a manner that would prejudice her response. This, of course,

---

21   The quotation (my translation) is from a portion of *A Record for Practice* not included in the present volume. Compare Wing-tsit Chan, *Instructions for Practical Living*, p. 94.

in no way denies the importance, much less the reality of the music. We cannot perceive or understand the sadness or foreboding of a composition simply by turning inward. We must listen to an actual performance, but our attention and awareness needs to be focused upon the responses of our heart-minds. When we come to understand our responses to such music, we understand not just something about the music but also something about ourselves and about the human heart-mind.

Culinary pursuits offer a variety of equally helpful examples. Consider what it is like to learn or teach someone what makes *crème brûlée* so delicious. Will it help to study or encourage the study of the chemical composition of *crème brûlée,* recipes for this dish, pictures of it, or menus that list it? Will it help to watch other people savor *crème brûlée* or read reviews about who makes the best *crème brûlée?*[22] None of these pursuits will bring us any closer to understanding and appreciating the wonderful taste of *crème brûlée.*[23] Wang's point is that in a certain respect all knowledge is like this. When we understand anything, *we* must grasp the point. In the case of ethical knowledge, where affective, volitional, and dispositional issues play a role in determining how well one understands and appreciates a point, Wang's claim and overall perspective make a good deal of sense.

This emphasis upon the role the heart-mind plays in understanding might lead one to think that Wang is not wholly unlike Kant in that both advocate a Copernican turn in regard to the mind. But the similarity here does not run deep; their views are profoundly different in a number of respects concerning the nature of the mind and its relationship to the world. Kant insists that we do not know things in themselves

---

22   In making a similar point, the Qing dynasty Confucian Zhang Xuecheng 章學誠 (1738–1801) asked whether we can teach someone about the delicious flavor of a roast we are eating by spitting some of it up into his mouth. See his essay "The Principles of Literature" ("Wenli 文理"). For a translation, see my *The Essays and Letters of Zhang Xuecheng.* For a discussion, see David S. Nivison, *The Life and Thought of Chang Hsüeh-ch'eng (1738–1801)* (Stanford, CA: Stanford University Press, 1966), pp. 111–15.

23   One could make a case that reading careful accounts by connoisseurs about their own experience of eating *crème brûlée* can help us savor it. Wang makes *some* allowance in this regard but insists, rightly, that no account can take the place of experience. The right thing to say is that such accounts can supplement and enhance reflective experience.

(*Ding an sich*), only how they are taken in and apprehended by the mind. The mind processes reality and makes it intelligible. Wang would only agree that the heart-mind is what allows the world to be known. But while Kant believed the mind contributes the categories, which orient and inform our perception and thought, Wang believed the heart-mind is itself the principle that structures, orders, and gives meaning to the phenomena of the world. What makes the principles of the heart-mind unique is their capacity to be consciously entertained; indeed, Wang sometimes describes the heart-mind as the conscious, knowing aspect or mode of principle.

Many of the quite subtle and often slippery aspects of Wang's philosophy that we have reviewed can be seen as culminating in his most famous and influential teaching, the unity of knowing and acting (*zhi xing he yi* 知行合一),[24] and pointing toward his ultimate ideal of regarding Heaven, earth, and the myriad creatures as one body (*tian di wan wu wei yi ti* 天地萬物為一體). Let us bring to a close this brief introduction to Wang's philosophy by exploring these two teachings and noting some of the ways in which they relate to the views we have discussed.

As we have seen, Wang believed that all human beings are endowed with a complete repertoire of "principles" that enable them to understand how things are and should be in the world. The heart-mind of human beings is principle in its knowing, conscious mode, and by bringing the principles of the heart-mind into play we can understand the world around us as well as our proper place within it. Such a view solves a number of vexing philosophical problems; for example, Wang had a coherent account of how it is we could ever *come to see* that something is true. Every act of understanding is the unimpeded operation of a faculty of sapience: "pure knowing." It is the unfolding of knowledge we already possess, a matching up or tallying of the principles of the heart-mind with some phenomenon in the world. Such a view is similar to our own notions about how the right view of theory "fits" the phenomena it purports to explain and our sense that understanding is a kind of "seeing," which we experience when "things become clear."

---

24   Since Wang often describes knowledge and action in terms of the *activities* of knowing and acting, I translate his doctrine as "the unity of knowing and acting" rather than the more common "unity of knowledge and action." For a discussion, see my *Ethics in the Confucian Tradition*, pp. 78–80 and elsewhere.

As noted earlier, however, human beings are embodied creatures, and the various types of *qi* that constitute our physical forms interfere with the principles of our heart-minds and lead us to mistakenly see ourselves as separate and cut off from the myriad principles that inform, structure, and give meaning to the rest of the world. This inclines us to be overly self-centered, which generates selfish desires; these mislead us into acting badly, thereby reinforcing and intensifying our sense of isolation and alienation. In order to overcome these pernicious tendencies, we must learn to "rectify our heart-minds" by "extending pure knowing" as we interact with and act in the world each day. Rather than thinking about ethics, we are to think ethically about everything we do. Wang thought that even hardened criminals could hear and heed the guidance of pure knowing; the challenge was to pay attention and to cultivate a vigilant awareness of the promptings of one's own heart-mind. "Even robbers and thieves know that they should not steal. When they steal, they still feel shame within them."[25]

Once we begin to cultivate the required awareness and attentiveness, our pure knowing will start to inform and guide us. Like sun shining on thin ice, pure knowing has the power to melt away and loosen the grip of selfish desires and light our path toward the Way. This process will move us from what Wang called "ordinary knowledge" (*chang zhi* 常知) to "real knowledge" (*zhen zhi* 真知).[26] Roughly speaking, we will move from *knowing about* ethics to ethical *knowledge*. The latter is substantially con-stituted by a strong disposition to attend and respond affectively to ethical situations and act properly and without hesitation. This is the crux of Wang's teaching of the "unity of knowing and acting."[27] There is no *real* moral knowledge that does not lead one to act; one cannot *really* possess moral knowledge if one has not properly engaged in moral activity.

---

25   The quotation (my translation) is from a portion of *A Record for Practice* not in this volume. Compare Wing-tsit Chan, *Instructions for Practical Living*, p. 194.

26   For a discussion of this distinction and Wang's general approach to ethics, see my *Ethics in the Confucian Tradition*, pp. 78–80 and elsewhere.

27   For a more detailed account of this teaching, see my *Ethics in the Confucian Tradi-tion*, pp. 98–100 and elsewhere. For a splendid study of the history of the relationship between knowledge and action, see David S. Nivison, "The Problem of 'Knowledge' and 'Action' in Chinese Thought Since Wang Yangming," in Arthur F. Wright, ed., *Studies in Chinese Thought* (Chicago: University of Chicago Press, 1967), pp. 112–45.

Wang deployed his teaching about the unity of knowing and acting to make a variety of different points, and this wide and varied use of a doctrine to effect moral improvement in students is another clear example of the point made earlier concerning the emphasis on therapy over theory. Wang's ultimate goal—one might say his ideal of spiritual health—was overcoming the sense of isolation and alienation, which is the shadow of a self-centered view of one's relationship to the world. The unity of knowing and acting played a subtle but vital role in effecting a cure for the malady of an excessive concern for the self. The more readily and regularly one's actions flowed spontaneously out of pure knowing, the less distance and separation one felt between the self and the world. The operation of pure knowing leads to hooking oneself up with world; one responds to it in a seamless process of perception, weighing, judging, willing, and acting. In the course of this process, one comes to see that the principles of one's heart-mind are the principles that one encounters everywhere in the world. One comes to realize the truth of what Lu said: "The universe is my heart-mind. My heart-mind is the universe."

Wang, though, expressed Lu's earlier idea in his own distinctive fashion, proclaiming that we should "regard Heaven, earth, and the myriad creatures as our own bodies."[28] Here again, it is easy to misconstrue what Wang is saying. He is not claiming that we are physically coextensive with all the things of the world (an odd thing for an "idealist" of any stripe to claim). Rather, he is invoking the notion that there is a deep and undeniable connection between each of us and every aspect of reality. We are "one" in the sense of sharing a common stock of principles, which link us and lead us to care, in varying ways and degrees, about the world. It is not that the world would not *exist* without the human heart-mind, but rather that it would not be what it is without the shared interaction between it and human beings.

> The pure knowing of human beings is the pure knowing of grass, wood, tiles, and stones. If grass, wood, tiles, and stones lacked the pure knowing of human beings, they could not be what they are. How could it be that this is

---

28   Wang presents this idea in its most developed form in his *Questions on the Great Learning,* which is included in this volume. For a discussion of this teaching, see my *Ethics in the Confucian Tradition,* pp. 27–30 and elsewhere.

true only of grass, wood, tiles, and stones? If Heaven and earth lacked the pure knowing of human beings, they could not be what they are. Heaven, earth and the myriad creatures have always been of one body with human beings.[29]

For Wang, the teaching that we are one body with the myriad creatures was not just true but of ultimate significance; realizing this state defined and constituted the goal of his spiritual practice. Those who *really* understand, who themselves *embody* this fact about the world, will feel and act accordingly. Knowing and acting will form a unity and lead them to care in the right ways, to the right degree, and for the right reasons for everything in the universe.

---

29   The quotation (my translation) is from a portion of *A Record for Practice* not included in the present volume. Compare Wing-tsit Chan, *Instructions for Practical Living*, p. 194.

LETTERS

For My Students in Chen Zhou[30]

During my two years in exile, I had no one with whom I could talk. Upon my return, I have enjoyed the company of all you friends—how fortunate! How fortunate indeed! But just as I experience this happiness, I find I suddenly must leave you—this is most dissatisfying and distressing!

There are many who forsake the path of learning and few who seek the Way. If someone from the state of Qi is surrounded by people from Chu, it is easy for him to be overcome and overwhelmed. With the exception of those who possess heroic resolve, few can remain steadfast and unchanged [under such circumstances].[31] You friends should burnish and polish one another, supporting one another in your shared aspiration to perfect yourselves.

In the present age, there are a few insightful officials who to some degree understand about seeking the Way, but before they have perfected any real virtue, they show off their abilities and incur the criticism of the vulgar people of the world. As a result, they often stumble and fall, failing to establish themselves, and even become obstacles to the practice of the Way. You, my friends, should take them as a warning, as a cautionary tale. Cut off the desire for reputation and glory and apply real effort [to] working on your inner selves.

---

30 This letter was written sometime in 1510. Chen Zhou 辰州 was located in what is now Yuan Ling 沅陵 County in present-day Hunan Province.

31 Wang's point is that in the present age, when so few people provide support and encouragement to follow the Way, it is particularly difficult for students to remain committed. Wang alludes to *Mengzi* 3B6, which describes a great official of the state of Chu who wanted to teach his son the language of Qi. Mengzi notes that the officer first must get a man of Qi to teach his son, but that the lessons will not take if the son is regularly surrounded by people who speak the language of Chu.

What I said in the temple earlier about quiet sitting should not be taken to imply sitting in meditation in order to enter *samādhi*.[32] Since many in our age are fully absorbed in and distracted by the things and affairs of daily life and do not work on themselves,[33] my intention is to use this practice [of quiet sitting] as a way to supplement what is said in the *Elements of Learning* about gathering in the wayward heart-mind.[34] Cheng Mingdao said, "As one enters upon the course of learning, one must know where to apply one's efforts. Once one is engaged in learning, one must understand where one has gained strength."[35] You, my friends, should apply yourselves in this way. Once you have made some progress, at a later time, you will gain strength.

"Learning requires that you drive yourself on with a whip to advance toward your inner self."[36] "The Way of the gentleman is hidden but each day becomes more manifest."[37] "While effort directed at gaining a name

---

32   Wang is warning his disciples not to mistake his endorsement of quiet sitting (*jingzuo* 靜坐) for the Chan Buddhist practice of seated meditation (*zuochan* 坐禪), the aim of which is to enter into and maintain a state of meditative stability or calm (*ding* 定, or *samādhi*). Neo-Confucians also advocated cultivating a state of *ding,* but distinguished it from the Buddhist ideal. (See the reference to Cheng Mingdao's "Letter on Calming One's Nature" ("Dingxingshu 定性書") in Wang's "Letter to Liu Yuandao," included here) Compare the passages about *samādhi* in the selections from the *Platform Sutra* that appear in this volume. For a revealing study of the neo-Confucian practice of quiet sitting, see Rodney L. Taylor, *The Confucian Way of Contemplation: Okada Takehiko and the Tradition of Quiet Sitting* (Columbia: University of South Carolina Press, 1988).

33   Compare *Analects* 14.23: "In ancient times, students worked for themselves; today, students work for others." The idea is that one should work to improve oneself, not to impress and curry favor with others.

34   Some say that the *Elements of Learning* (*Xiaoxue* 小學) was edited by Zhu Xi, but it is the work of his disciple Liu Zicheng 劉子澄, who compiled the text under Zhu's guidance. The "Splendid Sayings" ("Jiayan 嘉言") chapter of this work talks about "gathering in the wayward heart-mind." The latter expression is taken from *Mengzi* 6A11 and refers to those who lose sight of their innate moral sense.

35   See the *Extant Works of the Cheng [Brothers] from Henan*, chap. 12. The quotation is also recorded in *A Record for Reflection*, chap. 2. Compare Wing-tsit Chan, trans., *Reflections on Things at Hand* (New York: Columbia University Press, 1967), p. 59.

36   This is another saying from Cheng Hao; see the *Extant Works of the Cheng [Brothers] from Henan*, chap. 11. It is also recorded in *A Record for Reflection*, chap. 2; see Chan, *Reflections on Things at Hand*, p. 58.

37   *Doctrine of the Mean* 33.1.

differs in purity from effort directed at gaining profit, they equally are expressions of acquisitiveness."[38] "Humility brings benefit."[39] "Do not seek to distinguish yourself from others; seek to accord with principle."[40] These various lines should be written on the wall so that our eyes regularly rest upon them.

"Preparing for the official examinations need not threaten the effort to learn, though it may pose a threat to the nature of one's commitment."[41] If you regularly and methodically apply yourselves to vows you made earlier, the two tasks will not interfere with each other. When one understands how to sprinkle water upon the ground and sweep the floor and how to respond to inquiries and answer questions,[42] the most refined meaning and significance will have entered one's spirit.[43]

Reply to Huang Zongxian and Ying Yuanzheng[44]

I feel that last night I talked too much, but on the occasion of meeting you two gentlemen, I could not but talk too much! Since I am not very advanced in the course of my learning, some of what I said was highly unpolished. Nevertheless, it concerned part of the real spiritual effort

38   This saying is attributed to Cheng Yi. See *A Record for Reflection,* chap. 2; see Chan, *Reflections on Things at Hand,* p. 67.

39   The "counsels of the Great Yü" chapter of the *Book of History;* see James Legge, trans., *The Shoo King,* vol. 3 of *The Chinese Classics,* reprint (Hong Kong: University of Hong Kong Press, 1970), p. 65.

40   *Mengzi* 6A7.

41   Quoting Cheng Yi. See the *Outer Works of the Cheng [Brothers] from Henan,* chap. 11. See also *A Record for Reflection,* chap. 7; Chan, *Reflections on Things at Hand,* p. 199.

42   The reference is to *Analects* 19.12, where the disciple Zixia argues that the gentleman sees value in every aspect of learning, even mundane and elementary practices such as sprinkling water on the ground (to keep the dust down) and sweeping the floor. Compare *Recorded Sayings of the Two Cheng [Brothers]* (Er Cheng yulu 二程語錄), chap. 9.

43   The reference is to the fifth section of the second part of the *Great Appendix.*

44   Huang Zongxian 黃宗賢 (1477–1551), whose personal name was Wan 綰, was originally a friend of Wang who became a disciple upon hearing Wang's teachings regarding the extension of pure knowing. Through the marriage of his daughter to Wang's son, Huang became a relative as well. Ying Yuanzheng's 應原忠 personal name was Liang 良. This letter was written sometime in 1511.

(*gongfu* 功夫) that we share in common. If at first what I said does not make sense to you, please do not dismiss it lightly, for you surely will see pieces that suddenly fall into place.

The heart-mind of a sage does not contain even the slightest obscuration, and so there is no need to eliminate or polish away anything. But the heart-mind of the ordinary person is like a dirty and stained mirror.[45] One needs to make a concerted effort at cutting away and polishing in order to completely eliminate the various defilements covering it. After such an effort, even the smallest speck of dust will easily be seen [upon the mirror's surface], and brushing it off will require little effort. At such a stage, one already has realized the true nature of benevolence. Even before defilements are eliminated, there naturally will be small spots of clarity [on the mirror's surface]. If dust or dirt falls upon such places, they certainly will be seen and easily can be brushed away. But when defilements are piled upon such dirt and dust, there comes a point when they no longer can be seen. Here lies the difference between those who "know through study and practice for the advantage it brings" and those who "struggle to understand and practice through strenuous effort."[46]

I hope that you will not doubt what I say simply because these ideas are so difficult and challenging. Human beings are disposed to delight in ease and dislike difficulty; many also labor under layers of obscuration because of selfish thoughts and accumulated [bad] habits. However, once one sees through these impediments, naturally the task will no longer seem difficult. Among the ancients, some risked their lives ten thousand times and were happy to do so in order to attain this realization. Earlier, we did not grasp the idea that we had to direct our attention inward, and so naturally we had no way of talking about this kind of spiritual effort. Now that we have reached this stage of understanding, we must be on guard not to allow our delight in ease and dislike of difficulty to lead us to slide into Chan Buddhism. Eighty to ninety percent of what we discussed yesterday, concerning the differences between Confucianism

---

45 Wang's use of the "mind as a mirror" metaphor draws heavily upon what we find in the *Platform Sutra*. Compare the selections from that text in this volume.

46 The quotations are paraphrases from *Doctrine of the Mean* 20.9. The idea is that those who make an initial effort to clean their spiritual mirror—a metaphor for the heart-mind—have an easier time than those who let defilements pile up.

and Buddhism, was explained by Cheng Mingdao when he said that Buddhists exert "reverential attention to straighten out the inner life" but lack "righteousness to rectify the exterior life," and so in the end they fail in their efforts to use "reverential attention to straighten out the inner life."[47]

To My Younger Brothers[48]

I have received a number of your letters and all of them show that you are aware of and contrite about your shortcomings and possess an abundance of enthusiasm. This gives me boundless delight and comfort! And yet, I do not know whether your words express sincere feelings or are said simply to provide a nice impression.

The brightness of our original heart-mind (*benxin* 本心) is as brilliant as the noonday sun.[49] There are none who have done wrong who fail to know that they are wrong; the only problem is that they are unable to correct themselves. The moment there is a single thought to correct [oneself], the original heart-mind is attained.

Who is without fault? "The important thing is to correct [ourselves]."[50] Ju Boyu was a great worthy, and yet he said he "wished to correct his faults but had been unable to do so."[51] King Tang and Kongzi were great sages and yet the former said, "I willingly correct my faults," while the latter said, "I wish to be without major faults."[52] People all say, "If one is not a Yao or a Shun, how can one be without faults?" Even though this is a saying that has been handed down through time, it does not help us understand the heart-mind of Yao or Shun. Had Yao or Shun

---

47   For the quotation, see *the Extant Works of the Cheng [Brothers] from Henan*, chap. 4. These lines can also be found in *A Record for Reflection*, chap. 2; see Chan, *Reflections on Things at Hand*, p. 281.

48   This letter was written sometime in 1518. Wang had three younger brothers: Shoujian 守儉, Shouwen 守文, and Shouzhang 守章.

49   Wang uses the term *benxin* less frequently than did Lu, though he had other ways of referring to the original and perfect moral mind. For Lu's views, see the selections of his work in this volume.

50   See *Analects* 9.23. Compare Lu's "Explaining the *Analects*" in this volume.

51   See *Analects* 14.26.

52   For the first quotation, see "The Announcement of Zhonghui" section of the *Book of History* in Legge, *The Shoo King*, p. 180; for the second quotation, see *Analects* 7.16.

thought or felt that they were completely free of faults, they would have lacked the very thing needed to be a sage. The maxim that they shared between them was, "The human heart-mind is precarious. The heart-mind of the Way is subtle. Be ever refined and single-minded in order to hold fast to the mean!"[53] Since they thought that the human heart-mind was precarious, this shows their heart-minds were the same as other human beings'. To be "precarious" is to be [prone to commit] faults. Only because they remained "cautious and apprehensive"[54] and worked to be "refined" and "single-minded" were they able to "hold fast to the mean" and avoid faults.

The sages and worthies of ancient times always saw their own faults and corrected them. This is how they were able to be without faults. It was not that their heart-minds really were different from other human beings'. To be "careful about what is not yet seen and apprehensive about what is not yet heard" is the spiritual effort (*gongfu* 功夫) of always being able to see one's own faults.[55] Recently, I have seen places in my own life where I need to exert this kind of effort, but because the bad habits I picked up every day have accumulated to the point where they are now deep-seated flaws, I lack the courage to rectify these faults. And so, I am eager to inform you early on, my younger brothers, about this. Do not be like me and allow bad habits to accumulate to the point where they become deep-seated and are difficult to rectify.

When young, people have the energy and spirit to rally to a cause and the obligations of family life do not yet weigh upon their heart-minds. Therefore, it is very easy for them to apply themselves. As they mature, their worldly obligations grow more onerous and their energy and spirit gradually diminish with each passing day. Nevertheless, if they earnestly make an effort and commit themselves to learning, they still can achieve something of note. When they reach the age of forty or fifty years old, they are like the sun setting behind the hills; they gradually fade and are extinguished, and nothing can bring them back. This is why Kongzi said, "If

---

53   See the "Counsels of the Great Yu" section of the *Book of History* in Legge, *The Shoo King*, pp. 61–62.

54   The quotation is from the "Counsels of Gao Yao" section of the *Book of History* in Legge, *The Shoo King*, p. 73.

55   See *Doctrine of the Mean* 1.2–3.

someone reaches the age of forty or fifty years old and you have not heard of him, then there is no need to hold him in awe."[56] He also said, "When one reaches old age and one's physical powers begin to decline, one should guard against acquisitiveness."[57] I recently have observed this infirmity in my own life. And so, I am eager to inform you early on, my younger brothers, about this. Take advantage of this time in your lives to exert yourselves! Do not let this time pass and leave you with only regrets.

Letter to Liu Yuandao[58]

In your last letter you said, "[I] want to enter into sitting meditation on some desolate mountain in order to cut myself off from the affairs of the world, shield myself from thoughts and feelings, and cultivate my spiritual awareness. I must examine myself until I can maintain a comprehensive understanding, day and night, without cease; then, I can respond to the world [untainted] by emotions." You also said, "I want to pursue this goal through stillness, as it seems to be the shortest and most direct route, but I cannot slide into an empty lassitude." These aspirations suffice to show your remarkable commitment to the Way and your uncommon resolve.[59] The other things you said in your letter reveal that you are a person of insight. This is wonderful, wonderful indeed!

Now, the way that good doctors cure an illness is to match the treatment to the ailment, taking into consideration the various symptoms and, whenever appropriate, adjusting or augmenting the treatment.[60] The sole aim is to eliminate the disease. They do not start out with a fixed prescription, which without asking about the particular symptoms they apply to every patient. Why should a gentleman's learning differ in any way from this? Yuandao, you can assess the severity of your own

---

56   See *Analects* 9.22. The thought is that one need not accord this type of older person the high regard one normally would have toward an elder, not, as some translations imply, that one not *respect* them as persons.

57   See *Analects* 16.7.

58   Liu Yuandao's 劉元道 personal name was Junliang 君亮. For more about him, see Chan, *Instructions for Practical Living*, p. 214. This letter was written sometime in 1523.

59   Compare *Analects* 8.7.

60   This parable of the good doctor is picked up by Xu Ai in his preface to the *A Record for Practice*, a translation of which is contained in this volume.

illness, ascertain your own symptoms, and in light of these determine your own treatment. In this way, you will avoid harming yourself. I fear that your single-minded desire to cut yourself off from the affairs of the world, shield yourself from thoughts and feelings, and incline to an amorphous stillness already has led you to develop a nature of empty lassitude. Even though you desire to avoid sliding into empty lassitude, this is something you cannot avoid.

At the end of the day, though there is no fixed prescription for curing illness, the principle of getting rid of the illness does constitute a fixed approach. If you only understand the idea of applying medicine according to the disease and do not understand that the application of certain medicines can itself *cause* disease, your loss will be equally grave. When you have time, you should familiarize yourself with Cheng Mingdao's "Letter on Calming One's Nature."[61] When you do, your views will change.

I am sorry that I have not gone into greater detail on the topic of illness and just dashed this singularly poor response off in a hurry.

Reply to Inquiries Made by a Friend[62]

[In your letter,] you asked, "Up until now, former scholars all took 'study, inquiry, reflection, and discrimination' as pertaining to knowing while 'sincere practice' pertained to acting.[63] They clearly distinguished between these two things [i.e., knowing and acting]. Now, though, you alone say that knowing and acting form a unity (*zhi xing he yi* 知行合一). I cannot but have doubts about this."

My answer is as follows: "I have spoken about this on many occasions. Everything that is referred to as 'acting' is simply the actual performance of some affair. If one actually engages in the effort of study, inquiry, reflection, and discrimination, then study, inquiry, reflection, and discrimination are examples of acting. Study is studying some affair; inquiry is inquiring about some affair; reflection and discrimination are reflecting

---

61   For a complete translation of this letter, see Wing-tsit Chan, trans., *A Source Book in Chinese Philosophy*, reprint (Princeton, NJ: Princeton University Press, 1973), pp. 525–26.

62   The friend is not identified by Wang. This letter was written sometime in 1526.

63   See *Doctrine of the Mean* 20.19.

upon and discriminating in regard to some affair. And so, acting is studying, inquiring, reflecting, and discriminating. If you say that you first
study, inquire, reflect, and discriminate about some affair and afterward
you go on to act, how do you carry out this initial study, inquiry, reflection, and discrimination while suspended in a vacuum? When it is time
to act, how can you carry out study, inquiry, reflection, and discrimination? The intelligent, conscious, refined, and discerning aspects of acting
are knowing. The authentic, direct, sincere, and substantial aspects of
knowing are acting. If in acting, one is incapable of being refined, discerning, intelligent, and conscious, then one acts wantonly. This illustrates why 'study without reflection is waste';[64] one must then go on to
talk about the need for knowing. If in knowing, one is incapable of being
authentic, direct, sincere, and substantial, then one's thinking is reckless.
This illustrates why 'reflection without study is perilous'; one must then
go on to talk about the need for acting. From the beginning, there has
only been a single task.[65] Whenever the ancients talked about knowing
and acting, it was always with the aim of correcting or explaining some
problem in regard to this single task; they never split off and separated
them into two different affairs, as people do today. My theory that
knowing and acting form a unity, on the one hand, is simply a theory
aimed at correcting and explaining a contemporary problem; on the
other hand, this is how knowing and acting are and always have been in
both essence and structure. My friend, you simply must experience this
for yourself in reference to some actual affair, and in that moment you
will grasp the truth. Now, instead, you only look for understanding from
the meaning of words, and so you are pulled this way and that, wandering in every direction, and the more you talk, the more confused you
become. This is precisely a failure resulting from an inability to maintain
the unity of knowing and acting."

You also said, "Lu Xiangshan's discussions of learning share both many
similarities and many differences with those of Zhu Xi. You have said,
'Xiangshan saw directly and clearly where to begin one's learning.' But

---

64   For this and the following quotation, see *Analects* 2.15.

65   The word translated here and in the following as "task" is *gongfu* 功夫, which
connotes a spiritual effort or task. In other contexts, I have rendered it "spiritual effort"
or "spiritual task."

when I look at Xiangshan's writings, I find he says that learning consists of clear explanation and concrete practice and that the extension of knowledge (*zhi zhi* 致知) and the investigation of things (*gewu* 格物) pertain to clear explanation.[66] Given this, I see no difference between Xiangshan's views and Zhu Xi's, but, on the contrary, see dissimilarity between his views and your theory about the unity of knowing and acting."

My answer is as follows: "In regard to learning, the gentleman pays no mind to similarities or differences but only to what is correct. The similarities between my views and those of Lu Xiangshan are not the result of a lack of independence on my part or a desire to agree with him. The places where we disagree, I do not try to cover up. The differences between my views and those of Zhu Xi are not the result of a desire on my part to differ with him. The fact that we agree about some points takes nothing away from our agreement. Suppose Bo Yi, Liuxia Hui, Kongzi, and Mengzi were to gather together in some hall; just because their views would in some respects be partial and in others complete and their deliberations, discussions, and opinions would not in every respect be alike would not take anything away from the fact that they all are equally sages and worthies.[67] When scholars in later ages discuss learning, they always agree with whatever their faction advocates and attack whatever is different; this is the result of their selfish dispositions and frivolous feelings. In behaving like this, they treat the work of sages and worthies as if it were some child's game.

You also asked, "The theory of the unity of knowing and acting is the most commanding feature of your view about learning. Since in this respect you differ from Lu Xiangshan, may I please ask in what respects your views are alike?"

My answer is as follows: " 'Knowing' and 'acting' in fact are two words referring to a single spiritual task. This spiritual task requires both words in order to be explained perfectly and completely, without omission or

---

66   These are steps in the process of learning described in the second and third sections of the old text of the *Great Learning*; see James Legge, trans., *Li Chi: Book of Rites*, reprint (New York: University Books, 1967), vol. 2, pp. 411–12. The interpretation of these and related teachings constituted a rich and lively debate among neo-Confucians. For Wang's views, see the following and especially the selections from *A Record for Practice* translated in this volume.

67   Bo Yi and Liuxia Hui were famous worthies. See *Mengzi* 5B1.

flaw. If one sees clearly and precisely where to begin—that in fact there is only one place to begin—then even though knowing and acting are separated and explained as if they were two different things, in the end they always will be in the service of the one spiritual task. If at first the two are not well integrated and brought together, in the end, as they say, 'a hundred thoughts will come to the same conclusion.' Those who do not see clearly and precisely where to begin and in fact treat knowing and acting as two separate things, even if they take up the theory of the unity of knowing and acting, I am afraid they will never find a way to bring them together. Moreover, since they work at them as two separate things, then from start to finish they will be unable to find a place to set to work."

You also asked, "The theory of the extension of pure knowing (*zhi liangzhi* 致良知) truly is a teaching one could hold, 'waiting a hundred generations for a sage to appear [and confirm it] without being misled.'[68] Since Xiangshan saw clearly and precisely where to begin, how is it that his views on this topic differ [from yours]?"

My response is as follows: "Over time, Confucians have handed down this kind of interpretation about the 'extension of knowledge' and the 'investigation of things.' Xiangshan received these teachings and did not scrutinize or doubt them in any way. As a result, these are places where his views are not wholly refined, which is something that should not be covered up."

I would add, "Knowing that is authentic, direct, sincere, and substantial is acting. Acting that is refined, discerning, intelligent, and conscious is knowing. If in moments of knowing, one's heart-mind is unable to be authentic, direct, sincere, and substantial, one's knowing will be incapable of being intelligent, conscious, refined, and discerning. But it is not that in periods of knowing one only aims at being intelligent, conscious, refined, and discerning and not authentic, direct, sincere, and substantial. If in moments of acting, one's heart-mind is unable to be intelligent, conscious, refined, and discerning, one's actions will be incapable of being authentic, direct, sincere, and substantial. But it is not that in moments of acting, one aims only at being authentic, direct, sincere, and substantial and does not want to be intelligent, conscious, refined, and discerning. The heart-mind in itself always 'knows the transforming

---

68   The quotation is from *Doctrine of the Mean* 29.3.

and nurturing operations of Heaven and earth.'[69] 'Heaven knows the great beginning,'[70] and so does the heart-mind in itself."

Reply to Wei Shiyue[71]

Shi Yi arrived and provided me with an account of your efforts at "daily renovation,"[72] and I also received your letter. Your commitment and earnestness are a source of boundless joy and comfort for me. In your letter, when you talk about those who claim that they are acting on pure knowing, but instead rely on personal feelings or thoughts (*yi* 意),[73] take these to be pure knowing, and act upon these feelings or thoughts rather than their innately endowed pure knowing—this shows that you already have recognized and explored this shortcoming. Thoughts should clearly be distinguished from pure knowing. Whenever an idea arises in response to any thing or affair, this is called a "thought."[74] Thoughts can be either correct or incorrect. That which is able to know which thoughts are correct and which incorrect is called pure knowing (*liangzhi* 良知). If one relies upon pure knowing, then one will never act incorrectly.

---

69   See *Doctrine of the Mean* 33.1.

70   See the first section of the first part of the *Great Appendix*.

71   Wei Shiyue 魏師說 (1492–1575) was a native of Xinjian 新建 County in what is now the southwest portion of Chongren 崇仁 County in Jiangxi Province. His personal name was Liangbi 良弼. This letter was written sometime in 1527.

72   Shi Yi 師伊 is the courtesy name of Wei Liangzhi 魏良致, the younger brother of Wei Shiyue. The expression "daily renovation" is taken from the *Great Learning* and refers to the regular effort needed to succeed in self-cultivation. It is from the tenth section of the old text of the *Great Learning*; see Legge, *Li Chi*, vol. 2, p. 415. It can also be found in the second section of the commentary in Zhu Xi's revision; see James Legge, trans., *Confucian Analects, the Great Learning, and the Doctrine of the Mean*, vol. 1 of *The Chinese Classics*, reprint (Hong Kong: University of Hong Kong Press, 1970), p. 361.

73   The word "thought" is a term of art for Wang. As is clear further on, it refers to one's response to some thing or event—real or imagined—and can be either in accord with pure knowing and hence correct or aligned with personal preference and hence selfish. See the discussion on this and related terms in the selections from *A Record for Practice* included in this volume.

74   I have rendered the single word *wu* 物 as "thing or affair" when literally it should just be "thing." But for Wang, the word *wu* has this much broader meaning. See the discussion of the term *gewu* 格物 in the selections from *A Record for Practice* included in this volume.

Your doubts in regard to being in the grip of a desire for fame or swayed by circumstances etc. all concern cases in which the intention to extend pure knowing is not yet wholly sincere and perfect. If it were wholly sincere and perfect, there naturally would be no such problems. Those who find it difficult to begin a task or who suffer from being negligent or compromising do so because their intention to extend pure knowing is not yet sincere and perfect and their perception of pure knowing is not yet penetrating and complete. If their perception of pure knowing were penetrating and complete, then in their encounters with fame or circumstances there would be nothing but the marvelous operation of pure knowing. Since apart from fame or circumstances there is no pure knowing, how could one possibly be constricted by fame or swayed by circumstances?[75] This can occur only if one is moved by selfish thoughts and fails to accord with the original state of pure knowing.

Those who share our aims in the present age, although they all know that pure knowing operates everywhere, as soon as they enter the realm of social relationships and interactions, they immediately separate human feelings and the principles of things from pure knowing and regard them as two separate affairs. This is something that one absolutely must examine.

To Huang Zongxian[76]

Engaging in the spiritual task [of self-cultivation] is ten times more difficult when one holds an official position than when one retires to the mountains and forest glens. If someone in office is without good friends to admonish and correct him on a regular basis, his normal, everyday aspirations only rarely can avoid silently shifting and secretly being carried off; as his determination weakens, it deteriorates and dissipates

---

75   Pure knowing only operates *in response to* actual things and affairs such as the fame and circumstances described by Wei. It responds to such things as a mirror "reflects" the objects that come before it, "illuminating" the ethical features of these things and events. Once these pass, there is nothing left behind. Compare the description of how the enlightened mind responds to the things and affairs of the world and avoids attachment in the selections from *Platform Sutra* in this volume.

76   For Huang Zongxian, see the second letter in this section ("Reply to Huang Zongxian and Ying Yuanzheng"). This letter was written sometime in 1527.

with each passing day. Recently, I said to Huang Chengfu[77] that since neither of you have many friends in Beijing, the two of you should agree between yourselves that whenever one sees the other unsettled in any way, he will uphold the need to extend pure knowing; in this way, you can keep each other on course and in line.

Only the most courageous people can resolve to remain silent just as their speech waxes most eloquent, can tightly collect and restrain themselves as their passions are on the brink of bursting forth, or can quietly dissipate their anger and desire just as these are about to boil over. Nevertheless, when one has a direct and intimate understanding of pure knowing, such tasks naturally are not difficult. If we look for the source of these various shortcomings [i.e., in regard to speech, passion, and anger and desire], it does not lie in the original state of pure knowing; they only arise when pure knowing has become obscured and blocked up. When pure knowing arises, it is like the sun shining forth; all ghosts and demons dissolve and disappear [in its light]. When the *Doctrine of the Mean* says, "A sense of shame is close to courage,"[78] the "sense of shame" referred to is simply the shame one feels when one is unable to extend one's pure knowing. Many people today feel ashamed when they are unable to force others to accept what they say, when they are unable to overwhelm others with their passions, or when they are unable to give full reign to their anger and desires. They do not understand that these various shortcomings all are things that obscure and block up their pure knowing and are precisely the kind of thing about which a gentleman should be most ashamed. And so, contrary to what is right, people today take it as shameful that they are unable to obscure and block up their pure knowing. This is precisely to be ashamed of something that is not shameful and to have no shame about what is truly shameful.[79] Is this not lamentable indeed?[80]

You two gentlemen are my intimate friends, and nothing is more important to me than helping you in some way. My wish is that you

---

77   Huang Chengfu 黃誠甫 died in 1536. His personal name was Zongming 宗明.

78   See *Doctrine of the Mean* 20.10.

79   Compare *Mengzi* 7A6–7.

80   This is a close paraphrase of a line from *Zhuangzi*, chap. 2.

both become like the so-called great ministers of ancient times. Those in ancient times who were known as great ministers were renowned, not because of their intelligence and resourcefulness, but only because they were "plain and sincere, lacking other abilities, mild and straightforward, with a generous spirit."[81] In terms of intelligence and resourcefulness, you gentlemen are exceptional and far surpass the vast majority of people. The only reason you lack confidence in yourselves is because you are not yet able to extend your pure knowing and have not yet attained the state of being "plain and sincere, mild and straightforward."

The present state of the world may be compared to a person suffering numerous grave maladies. The only real hope of bringing the dead back to life in this case lies with you gentlemen. But how can you treat the ills of the world before curing yourselves? In the depths of my heart, I have an idea that I feel compelled to share with you in every detail. Whenever the two of you meet, I hope you secretly will invoke this thought to help keep each other on course and in line. You must conquer and expel every vestige of selfishness, really become one with Heaven, earth, and the myriad creatures, truly "pacify and save"[82] the world, and return it to the ideal state of rule that existed during the Three Dynasties.[83] Then, you will prove yourselves worthy of our sagely and enlightened emperor, repay the favor he has shown you, and by contributing to this great enterprise not waste your time on earth.

I lie here on my sickbed among the mountains and forest glens and can only prepare medicines and drugs in an effort to prolong my life. But I am in profound sympathy with you gentlemen out there [serving as officials], and so, before realizing what was happening, I find that I have gone into such extensive detail. I hope you will make allowances for my excessive show of emotion.

---

81   See the "Declaration of the Duke of Qin" section of the *Book of History* in Legge, *The Shoo King*, p. 629. This passage is quoted in the thirtieth section of the old text of the *Great Learning*; Legge, *Li Chi*, vol. 2, p. 421. Compare Lu's appeal to the same passage in his "(Eighth) Letter to Wu Zisi," which is presented in this volume.

82   See "The Charge to Zhong of Cai" section of the *Book of History* in Legge, *The Shoo King*, p. 491.

83   The golden age of the Xia, Shang, and Zhou dynasties.

A RECORD FOR PRACTICE
(CHUANXILU)

Xu Ai's Preface[84]

Among the disciples was one who, on his own, had written down Master Wang's teachings. Hearing of this, the Master said, "Sages and worthies teach in the same way that physicians prescribe medicine.[85] They always match the treatment to the ailment, taking into consideration the various symptoms and, whenever appropriate, adjusting the dosage. Their sole aim is to eliminate the ailment. They have no predetermined course of action. Were they indiscriminately to stick to a single course [of treatment], rarely would they avoid killing their patients. Now, with you gentlemen, I do nothing more than diagnose and polish away each of your particular prejudices or obsessions. As soon as you manage to make these changes, my words become nothing but useless tumors. If, subsequently, you preserve my words and regard them as dogma, you will one day mislead yourselves and others. Could I ever atone for such an offense?"

Since I had carefully written down some of the Master's teachings, one of my fellow students remonstrated with me. I then said to him, "In taking your position, you are indiscriminately sticking to a single course and have lost the Master's meaning. Kongzi once said to Zigong, 'I prefer not talking.'[86] Yet on another day, he said, 'I have talked with Yan Hui all day long.'[87] Now, why

---

84 This preface is the first to appear in the *Complete Works of Wang Yangming* (*Wang Wenchenggong quanshu* 王文成公全書) edition and is referred to as the "Old Preface." The translation here is based upon my earlier work for *Ethics in the Confucian Tradition*, pp. 143–44. Additional annotation and discussion can be found there.

85 Compare the earlier example of this metaphor in "Letter to Liu Yuandao," appearing in this volume.

86 Quoting *Analects* 17.17.

87 Quoting *Analects* 2.9.

wasn't he consistent in what he said? Since Zigong sought sageliness only in words, Kongzi used 'not talking' as a warning to him, to help him feel for it with his heart-mind and seek a personal attainment. Yan Hui listened in silence to what Kongzi said, and in his heart-mind he understood.[88] In him, there was nothing lacking. Therefore, Kongzi talked to him all day long—like a river bursting its banks and rushing to the sea. Thus, Kongzi's not talking to Zigong was not [speaking] too little, and his talking to Yan Hui all day long was not [speaking] too much. Each received what was appropriate to him."

In our present situation, writing down what the Master says, as I have done, is surely contrary to his wishes. Since we disciples continue to enjoy his company, what possible purpose could this serve? However, on some occasions we must be away from the Master's side, and at some point we all must live apart from the group. At such times, the Master's inspiring example is far away, and we are unable to receive his admonitions. If one of limited abilities, such as I, did not receive the Master's teachings and was unable, regularly, to receive his admonitions and instructions, it would be rare indeed if one were not overcome [by the task] and lost.

Regarding the Master's teachings, if we disciples only let them "enter our ears and pass out our mouths"[89] and do not ourselves personally embody these teachings, then in writing them down I have indeed committed a crime against our teacher. However, if from this record we can grasp the general idea of his teachings and sincerely realize them in concrete action, then this record is truly the heart-mind of the Master, which can *talk [to us] all day long*.[90] Can one do without any part of it? Having completed my record, I wrote this down as a preface to the first section in order to make [my intention] clear to my fellow students.

Xu Ai's Introduction[91]

Concerning "rectifying one's thoughts [in regard to things]" and all the other theories of the *Great Learning,* the Master regarded [the presentation

---

88   The reference is to *Analects* 7.2.

89   Quoting the "Encouraging Learning" chapter of the *Xunzi.*

90   See the previous quotation of *Analects* 2.9.

91   This introduction precedes the fourteen sections of the present version of *A Record for Practice,* which were recorded by Wang's disciple Xu Ai.

of these] that is found in the old version [of the text] to be correct—that is, the version that former scholars regarded as mistaken.[92] When I first heard this, I was startled and ended up in doubt. I used every ounce of my strength to reflect upon these teachings and consulted with various [fellow] disciples in order to raise questions for the Master. This led me to see that the Master's teachings are like the coolness of water or the heat of fire; surely, I can "wait a hundred generations for the coming of [a new] sage without harboring the slightest doubt."[93]

Heaven endowed the Master with intelligence and wisdom. He is congenial, happy, contented, easygoing, and does not pay attention to outward appearances. People know that as a youth he was unconstrained and unconventional and that he drifted into the practice of writing flowery compositions and in and out of the study of Buddhism and Daoism; so, when they first hear his teachings, they regard them simply as attempts to say something different or revealing a fascination with what is strange, wholly lacking in careful reflection or inquiry. People do not know that by living for three years in a barbarous region,[94] overcoming difficulties and cultivating tranquility, our Master became "[wholly] refined and [wholly] focused."[95] He surely has passed beyond [ordinary men] and entered the realm of the sages, where everything is perfectly in accord with the grand mean and what is absolutely correct.[96]

I have studied closely with the Master, day and night. When I first encountered his Way, it seemed so easy, but gazing upon it, I found it

---

92   Wang insisted on following the original text of the *Great Learning* as it appears in the thirty-ninth chapter of the *Book of Rites*. As mentioned in Part Two, note 76, Zhu Xi, extending a process begun by Cheng Yi, rearranged and augmented the original text.

93   Quoting *Doctrine of the Mean,* chap. 29; see Legge, *Confucian Analects, the Great Learning, and the Doctrine of the Mean,* p. 426.

94   This refers to Wang's banishment to Guizhou in southwestern China, roughly from 1508 to 1510.

95   The reference is to the well-known passage from the "Counsels of the Great Yu" chapter of the *Book of History,* which describes the difference between the wayward "human heart-mind" and the ideal "heart-mind of the Way"; see Legge, *The Shoo King,* pp. 61–62.

96   The grand mean (*dazhong* 大中) is mentioned in the first line statement of hexagram 15 of the *Book of Changes*. The expression "absolutely correct" (*zhizheng* 至正) is seen in several classical sources. See, for example, the "Evolution of the Rites" chapter of *Sayings from Kongzi's School.*

rose ever higher [before me]. [In the beginning,] it seemed crude, but exploring it, I found it ever more refined. On first approach, it seemed familiar and limited, but as I made progress along it, I found it offered ever more benefit and proved inexhaustible.[97] After more than ten years of study, I still have not been able to peer over the Master's outer fence.[98] And yet, among contemporary gentlemen, some, who have met the Master only once, some, who have never even heard his voice, and some, who [simply] are predisposed to being dismissive or growing indignant, advance prejudiced conclusions and groundless speculations on the basis of an idle conversation or hearsay. What kind of understanding could they possibly possess? Even the Master's followers, when they listen to his teachings, often grasp only one point in every three. They see that the horse is a stallion or mare and that it is black or palomino but fail to see that it is, as they say, "a thousand-league horse."[99] And so, I prepared a record of the teachings that I heard on a regular basis. On my own, I showed these to fellow students in order to compare and correct what I had recorded, so that I would not turn my back upon the Master's teachings.

1. I asked, "Zhu Xi says that the phrase 'loving the people' (*qin min* 親民) in the line from the *Great Learning* that reads '[Making bright one's bright virtue] lies in loving the people' should be changed to 'renovating the people' (*xin min* 新民).[100] Since a later passage in the text says 'Encourage

---

97   Xu Ai's description of Wang's teaching here echo Yan Hui's well-known remarks about Kongzi's Way in *Analects* 9.11.

98   Xu Ai is making another allusion to the *Analects* (see 9.23). The idea is that he has not even begun to see the more esoteric aspects of Wang's teachings, the true treasures, which lie deep within Wang's inner palace.

99   Literally, the text reads, "a thousand-*li* horse," with a *li* being around a third of a mile. The expression and reference is to a story that first appears in the *Huainanzi* about a man who could discern the most essential and important features of a horse— whether or not it could run for a thousand *li*—but who did not pay attention to and hence was not reliable when it came to reporting on nonessential features—such as its sex or color. See Evan Morgan, trans., *Tao: The Great Luminant,* reprint (New York: Paragon Books, 1969), pp. 118–19.

100   Zhu Xi explicitly adopts this idea from Cheng Yi. Much of the following discussion turns on the grammar and sense of the word "new" (*xin* 新), which is translated here as "renovating" (i.e., "making new").

the people to renovate themselves' (*zuo xin min* 作新民),[101] it seems as though there is good evidence for his claim. But you, Master, are of the opinion that it is proper to follow the old version of the text, which has 'loving the people.' Do you, too, have good evidence for your view?"

The Master said, "The word *xin* ['renovate'] in the expression 'Encourage the people to renovate themselves' refers to the people renovating *themselves* [i.e., not *being* renovated].[102] The word *xin* is not being used in the same way in the expression 'lies in *renovating* the people' (*zai xin min* 在新民). How can the former [use of *xin*] be regarded as evidence? The word 'encourage' (*zuo*) is parallel to the word 'loving' (*qin*), but they do not mean the same thing.[103] The passages that follow, which talk about 'ordering the state' and 'bringing peace to the world,' do not expand upon the meaning of the word *xin*.[104] When the text says things like, '[Oh! The former kings are not forgotten!] The gentleman regards as worthy what they regarded as worthy and loves what they loved; the common man enjoys what they enjoyed and benefits from what benefited them,' or '[Watch over the people] as though you were caring for an infant,' or '[The ruler] loved what the people loved and loathed what the people loathed. This is what it means to be mother and father to the people', all of these express the idea of *loving*.[105] The [sense of love] in the expression 'loving the people' (*qin min*) is like Mengzi's teaching that '[the gentleman] *loves* his parents and is benevolent toward people.'[106] To love is to be benevolent toward. It was because "the people are lacking in love" that Emperor Shun employed Xie as minister of education and

---

101   This line is from the tenth section of the old text of the *Great Learning;* see Legge, *Li Chi,* vol. 2, p. 415. It is found in the second section of the commentary in Zhu Xi's revision; Legge, *Confucian Analects, the Great Learning, and the Doctrine of the Mean,* p. 361. It is a quotation from the "Announcements to [the Prince of] Kang" chapter of the *Book of History;* see Legge, *The Shoo King,* p. 388.

102   Wang is quoting Zhu Xi's own gloss on this phrase.

103   Wang's point is that *qin* in the original text is the main verb of the clause, while *zuo* serves this function in Zhu Xi's version.

104   These lines are from the second and fourth sections of the old text of the *Great Learning;* Legge, *Li Chi,* vol. 2, p. 411–12.

105   The quotations are from the eighth, seventeenth, and twenty-fourth sections of the old text of the *Great Learning;* see Legge, *Li Chi,* vol. 2, pp. 414, 417, and 420, respectively.

106   See *Mengzi* 7A45.

had him reverently disseminate the Five Teachings.[107] This was how [Shun] loved the people. In the 'Canon of Yao,' the line that reads '[He] was able to make bright his resplendent virtue' describes 'making bright one's bright virtue.'[108] The following lines [in the 'Canon of Yao'], that talk about 'loving the nine classes of his kin,' 'pacifying and cultivating [the people of his domain],' and 'unifying and harmonizing [the myriad states]' describe 'making bright one's bright virtue throughout the world.' This idea also is seen in Kongzi's teaching that "the gentleman cultivates himself in order to bring peaceful repose to the people.'[109] 'Cultivating himself' describes 'making bright one's bright virtue,' while 'to bring peaceful repose to the people' describes loving the people.[110] Reading [the opening line in the *Great Learning* as] 'loving the people' combines the ideas of educating and nurturing [the people]. Reading it as 'renovating the people' would seem to be one-sided [and incomplete]."

2. I asked, "Concerning the line 'When one knows where to abide, there is stability,'[111] Zhu Xi thought that 'each thing and every affair has its own fixed principle.'[112] This seems to conflict with your explanation [of the text]."

---

107   The quotation and story are from the "Canon of Shun" chapter of the *Book of History;* see Legge, *The Shoo King,* p. 44. The Five Teachings concern the proper relationship between father and son, ruler and minister, husband and wife, old and young, and friend and friend. Compare *Mengzi* 3A4.

108   Here, Wang draws a parallel between this section of the *Book of History* and the opening lines of the *Great Learning,* arguing that the former testifies to the relationship between the ideas of "making bright one's bright virtue" and "*loving* the people."

109   *Analects* 14.45.

110   Wang draws a parallel between this section of the *Analects* and the opening lines of the *Great Learning,* arguing that this similarity provides additional evidence for his interpretation.

111   Quoting the first section of the old text of the *Great Learning;* see Legge, *Li Chi,* vol. 2, p. 411, which in the previous line identifies "the highest good" as "where to abide."

112   See the first section (*shang* 上) of Zhu's *Some Questions on the Great Learning* (*Daxue huowen* 大學或問) in the *Complete Works of Master Zhu* (*Zhuzi quanshu* 朱子全書; Shanghai: Shanghai guji chubanshe, 2002), vol. 6, p. 510. Zhu's view is that one first must investigate things and understand their principles; this knowledge shows one "where to abide." He illustrates the point by drawing an analogy with archery: an archer first must know what his target is; only then can he hit it.

The Master said, "To seek for the highest good in things and affairs is to treat righteousness as external.[113] The highest good is the original state of the heart-mind; it is simply what results when the effort of making bright one's bright virtue reaches the point of being 'wholly refined and wholly focused.'[114] This being so, it is never separated or found apart from things and affairs.[115] Zhu Xi got it right when in his commentary on the *Great Learning* he said that '[making bright one's bright virtue] is fully realizing Heavenly principle without the presence of even the slightest human desire.'"[116]

3. I asked, "If one seeks for the highest good only in the heart-mind, I fear that one will not fully grasp the principles of all the world's affairs."

The Master said, "The heart-mind *is* principle. Is there any affair outside the heart-mind? Is there any principle outside the heart-mind?"

I said, "For example, in the filial piety with which one serves one's parents, the loyalty with which one serves one's ruler, the trust with which one interacts with one's friends, or the benevolence with which one governs the people—in each of these [activities], there are many principles. I fear that all of them must be carefully investigated."

The Master sighed and said, "This way of explaining things has impeded understanding for a long, long time. How can I bring forth enlightenment with just a single word? Suppose, though, that I talk about it along the lines of the question you asked. For example, in serving one's parents, it will not do to go and seek the principle of filial piety in one's parents. In serving one's ruler, it will not do to go and seek the principle of loyalty in one's ruler. In one's interactions with one's friends

---

113   Wang is referring to Mengzi's criticism of Gaozi in *Mengzi* 6A4. The purported error, roughly, is to think that moral qualities inhere wholly in external objects.

114   The reference is to the "Counsels of the Great Yu" chapter of the *Book of History*. See note 95 in this part of the volume.

115   The idea is that "making bright one's bright virtue" is simply the activity of responding to things and affairs, which is the "function" of the heart-mind in its original state.

116   See Zhu's commentary on the opening line of the *Great Learning* in the *Great Learning in Sections and Sentences* (*Daxue zhangju* 大學章句) in *Collected Comments on the Four Books* (*Sishujizhu* 四書集註).

or in governing the people, it will not do to seek the principle of trust or benevolence in one's friends or in the people. All of these [principles] are only found here in 'this heart-mind.'[117] The heart-mind is principle. When this heart-mind is kept completely free of the slightest impediment from selfish desire, then it is Heavenly principle. There is no need to add anything from outside. When the pure Heavenly principle of the heart-mind is applied in serving one's parents, it is filial piety. When it is applied in serving one's lord, it is loyalty. When it is applied in interactions with one's friends or in governing the people, it is trust or benevolence, respectively. The only thing one needs to do is to exert oneself to keep this heart-mind free of human desires and preserve Heavenly principle."

I said, "Hearing you explain it in this way, I feel that I have gained some understanding, but the old explanation remains coiled up within my breast. I still can't fully cast it out. For example, in serving one's parents, one is to do things such as 'warm their bed in winter and cool it in summer, to adjust everything for their comfort, and to inquire about their health each morning.'[118] There are so many aspects and details; shouldn't these be explored and investigated?"

The Master said, "Why would one not explore and investigate [such things]? One just needs some definite way to proceed. One just needs to explore and investigate them by keeping this heart-mind free of human desires and preserving Heavenly principle. For example, when one explores and investigates providing warmth for one's parents in the winter, one simply needs to fully express the filial piety of this heart-mind; one's only fear is that some trace of human desire gets mixed in. When one explores and investigates providing cool comfort to one's parents in the summer, one simply needs to fully express the filial piety of this heart-mind; one's only fear is that some trace of human desire gets mixed in. One just needs to explore and investigate this heart-mind. If this heart-mind is completely free of human desire and is pure Heavenly principle, then one has a heart-mind that is sincere in its filial piety

---

117   Wang adopts the expression "this heart-mind" (cixin 此心) from the Mengzi and uses it here and elsewhere as a term of art. For Wang, it refers to the "original heart-mind," or the heart-mind in its pure and unadulterated state. Compare Mengzi 1A7.

118   From the "Summary of the Rites" chapter of the Book of Rites. Compare Legge, Li Chi, vol. 1, p. 67.

toward one's parents. In winter, it will naturally think about one's parents being cold and explore ways to provide them with warmth; in summer, it will naturally think about one's parents being hot and explore ways to provide them with cool comfort. These are all just the detailed expressions of a sincere, filial heart-mind. But one first must have this sincere, filial heart-mind; only then will one have these detailed expressions. If we compare [the expression of filial piety] to a tree, then the sincere, filial heart-mind corresponds to the roots and the detailed expressions are the branches and leaves. One first must have the roots; only then will one have branches and leaves. One cannot first go looking for branches and leaves and only then plant the roots. The *Book of Rites* says, 'A filial son, cherishing profound love [for his parents], will always have a harmonious air about him. One with a harmonious air about him will always have a pleasant countenance. One with a pleasant countenance will always be compliant and accommodating.'[119] One must have profound love as the root, then naturally one will be like this."

4. Zheng Zhaoshuo 鄭朝朔[120] asked, "[Aren't there] some cases in which the highest good must be sought in things and affairs?"

The Master said, "The highest good is simply this heart-mind [in the state where] the purity of Heavenly principles is fully attained. Why would one seek [for the highest good] in things and affairs? But perhaps you could offer some examples."

Zhaoshuo said, "For example, when serving one's parents, the particular way in which one should provide warmth or cooling comfort to them [as required] or the proper way in which to serve or nurture them[121]—the appropriate methods for such things must be sought and only then can one attain the highest good. This is why one must engage in 'the effort of inquiry, study, thought, and discrimination.'"[122]

---

119 Compare Legge, *Li Chi*, vol. 2, pp. 215–16.
120 Zheng's personal name was Yichu 一初. He was a native of the Qiyang 揭陽 District in Guangdong Province, won the presented scholar degree in 1505, and became a disciple of Wang.
121 Zhu attributes this description of the proper care of one's parents to Cheng Yi. See Zhu's *Some Questions on the Great Learning*; see *Zhuzi quanshu*, vol. 6, p. 525.
122 Quoting *Doctrine of the Mean* 2.20; see Legge, *Li Chi*, vol. 2, p. 318.

The Master said, "What you describe are simply the various details about how to provide warmth or cool comfort to [one's parents] or the proper way to serve or nurture [them]; such things can be explored and fully understood in a day or two. What need is there for inquiry, study, thought, and discrimination? It is just that if one wants this heart-mind to be [in the state where] the purity of Heavenly principles is fully attained when one provides warmth or cool comfort [to one's parents] or when one is serving or nurturing [them], one must engage in inquiry, study, thought, and discrimination or one will commit a minute error in the beginning that leads to an major mistake in the end. This is why even sages need the teaching about being '[wholly] refined and [wholly] focused.'[123] If the highest good only meant getting the details of behavior correct, then an actor who was able to perform correctly the various details of behavior concerning how to provide warmth or cool comfort [to one's parents] or the proper way to serve or nurture [them] could be said to have attained the highest good.

This day provided me with greater understanding.

5. I did not understand the Master's teaching about the unity of knowing and acting. Having debated it back and forth with Huang Zongxian[124] and Gu Weixian 顧惟賢[125] without coming to any resolution, I asked the Master about it.

The Master said, "Try offering an example and let us see."

I said, "For example, there are people who despite fully knowing that they should be filial to their parents and respectful to their elder brothers, find that they cannot be filial or respectful. From this it is clear that knowing and acting are two separate things."

The Master said, "They already have been separated by selfish desires; this is not the original state of knowing and acting. There never have been people who know but do not act. Those who 'know' but do not act simply do not yet know. Sages and worthies taught people about

---

123   See note 95 in this part of the volume.

124   See Part 3, note 44.

125   Weixian is the courtesy name of Gu Yingxiang 顧應祥 (1483–1565). Although he was a disciple of Wang, he came to reject Wang's teaching about the unity of knowledge and action.

knowing and acting so that people would return to the original state of knowing and acting and not just do what they could and quit. Thus, the *Great Learning* gives us examples of true knowing and acting, saying it is 'like loving a beautiful color or hating a bad odor.'[126] Seeing a beautiful color is a case of knowing, while loving a beautiful color is a case of acting. As soon as one sees that beautiful color, one naturally loves it. It is not as if you first see it and only then, intentionally, you decide to love it. Smelling a bad odor is a case of knowing, while hating a bad odor is a case of acting. As soon as one smells that bad odor, one naturally hates it. It is not as if you first smell it and only then, intentionally, you decide to hate it. Consider the case of a person with a stuffed-up nose. Even if he sees a malodorous object right in from of him, the smell does not reach him, and so he does not hate it. This is simply not to know the bad odor.

The same is true when one says that someone knows filial piety or brotherly respect. That person must already have acted with filial piety or brotherly respect before one can say she knows them. One cannot say she knows filial piety or brotherly respect simply because she knows how to *say* something filial or brotherly. Knowing pain offers another good example. One must have experienced pain oneself in order to know pain. [Similarly,] one must have experienced cold oneself in order to know cold, and one must have experienced hunger oneself in order to know hunger. How can knowing and acting be separated? This is the original state of knowing and acting, before any selfish thoughts have separated them. The sages taught people that this is how things must be in order to have [real] knowledge. If this is not how things are, one simply does not know. This is a critical, practical form of spiritual training. What is the point of earnestly insisting that knowing and acting are two separate things? What is the point of my insisting that they are one? If one does not understand the guiding aim behind these different explanations and just insists on saying they are one or they are two—what is the point?"

I said, "The ancients talked about <u>knowing</u> and <u>acting</u> as two things, and they did so because they wanted people to distinguish them clearly.

---

126   See the fifth section of the old text of the *Great Learning;* see Legge, *Li Chi,* vol. 2, p. 413.

Change maker. thinking about yourself.

On the one hand, one was to work at knowing; on the other hand, one was to work at acting. In this way, one would have a place to begin one's spiritual training." What reform 1st?, individual? Society?.

The Master said, "This [interpretation] loses the guiding aim of the ancients. I have said that knowing is the intent of acting and that acting is the work of knowing and that knowing is the beginning of acting and acting is the completion of knowing. Once one understands this, then if one only talks about knowing, [the idea of] acting is already present, or if one only talks about acting, [the idea] of knowing is already present. The reason that the ancients first talked about knowing and then talked about acting is only because there is a type of person in the world who foolishly acts upon impulse without engaging in the slightest thought or reflection. Because they always act blindly and recklessly, it is necessary to talk to them about knowing; only then can their actions be made correct. There is also a type of person who is vague and irresolute; they engage in speculation while suspended in a vacuum and are unwilling to apply themselves to any concrete actions. Because they only grope at shadows and grab at echoes, it is necessary to talk to them about acting; only then can their knowing be made real. The ancients could not but talk in this way, in their effort to augment deficiencies and remove obscurations. If one grasps this underlying aim, then talking about either [knowing or acting] will suffice.

"But people today instead separate knowing and acting into two distinct tasks to perform and think that one must first know and only then can one act. They say, 'Now I will perform the task of knowing, by studying and learning. Once I have attained real knowledge, I then will pursue the task of acting.' And so, till the end of their days, they never act, and till the end of their days, they never know. This is not a minor malady, nor did it arrive just yesterday. My current teaching regarding the unity of knowing and acting is a medicine directed precisely at this disease. It is not something I simply conjured up out of thin air; the original state of knowing and acting has always been like this. Now if one understands the underlying aim [of this teaching], then there is nothing wrong with saying that they are two, for they are only one. If one says that they are one but fails to understand the underlying aim [of this teaching], then how will that help? One would only be speaking idle words."

6. I asked, "Yesterday when I inquired about the Master's teachings concerning abiding in the highest good, I felt as though I was beginning to get a handle on this task. But when I thought about it in connection with Zhu Xi's view concerning *gewu*[127] I could not, in the end, reconcile the two [views]."

The Master said, "The rectification of [thoughts in regard to] things (*gewu*) is the work of abiding in the highest good. If one understands the highest good, one understands the rectification of [thoughts in regard to] things."

I said, "Yesterday, when I thought about Zhu Xi's views concerning *gewu* in light of your teachings, I seemed to get the general idea. But Zhu Xi's views are supported by the line from the *Book of History* about being '[wholly] refined and [wholly] focused,'[128] the line from the *Analects* about 'pursuing an expansive study of culture and restraining oneself with the rites,'[129] and the line from the *Mengzi* that says 'by fully developing one's heart-mind, one comes to fully understand one's nature.'[130] Under the weight of this evidence, I have not been able to break free of Zhu Xi's view."

The Master said, "Zi Xia had devout faith in Kongzi, while Zengzi turned to look [for the truth] within himself.[131] Devout faith surely is good, but it is not as genuine as turning to look within oneself. Now since you have not 'grasped it with your own heart-mind,'[132] why do you not seek the truth rather than simply remaining habituated to what you have heard in the past? For example, even though Zhu Xi had great

---

127   As previously discussed, Zhu understood *gewu* 格物 as involving the study and understanding of the principles of various things and events. Wang insisted that it meant the rectification of one's thoughts and ideas in response to things and events. For an elucidation of this difference, see Wang's explanation in question 6 in *Questions on the Great Learning* as presented here.

128   See note 95 in this part of the volume.

129   *Analects* 6.25.

130   *Mengzi* 7A1.

131   Quoting Zhu Xi. See the commentary on *Mengzi* 2A2 in his *Collected Comments on the Mengzi* (*Mengzi jizhu* 孟子集註). Zhu had in mind passages in the *Analects* that seem to imply this difference between the disciples. For example, see *Analects* 1.4, which describes Zengzi's proclivity toward self-reflection, and 19.3–19, which depicts Zi Xia as someone who tended to follow Kongzi's teachings.

132   Alluding to Mengzi's teachings in *Mengzi* 2A2.

respect for and faith in Cheng Yi, when he encountered a point that he could not grasp with his own heart-mind, did he ever just follow him? [The teachings concerning] being '[wholly] refined and [wholly] focused,' 'pursuing an expansive [study of culture] and restraining [oneself with the rites],' and 'fully developing one's heart-mind [and fully understanding one's nature]' are consistent with my views. The only problem is that you have not reflected sufficiently upon these matters.

"Zhu Xi's views concerning *gewu* cannot avoid being forced and contrived and do not represent the original aim of this doctrine. Being 'wholly refined' is the work of 'being wholly focused.' 'Pursuing expansive study is the work of restraining oneself.'[133] Since you already understand my teaching about the unity of knowing and acting, then when either [knowing or acting] is mentioned, you know [that the other is implied]. 'By fully developing one's heart-mind, one comes to fully understand one's nature and Heaven';[134] this is what those who are 'born with knowledge and practice it easily'[135] do. 'Preserving one's heart-mind and nurturing one's nature in order to serve Heaven'[136] is what those who 'know through study and practice for good effects'[137] do. 'To maintain singleness of purpose regardless of whether one suffers an early death or enjoys a long life and to cultivate one's self and await [Heaven's decree]'[138] is what those who 'gain knowledge through difficulties and practice with diligence'[139] do. The mistake in Zhu Xi's teachings about *gewu* lies in reversing this hierarchy. He thought that 'fully developing one's heart-mind and fully understanding one's nature' concern '*gewu* and knowledge being extended.' This is to require a beginning student to do what those who are 'born with knowledge and practice it easily' do. How can they possibly do that?"

---

133   Wang is referring to the classical teachings mentioned previously. His point is that these are not distinct tasks but merely different aspects of a single, unified effort: to express the pure Heavenly principles within the heart-mind as one encounters things and events in the world.

134   *Mengzi* 7A1.

135   *Doctrine of the Mean*, chap. 20. Compare *Analects* 16.9.

136   *Mengzi* 7A1.

137   *Doctrine of the Mean*, chap. 20. Compare *Analects* 16.9.

138   *Mengzi* 7A1.

139   *Doctrine of the Mean*, chap. 20. Compare *Analects* 16.9.

I asked, "Why is it that 'fully developing one's heart-mind and fully understanding one's nature' are things that those who are 'born with knowledge and practice it easily' do?"

The Master said, "The nature is the embodied state of the heart-mind. Heaven is the source of the nature. To fully develop the heart-mind is simply to fully develop the nature. 'Only the most perfectly sincere people in the world are able to fully develop their nature and understand the transforming and nourishing [processes] of Heaven and earth.'[140] Those who preserve their heart-minds have not fully developed them. To understand Heaven is to understand in the way that those responsible for a district or county understand that the affairs [of their district or county] are *their* affairs. This is to be one with Heaven. To serve Heaven is comparable to how children serve their parents or ministers serve their lords. Only if one fulfills one's service with respect and reverence can one avoid error. Even so, this is to be at one remove from Heaven. Herein lies the difference between sages and worthies.[141]

"As for 'not allowing [the possibilities of] an early death or long life to cause one to be of two heart-minds,'[142] this [maxim] is designed to teach students to single-mindedly work at doing good without allowing a concern for failure or success, early death or long life to shake their commitment to do good. Students should just work at 'cultivating one's self and awaiting [Heaven's] decree,'[143] knowing that failure or success, early death or long life are matters of [Heaven's] decree and that such things need not unsettle one's heart-mind.[144] Although those who serve Heaven are at one remove from Heaven, they already see the

---

140   Quoting *Doctrine of the Mean,* chap. 22.

141   Sages know Heaven and hence, like a good magistrate or prefect, see whatever must be done as their personal responsibility. In this sense they are one with Heaven. Worthies, like children and ministers, make an effort to serve Heaven but are not in full communion with Heaven. The former develop their heart-minds fully, while the latter merely preserve their heart-minds.

142   Quoting *Mengzi* 7A1.

143   Paraphrasing *Mengzi* 7A1.

144   "Unsettle one's heart-mind" translates *dongxin* 動心 and refers to the idea of attaining an "unsettled heart-mind" found in *Mengzi* 2A2. Compare *Mengzi* 6B15. For an analysis of this idea within the greater context of moral courage, see Philip J. Ivanhoe, "Mengzi's Conception of Courage," *Dao: A Journal of Comparative Philosophy* 5:2 (June 2006): 221–34.

Heavenly right before them. Those who 'await Heaven's decree' still have not seen [the Heavenly] before them in this way but are waiting for an experience like this. These are all [tasks] for beginning students and convey a sense of difficulty and diligence. But now what [Zhu Xi teaches] reverses the order [of learning] and leaves students with no place to begin."

I asked, "Yesterday, after listening to your instructions, I could dimly discern that one's spiritual training must be as you describe. Now, hearing your explanation, I no longer can doubt that this is true. Yesterday, it dawned on me that the word 'thing' (*wu* 物) in the expression 'rectifying [one's thoughts in relation to] things' (*gewu* 格物) has the same meaning as the word 'undertaking' or 'affair' (*shi* 事). Both words refer to the heart-mind."

The Master said, "That is so. The governor of the body is the heart-mind. What the heart-mind puts forth are thoughts. The fundamental nature of thoughts is knowledge. Where there is a thought, there is a thing (*wu*). If one's thoughts are on serving one's parents, then serving one's parents is a thing. If one's thoughts are on serving one's ruler, then serving one's ruler is a thing. If one's thoughts are on being benevolent to the people or caring for other creatures, then being benevolent to the people or caring for other creatures are things. If one's thoughts are on looking, listening, speaking, or acting, then looking, listening, speaking, or acting are things. This is why I say that there is no principle outside the heart-mind and no thing outside the heart-mind. The *Doctrine of the Mean*'s teaching that 'without sincerity, there is nothing'[145] and the task of 'making bright one's bright virtue' described in the *Great Learning* are nothing other than examples of making one's thoughts sincere. The task of making one's thoughts sincere is nothing other than 'rectifying [one's thoughts in relation to] things.'"

7. The Master also said, "The word *ge* in *gewu* is like the *ge* in the line from the *Mengzi*, which says, '[Only] a great man [is able to] rectify (*ge*) the ruler's heart-mind.'[146] It means to eliminate whatever is not

---

145   *Doctrine of the Mean,* chap. 25.

146   *Mengzi* 4A20. Compare Lu's "Second Letter (to Zhu Xi)" in Part Two of this volume and especially note 123 there.

correct in order to maintain the correctness of the original state of the heart-mind. Wherever there is a thought, one eliminates whatever is not correct in order to maintain what is correct. At all times and in every circumstance, one preserves Heavenly principles. This is what it means to fully realize principle. Heavenly principles are none other than bright virtue; fully realizing Heavenly principles is nothing other than making bright one's bright virtue."[147]

8. The Master also said, "Knowing is the original state of the heart-mind. The heart-mind naturally is able to know. When it sees one's parents, it naturally knows to be filial. When it sees one's elder brother, it naturally knows to be respectful. When it sees a child [about to] fall into a well, it naturally knows the feeling of compassion.[148] This is none other than pure knowing. There is no need to seek for such [knowledge] outside [the heart-mind]. If the operation of pure knowing is not blocked by selfish thoughts, then, as it is said, 'If one expands one's compassionate heart-mind, one's benevolence will be more than can be used.'[149] Nevertheless, most people are not able to avoid being blocked by selfish thoughts, and so they must engage in the tasks of extending their knowledge and rectifying their thoughts in regard to things in order to overcome selfishness and return to principle. Once their pure knowing is able to work its way through the obstruction and flow freely, this is extending their knowledge. When their knowledge is extended, their thoughts are made sincere."

9. I asked, "You, Master, take the 'extensive [study] of culture (*wen* 文)' to be the spiritual task of 'restraining oneself with ritual (*li* 禮).'[150] I have pondered this in depth but have been unable to understand it in the least. Please show me what you mean."

---

147 Wang refers to several steps in the process of self-cultivation described in the *Great Learning*.

148 The locus classicus of this example is *Mengzi* 2A6.

149 *Mengzi* 7B31.

150 *Analects* 6.25. These lines traditionally have been interpreted as referring to two distinct yet complementary types of effort: the extensive study of culture and restraining oneself through ritual practice.

The Master said, "The word 'ritual' refers to the same thing as the word 'principle' (*Li* 理).[151] [Those aspects of] principle that are manifested and can be seen are called 'culture' (*wen* 文).[152] [Those aspects of] culture that are hidden and cannot be seen are called 'principle.' This involves only one thing. Restraining oneself with ritual is simply to want this heart-mind (*cixin*) to remain pure Heavenly principle. If one wants this heart-mind to remain pure Heavenly principle, one must apply effort wherever principle is manifested. If it is manifested while serving one's parents, then one must study how to preserve Heavenly principle while serving one's parents. If it is manifested while serving one's ruler, then one must study how to preserve Heavenly principle while serving one's ruler. If it is manifested while living in wealth and honor or poverty and humble circumstances, then one must study how to preserve Heavenly principle while living in wealth and honor or poverty and humble circumstances. If it is manifested while living in difficulty and deprivation or among barbarians, then one must study how to preserve Heavenly principle while living in difficulty and deprivation or among barbarians.[153] The same practice should be followed whether one is active or at rest, speaking or silent; wherever [principle] is manifested—right there is where one must learn to preserve Heavenly principle. This is what I mean by saying that to engage in the extensive [study] of culture is the spiritual task of restraining oneself with ritual. The extensive [study] of culture is to be 'wholly refined'; restraining oneself with ritual is to be 'wholly focused.'"[154]

10. I asked, "[Zhu Xi said that] 'the heart-mind of the Way always is the governor of the self and the human heart-mind always obeys

---

151   Both words are pronounced the same way, and so I distinguish them by capitalizing the romanization of the second. Wang's argument in this section plays on the phonetic similarity between key terms of art in neo-Confucian philosophy.

152   Wang is further alluding to the more primary sense of *wen* as "pattern." His point is that every pattern has an underlying principle.

153   The last two lines draw directly upon *Doctrine of the Mean*, chap. 14.

154   Citing the well-known passage from the "Counsels of the Great Yu" chapter of the *Book of History*, which describes the difference between the wayward "human heart-mind" and the ideal "heart-mind of the Way"; see Legge, *The Shoo King*, pp. 61–62.

it.'[155] Seen in light of your teachings regarding being wholly refined and wholly focused, this claim seems flawed."

The Master said, "That is correct. The heart-mind is one. Before it is mixed with what is human, it is called the heart-mind of the Way. After being mixed with human artifice, it is called the human heart-mind. When the human heart-mind attains its correct state, it is the heart-mind of the Way. When the heart-mind of the Way loses its correct state, it is the human heart-mind. From the very start, there are not two heart-minds. Cheng Yi said, 'The human heart-mind is human desire; the heart-mind of the Way is Heavenly principle.'[156] While this way of putting it seems to divide [the heart-mind into two things], it succeeds in conveying the basic idea. Now, to say that the heart-mind of the Way is the governor and the human heart-mind obeys its commands, this is to posit the existence of two heart-minds. Heavenly principle and human desires cannot be in play at the same time, and so how could one have Heavenly principle as the governor and human desires subsequently obeying its commands?"

11. I asked about Wenzhongzi and Han Tuizhi.[157]

The Master said, "Han Tuizhi was a great literary man but nothing more, while Wenzhongzi was a worthy scholar. Because people of later ages only esteem literary talent, they have glorified Han Tuizhi. But the fact is that Han Tuizhi was vastly inferior to Wenzhongzi."

---

155   See Zhu's preface to the *Doctrine of the Mean* in *Sections and Sentences* (*Zhongyong zhangju* 中庸章句) in *Collected Comments on the Four Books.* For the "heart-mind of the Way" and the "human heart-mind," see note 154.

156   *Extant Works of the Cheng [Brothers] from Henan,* chap. 19.

157   Wenzhongzi 文中子 (584–617) is Master Wenzhong; his given name is Wang Tong 王通, and his courtesy name is Zhongyan 仲淹. An eminent Confucian and active commentator, much of whose work is now lost, he thought of himself as equal to Kongzi, which has lowered him in the eyes of most Confucians. Han Tuizhi 韓退之 (768–824), better known as Han Yu 韓愈 was one of China's greatest essayists and a vehement critic of Buddhism and Daoism. He is mentioned in Lu's "Second Letter to Senior Official Li," presented in this volume. See especially Part Two, note 172. Many Confucians consider him to be part of an orthodox tradition stretching back to Kongzi. Most modern scholars regard him as an important herald of and contributor to the Confucian revival that blossomed in the Song dynasty.

I asked, "Why then did [Wenzhongzi] commit the mistake of imitating the classics?"[158]

The Master said, "I am afraid that imitating the classics cannot wholly be condemned. Could you explain to me the difference between imitating the classics and the intent behind the writings of scholars in later ages?"

I said, "Scholars writing today are not without the intention of advancing their reputations, but their primary aim is to elucidate the Way. Imitating the classics, though, is purely aimed at [gaining] a reputation."

The Master asked, "In elucidating the Way, whom are people emulating?"

I replied, "Kongzi edited and transmitted the six classics in order to elucidate the Way."

The Master said, "Then why is not imitating the classics also emulating Kongzi?"

I replied, "Writing that [elucidates] reveals something about the Way, while imitating the classics seems only to imitate what has come down to us. I am afraid that this does not in any way augment the Way."

The Master said, "By 'elucidating the Way' do you mean to return to simplicity and purity and manifest these in one's actual practice, or do you mean to dress up and embellish one's words and just wrangle and contend with others? The great chaos found throughout the world today has arisen because vacuous writing has flourished while actual practice has declined. If the Way were elucidated throughout the world, there would be no need to transmit the six classics. Editing and transmitting the six classics was something that Kongzi could not but do. From the time when Fuxi[159] first drew the Eight Trigrams to the age of King Wen and the Duke of Zhou,[160] commentaries on the *Book of Changes,* such as the *Mountain Ranges* (*Lianshan* 連山) and *Returning to the Treasury*

---

158   Among Wenzhongzi's now lost works are various "supplements" to the classics.

159   Fuxi ("Tamer of Oxen") was the first of three mythical cultural heroes who were credited with inventing the rudiments of Chinese civilization. One of Fuxi's achievements was drawing and naming the sixty-four hexagrams of the *Book of Changes.*

160   King Wen was the virtuous vassal of Tyrant Zhou. While having ample reasons to revolt, he remained loyal. However, his son, King Wu, overthrew Tyrant Zhou and founded the Zhou dynasty. The Duke of Zhou was King Wu's brother. Tradition has it that when King Wu died, the duke served as wise and loyal regent for the king's young son. By so doing, he exhibited his virtuous character and devotion to the greater good.

(*Guicang* 歸藏),[161] were written. These came in every shape and form, varied in content, and no one knows how many were produced. [As a result,] the Way of the *Book of Changes* was thrown into great chaos. Kongzi saw that the fashion of indulging in superfluous writing was gaining strength with each day and the production of such explanations would never cease. And so, he took the commentaries provided by King Wen and the Duke of Zhou and added his own exposition to these, insisting that this was the only way to grasp the true meaning of the *Book of Changes*.[162] As a result, the proliferation of commentaries ceased and those who talked about the *Book of Changes* began to form a unified consensus.

"The same is true in the cases of the *Book of History, Book of Songs, Book of Rites, Book of Music,* and *Spring and Autumn Annals.* Following the opening four chapters of the *Book of History* and the first two chapters of the *Book of Songs,* no one knows how many thousands of reams of works such as the *Nine Hills* (*Jiuqiu* 九丘) and the *Eight Inquiries* (*Basuo* 八索) as well as various licentious and superfluous verses were written.[163] The names and institutions of rituals and music also were produced in inexhaustible abundance. It was only after Kongzi edited and eliminated these and transmitted orthodox versions [of these texts] that such commentaries ceased being produced. When did Kongzi ever add a single word to the *Book of History, Book of Songs, Book of Rites,* or *Book of Music?* The various teachings in the present *Book of Rites* are all things added by later Confucians; these are not part of Kongzi's original text. As for the *Spring and Autumn Annals,* while it is said that Kongzi "made" it, in fact it consists of the old text of the official history of the state of Lu.[164] When people describe Kongzi as "writing" [the classics], they

---

161   According to the third chapter of the *Rites of Zhou* (*Zhouli* 周禮), these were two versions of the *Book of Changes.*

162   Wang here is relying on traditional views about the composition of the text. The hexagram statements (*guaci* 挂辭) or judgments (*tuan* 彖) on each hexagram are ascribed to King Wen. The line statements (*yaoci* 爻辭) for each line of the hexagrams are ascribed to the Duke of Zhou. These comments along with the hexagrams themselves constitute the classic (*jing* 經) part of the received text.

163   The references are to the "Canons" of Yao and Shun and the "Counsels" of Yu and Gaoyao in the *Book of History* and the "Zhou" and "Shao Nan" chapters of the *Book of Songs.* The *Nine Hills* and the *Eight Inquiries* are now lost historical works.

164   See *Mengzi* 3B9 for the passage that ascribes the "making" of the *Spring and Autumn Annals* to Kongzi.

mean he wrote down the old texts. When they talk about him "editing" [the classics], they mean he eliminated all that was superfluous. He reduced and never added to the classics. When Kongzi transmitted the six classics, he feared that superfluous writings would cause chaos throughout the world. He only sought to simplify them so that they would not mislead the people. He worked to get rid of the words so that people could grasp the true meaning. He did not want to teach through words at all.

"After the Spring and Autumn Period [722–481 B.C.E.], superfluous writings grew ever more numerous and the world grew ever more chaotic. What was wrong with the first emperor's burning of the books was that he did this out of a selfish motivation, and it was improper to burn the six classics. If at the time his intent had been to make clear the Way and to burn all the books that opposed the classics and violated principle, then his actions would have been proper and would happen to have conformed to [Kongzi's] ideas about editing and transmitting [the classics]. Since the Qin and Han dynasties, writing has grown more numerous with each passing day. One could not possibly get rid of it all. The best that one can do is to take Kongzi as one's model: record what comes close to being correct and make it known. As a consequence, perverse theories will gradually be abandoned. I don't know what Wenzhongzi intended to accomplish when he imitated the classics, but I strongly endorse what he did and feel that if another sage were to arise, he would find nothing wanting [in Wenzhongzi's actions].

"The reason the world is not well ordered is simply because [superfluous] writing has increased so dramatically while actual practice has declined. There are those who set forth their personal opinions and play the novel off against the strange, all in order to seduce the average person and win fame for themselves. They do so only to disorder the understanding of the world and muddy the eyes and ears of the people so that they will waste their time competing with one another writing flowery compositions in order to win acclaim in their age and will no longer comprehend conduct that honors what is fundamental, esteems what is real, reverts to simplicity, and returns to purity. This all began with those who practiced writing."

I replied, "But some writing seems indispensable. For example, in the case of the classic *Spring and Autumn Annals,* were it not for the *Zuozhuan*,[165] [the classic] would probably be difficult to comprehend." The Master said, "To say that we must have the *Zuozhuan* before we can understand the *Spring and Autumn Annals* is to regard [the classic] as if it were a partially quoted phrase. Why would Kongzi exert such an effort to produce writing that is so difficult and obscure? Most of the *Zuozhuan* is simply the old text of the official history of the state of Lu. If we must read it before we can understand the *Spring and Autumn Annals,* why would Kongzi have felt a need to edit [the classic]?"

I replied, "Cheng Yi said that, 'The commentary to the *Spring and Autumn Annals* presents cases; the classic presents judgments.'[166] For example, the *Spring and Autumn Annals* says that a certain king was murdered or a certain state attacked. If these affairs are not described clearly, it would likely be difficult to reach a judgment."

The Master said, "In saying this, Cheng Yi probably was just according with the views of contemporary scholars; this does not reflect Kongzi's intention in composing the classics. For example, if the *Spring and Autumn Annals* says that a certain king was murdered, since we know that the murder of a king is a crime, what need is there to inquire about the details of the murder? Only the king can launch an attack of rectification.[167] If the *Spring and Autumn Annals* says that a certain state was attacked, since we know that attacking a state is a crime, what need is there to inquire about the details of the attack? Kongzi's sole intention in transmitting the classics was to rectify people's heart-minds, preserve Heavenly principle, and eliminate human desires. If some affair concerned the preservation of Heavenly principle or the elimination of human desires, then Kongzi often would speak about it, or if someone asked a specific question, he

---

165   The *Zuozhuan* is the *Commentary of Zuo*. Attributed to Zuo Qiuming, who was probably Kongzi's contemporary, it is more a complement than a commentary to the classic. The *Zuozhuan* provides a wealth of historical detail about events in the original text. See James Legge, trans., *The Ch'un Ts'ew with the Tso Chuen*, vol. 5 of *The Chinese Classics,* reprint (Hong Kong: University of Hong Kong Press, 1970).

166   This line is found in the *Extant Works of the Cheng [Brothers] from Henan,* chap. 16, and the "Extension of Knowledge" ("Zhi zhi 致知") chapter of *A Record for Reflection.* Compare Chan, *Reflections on Things at Hand,* p. 118.

167   An "attack of rectification" or "rectification campaign" (*zhengfa* 征伐) was a punitive assault led by the legitimate king to subdue an unruly vassal state. Any military action involving one vassal state attacking another was *ipso facto* illegitimate.

would explain things according to that person's ability to understand. But even in such cases, he would not go on at length, because he feared that people would only seek [the truth] within words. This is why he said, 'I would prefer not to speak.'[168] How could he allow himself to offer detailed descriptions of all those affairs that give rein to human desires and annihilate Heavenly principle? This is to aid chaos and abet villainy. This is why Mengzi said, 'No one in Kongzi's school talked about the affairs of Duke Huan or Duke Wen, and so these things have not been handed down to later ages.'[169] This approach is characteristic of the Confucian School. Contemporary scholars, though, talk only about the learning suited to a despot. And so, they want to know many subtle plans and crafty schemes. What they know all is aimed at gaining some profit or advantage, which is diametrically opposed to Kongzi's intention in composing the classics. How can such people understand?"

Thereupon, the Master sighed and said, "It is not easy to talk about this with those who are not 'advanced in Heavenly Virtue.'"[170]

He continued, saying, "Kongzi said, 'Even in my time, historians leave some things out of their accounts.'[171] Mengzi said, 'It would be better to be without books than to trust in them completely. In the "Completion of War" in the *Book of History,* I accept only two or three strips [of characters].'[172] When Kongzi edited the *Book of History,* he covered the four to five hundred years of the Tang, Yu, and Xia periods in several chapters.[173] Why did he not record at least one more affair [from this period]? Through this we can understand Kongzi's intention. His only aim was to eliminate superfluous writing. Scholars of later ages have worked to the contrary and only aim at adding more."

---

168   *Analects* 17.19.

169   A rough quote of *Mengzi* 1A7.

170   Quoting *Doctrine of the Mean,* chap. 32.

171   *Analects* 15.25. The idea is that even in the decadent age in which Kongzi lived, some historians would still do the right thing.

172   *Mengzi* 7B3. The "Completion of War" is the third book in the fifth part of the *Book of History.* It purportedly describes the triumph of King Wu over the tyrant Zhou. Mengzi could not accept its gory descriptions of this campaign. In his mind, an enlightened conqueror could never wreak such carnage. Compare Lu's reference to this passage in his "Letter to Zhu Yuanhui (Zhu Xi)" presented here; see Part Two, note 96.

173   "Tang" and "Yu" refer to the reigns of Yao and Shun, respectively. Xia refers to the Xia dynasty. This entire period is covered by the opening sections of the *Book of History.*

I said, "Kongzi's sole intention in transmitting the classics was to eliminate human desires and preserve Heavenly principle. This offers a perfect explanation for why he did not want to describe in detail the affairs in the period of the Five Despots and the time that followed.[174] But why did he not offer more details about the time before the reigns of Yao and Shun?"

The Master said, "In the age of Fuxi and Huangdi, affairs were few and far between; only in rare cases have they been handed down [to later generations].[175] This can help us to imagine how pure, graceful, modest, and simple their age was and how free it was of any air of ornamentation or embellishment. This was the method of governing practiced in high antiquity, something later ages are incapable of attaining."

I said, "There were records of the Three Emperors that were handed down to later ages.[176] Why did Kongzi edit them out?"

The Master said, "Even if such records did indeed exist, because of changes that arose over the course of generations, they would gradually have become inappropriate. As customs began to change [over the ages], ornamentation and embellishment became more and more dominant. Even by the end of the Zhou dynasty, one could no longer substitute the customs of the Shang or Xia dynasties, even if one wanted to, not to mention [the customs of] Yao or Shun—much less Fuxi or Huangdi! Nevertheless, while their methods of governing were different, they followed the same Way. Kongzi reverently passed down the ways of Yao and Shun and made clear the methods of Wen and Wu. But the methods of Wen and Wu are the Way of Yao and Shun. Because they adjusted their methods of governing in accordance with the times, their institutions, programs, policies, and laws naturally were not the same. Certain aspects of the administration of the Shang and Xia were inappropriate when handed down to the Zhou. This is why 'the Duke of Zhou aspired to combine the best of the Three

---

174   The Five Despots were five particularly bad rulers from the Spring and Autumn Period; see *Mengzi* 6B7.

175   Fuxi is described in note 159 of this part of the volume. Huangdi ("The Yellow Emperor") was the third of the three mythical cultural heros credited with inventing the rudiments of Chinese civilization. According to tradition, both Fuxi and Huangdi lived in the period prior to the reigns of Yao and Shun.

176   The Three Emperors are the two mythical cultural heroes described in note 175 along with Shennong ("The Divine Farmer").

Sovereigns . . . whenever he encountered something inappropriate [for his time], he would gaze toward the heavens and reflect until day passed into night.'[177] How much more difficult is it to appropriate the methods of government used in high antiquity! This certainly is why Kongzi endorsed reducing the records [of such times] to an absolute minimum."

He continued, saying, "To maintain a policy of 'nonaction' and prove incapable of adjusting one's methods of governing in accordance with the times, as the Three Sovereigns did, but instead insist on implementing the customs of high antiquity is the approach and method of Buddhists and Daoists. To adjust one's methods of governing in accordance with the times but prove incapable of rooting all one's practices in the Way, as the Three Sovereigns did, and instead to act with your heart-mind on profit and advantage is the policy of despots and those who follow them. Scholars in later ages have talked up and down and back and forth but all they ever talk about is the method and approach of despots."

12. [The Master] continued, saying, "The way of governing that was practiced before the time of Yao and Shun cannot be appropriated by later generations; it should be set aside. The way of governing followed by those who came after the Xia, Shang, and Zhou dynasties cannot serve as a proper model for later generations; it should be deleted. [Later generations] only can follow the way of the Three Dynasties.[178] However, the way contemporary scholars discuss the Three Dynasties—without understanding the root they only follow the tips of the branch—guarantees that they will not be able to appropriate it."

13. I said, "When former scholars discussed the six classics, they regarded the *Spring and Autumn Annals* as a work of history. But since works of history are only records of affairs, I am concerned that in the end this means that to some degree it differs in nature from the other five classics."

The Master replied, "If you talk about it in terms of affairs, it is a work of history; if you talk about it in terms of the Way (Dao), it is a classic. But affairs are the Way and the Way is affairs. The *Spring and Autumn*

---

177   *Mengzi* 4B20. The Three Sovereigns are the founders of the first three dynasties: Yu, founder of the Xia; Tang, founder of the Shang; and Kings Wen and Wu, regarded as the cofounders of the Zhou.

178   The Xia, Shang, and Zhou.

Annals is also a classic; the [other] five classics are also histories.[179] The *Book of Changes* is a history of Fuxi. The *Book of History* is a history of the times of Yao, Shun, and those who followed them. The *Book of Rites* and the *Book of Music* are histories of the Three Dynasties. They concern the same affairs; they concern the same Dao. Where lies their alleged difference?"

14. He continued, saying, "The [other] five classics also are just histories. Histories illuminate good and bad and offer instructions and prohibitions. The good can offer instruction when we preserve its traces to serve as a model. The bad can offer a warning when we preserve the warning while eliminating the [details of the bad] affairs in order to prevent wickedness."

I said, "Preserving its traces to serve as a model clearly is to preserve the original state of Heavenly principle. Is preserving the warning while eliminating the [details of the bad] affairs to nip human desires in the bud?"

The Master said, "Kongzi composed the classic certainly for no other reasons than these. Nevertheless, one need not get bogged down in words and sentences."

I further asked, "The bad can offer a warning when we preserve the warning while eliminating the [details of the bad] affairs in order to prevent wickedness. Why, then, does the *Book of Songs* offer the lone exception in that the odes of Zheng and Wei were not edited out?[180] A former scholar said that this was because the bad can serve to reprove one's flagging will.[181] Is that correct?"

The Master said, "The [extant version] of the *Book of Songs* is not the original text of the Confucian School. Kongzi said, 'Banish the songs of Zheng . . . The songs of Zheng are licentious!'[182] He also said, 'I detest the

---

179   Wang's idea, expressed here and in Section 14, that the classics can be understood as histories, influenced and was developed by the Qing dynasty Confucian Zhang Xuecheng. For a discussion of this aspect of Zhang's philosophy, see Nivison, *The Life and Thought of Chang Hsüeh-ch'eng (1738–1801)*, pp. 98–100, 201–4, and elsewhere.

180   These portions of the *Book of Songs* have long been considered licentious and a long, complex, and often convoluted commentarial tradition has focused on explaining their inclusion in the classic.

181   This represents the view of Zhu Xi as expressed, for example, in his preface to the *Collected Commentaries on the Book of Songs (Shi jizhuan* 詩集傳) and his note on *Analects* 2.2 in his *Collected Comments on the Four Books*.

182   *Analects* 15.10.

way the songs of Zheng corrupt elegant music![183] [And he said,] 'The sounds of Zheng and Wei . . . are the sounds of a benighted state!'[184] This is the view and approach of the Confucian School. The three hundred odes that Kongzi compiled all were what are called elegant music.[185] All could be performed at the suburban or ancestral sacrifices or in district or neighborhood rituals.[186] They all were a means for promoting peace and cultivating a virtuous nature. How can one reform customs and improve habits while the songs of Zheng and Wei are tolerated?[187] They promote licentiousness and induce wickedness. Contemporary scholars must have added these after the burning of the books by the Qin dynasty in order to bring the number of odes back up to three hundred. Most common people take delight in passing along licentious or lewd songs. Even today, you can hear them [sung] in every alley. But to say that 'the bad can serve to reprove one's flagging will' is simply what one might say when one seeks but fails to find the proper explanation."

Xu Ai's Postscript[188]

Since the old interpretation was lost long ago,[189] when I first heard the Master's teachings, I was startled and unsure. I did not know where to

---

183   *Analects* 17.18.

184   Quoting the "Record of Music" chapter of the *Book of Rites*. Compare Legge, *Li Chi*, vol. 2, p. 94.

185   For the idea that the *Book of Songs* contains three hundred odes, see *Analects* 2.2.

186   The emperor performed both the suburban and ancestral sacrifices. The former were the most important public sacrifices he would make, while the latter were the most important private ones. See the "Proceedings of the Government in the Different Months" chapter of the *Book of Rites* for a reference to these sacrifices; see Legge, *Li Chi*, vol. 1, p. 278. The idea of these remarks is that the odes were proper for every occasion and every place calling for ritual propriety.

187   The twelfth chapter of the *Classic of Filial Piety* says, "To reform customs and improve habits, nothing is better than [proper] music." Similar ideas are found in the *Book of Songs,* the *Xunzi,* and the *Book of Rites.*

188   This translation is based upon my earlier work, which appears as the first appendix of my *Confucian Moral Self Cultivation* (see pp. 145–46). Additional annotation and discussion can be found there.

189   That is, the interpretation based upon the old version of the *Great Learning,* which Wang insisted on following. The Cheng-Zhu School rearranged and augmented the original chapters of this work and gave the text a radically new interpretation. Compare the opening line of "Xu Ai's Introduction."

begin [to understand them]. Later, after listening to him for a long time, I gradually came to see that I must gain a personal understanding of these teachings and apply them in concrete situations. After this, I began to believe that the Master's teachings were the legitimate tradition of the Confucian school. If one departs from these, there is nothing but narrow paths and byways, cut-off harbors and blocked rivers, [which lead nowhere]. For example, his teachings that "rectifying one's thoughts [about things]" is the task of "making one's thoughts sincere,"[190] that "displaying goodness" is the task of "making one's self sincere,"[191] that "fully comprehending principle" is the task of "fulfilling one's nature,"[192] that "pursuing inquiry and study" is the task of "honoring the virtuous nature,"[193] that "extensive cultural study" is the task of "restraining oneself through the rites,"[194] and that "maintaining purity" is the task of "maintaining singleness"[195]—all these teachings were at first difficult to reconcile with one another. However, after contemplating them for a long time, [I discovered that] unconsciously my feet began to step in time to them and my hands began to dance [according to their rhythms].[196]

---

190   See the second and third sections of the old text of the *Great Learning;* see Legge, *Li Chi,* pp. 411–12.

191   See *Doctrine of the Mean*, chap. 20.

192   See the first section of the "Explanations of the Trigrams" commentary of the *Book of Changes.*

193   See *Doctrine of the Mean,* chap. 20.

194   See *Analects* 9.11.

195   From the "Counsels of the Great Yu" chapter of the *Book of Documents*; see Legge, *The Shoo King,* pp. 61–62.

196   The reference is to *Mengzi* 4A27, where Mengzi relates the spontaneous inclination human beings have for moral action to their spontaneous inclination to dance when they hear music. Both actions are motivated by and express natural feelings of joy. Compare the line in the seventeenth chapter of the "Record of Music" in the *Book of Rites.* For a translation, see Legge, *Li Chi,* vol. 2, p. 131.

QUESTIONS ON THE GREAT LEARNING (DAXUE WEN)[197]

Introduction by Qian Dehong

Whenever my teacher accepted a new student, he would always rely upon the first chapters of the *Great Learning* and the *Doctrine of the Mean* to show him the complete task of sagely learning and acquaint him with its proper path. I received and recorded the *Questions on the Great Learning* the night before the master set off to suppress a rebellion occurring in the area of Sien and Tianzhou.[198]

Questions on the Great Learning

1. [Question:] "A former scholar[199] considered the *Great Learning* to be 'the learning appropriate for a [morally] great person.' May I ask, how is it that the learning of such a great person lies in 'making bright [one's] bright virtue?'"[200]

[Master Yangming replied]: "Great people regard Heaven, earth, and the myriad creatures as their own bodies. They look upon the world as

---

197   The disciple Qian Dehong recorded this work in 1527, one year before Wang's death. As Qian's introduction suggests, the text explores the meaning of the opening sections of the old text of the *Great Learning*. The six questions follow the old text almost line by line. Compare Legge, *Li Chi,* vol. 2, pp. 411–24.

198   Sien 思恩 and Tianzhou 田州 were two prefectures in present-day Guangxi Province.

199   The reference is to Zhu Xi. See Zhu's comments on the first line of the text in the *Great Learning in Sections and Sentences.*

200   This is the opening line of the old text of the *Great Learning;* see Legge, *Li Chi,* vol. 2, p. 411.

one family and China as one person within it. Those who, because of the space between their own bodies and other physical forms, regard themselves as separate [from Heaven, earth, and the myriad creatures] are petty persons. The ability great people have to form one body with Heaven, earth, and the myriad creatures is not something they intentionally strive to do; the benevolence of their heart-minds is originally like this. How could it be that only the heart-minds of great people are one with Heaven, earth, and the myriad creatures? Even the heart-minds of petty people are like this. It is only the way in which such people look at things that makes them petty. This is why, when they see a child [about to] fall into a well, they cannot avoid having a sense of alarm and concern for the child.[201] This is because their benevolence forms one body with the child. Someone might object that this response is because the child belongs to the same species. But when they hear the anguished cries or see the frightened appearance of birds or beasts, they cannot avoid a sense of being unable to bear it.[202] This is because their benevolence forms one body with birds and beasts. Someone might object that this response is because birds and beasts are sentient creatures. But when they see grass or trees uprooted and torn apart, they cannot avoid feeling a sense of sympathy and distress. This is because their benevolence forms one body with grass and trees. Someone might object that this response is because grass and trees have life and vitality. But when they see tiles and stones broken and destroyed, they cannot avoid feeling a sense of concern and regret. This is because their benevolence forms one body with tiles and stones.

"This shows that the benevolence that forms one body [with Heaven, earth, and the myriad creatures] is something that even the heart-minds of petty people possess. Such a heart-mind is rooted in the nature endowed by Heaven and is naturally luminous, shining, and not beclouded. This is why it is called 'bright virtue.' The heart-minds of petty people have become cut off and constricted, and yet the benevolence that forms one body [with Heaven, earth, and the myriad creatures]

---

201   Paraphrasing the example of the child and well from *Mengzi* 2A6.

202   *Mengzi* 1A7 offers the example of King Xuan being "unable to bear" the anguished cries and frightened appearance of an ox being led to slaughter. Mengzi goes on to infer a general aversion to seeing any animal suffer.

is able to be as unbeclouded as what Heaven originally endowed. This occurs in those times when they have not yet been moved by desires or obscured by selfishness. Once they have been moved by desires or obscured by selfishness, beset by thoughts of benefit and harm and stirred by feelings of indignation and anger, they will then attack other creatures, injure their own kind, and stop at nothing. At the extreme, they will even murder their own kin and wholly lose the benevolence that forms one body [with Heaven, earth, and the myriad creatures]. And so, if only they are without the obscuration of selfish desires, even the heart-minds of petty people will have the same benevolence that forms one body [with Heaven, earth, and the myriad creatures] that great people possess. As soon as there is obscuration by selfish desires, then even the heart-minds of great people will become cut off and constricted, just like those of petty people. This is why the learning of the great person indeed lies only in getting rid of the obscuration of selfish desires, thereby making bright one's bright virtue and restoring the original condition of forming one body [with Heaven, earth, and the myriad creatures]. It is not anything that can be added to this original state."

2. [Question:] "In that case, why [does the learning of the great person] lie in loving the people?"

[Master Yangming] replied: "Making bright [one's] bright virtue is the state[203] of forming one body with Heaven, earth, and the myriad things. Loving the people universally extends the operation[204] of forming one body with Heaven, earth, and the myriad things.[205] And so, making bright [one's] bright virtue must find expression in loving the people, and loving the people simply is the way one makes bright one's bright

---

203   Literally, the "body" (*ti* 體).

204   Literally, the "use" or "function" (*yong* 用).

205   The terms *ti* (here, "state") and *yong* (here, "operation") are used to make a variety of distinctions in traditional Chinese philosophy. See note 15 in the introduction to the *Platform Sutra* in this volume. Here, the point is that making bright one's bright virtue is the goal of moral cultivation itself—its body or substance—while loving the people is the natural operation or function of such a virtuous state.

virtue.[206] This is why it is only when I love my father, the fathers of other people, and the fathers of everyone in the world that my benevolence truly forms one body with my father, the fathers of other people, and the fathers of everyone in the world. It is only when I truly form one body with them that the bright virtue of filial piety begins to be made bright. It is only when I love my elder brother, the elder brothers of other people, and the elder brothers of everyone in the world that my benevolence truly forms one body with my elder brother, the elder brothers of other people, and the elder brothers of everyone in the world. It is only when I truly form one body with them that the bright virtue of brotherly love begins to be made bright. It is the same in regard to rulers and ministers, husbands and wives, and friends; it is the same in regard to mountains and rivers, ghosts and spirits, birds and beasts, and grass and trees. It is only when I truly love them all and universally extend my benevolence that forms one body with them that my bright virtue will be made bright in every respect, and I can really form one body with Heaven, earth, and the myriad things. This is what it means to 'make bright one's bright virtue throughout the world.' This is what it means to 'regulate the family, order the state, and bring peace to the world.' This is what it means to 'fulfill one's nature.'"[207]

3. [Question:] "In that case, why [does the learning of the great person] lie in abiding in the highest good?"

[Master Yangming] replied: "The highest good is the ultimate standard for making bright one's bright virtue and loving the people. The nature endowed by Heaven is the highest good in its purest state. To be luminous, shining, and not beclouded are manifestations of the highest good. This is the original state of bright virtue or what is called 'pure knowing.' When the highest good is manifested, whatever is good will

---

206 Here, Wang is relying upon other senses of the terms *ti* and *yong*. First is the idea that the *ti* and *yong* of a given thing are only conceptually but never actually distinct from each other. Second is the idea that each thing or body (*ti*) has a natural function (*yong*). Recall the example of both these senses in Section 15 of the *Platform Sutra*, included here, which tells us that a lighted lamp (*ti*) is never found apart from lamplight (*yong*).

207 The quotations are from the first, second, and fourth sections of the old text of the *Great Learning*; see Legge, *Li Chi*, vol. 2, pp. 411–12.

appear as good and whatever is bad will appear as bad. We will respond to the weighty or the light, the substantial or the insubstantial as these affect us. Our changing postures and various actions will stick to no fixed principle, and yet none will fail to attain its Heavenly mean. This is the ultimate of what is 'admirable for human beings and proper for things.'[208] It admits neither the slightest deliberation or doubt nor the most miniscule addition or subtraction. If there is even the slightest deliberation or doubt or the most miniscule addition or subtraction, then this constitutes the petty cunning of selfish thought and is no longer the highest good. But of course, if one has not mastered being 'watchful over oneself when alone'[209] and is not 'wholly refined and wholly focused,'[210] then how could one have attained such a state?

"It is only because the people of later ages don't understand that the highest good is within their own heart-minds and instead use their selfish cunning to grope and search for it outside their own heart-minds that they mistakenly believe that each affair and every thing has its own fixed principle.[211] In this way, the proper standard for right and wrong becomes obscured; they [become preoccupied with] disconnected fragments and isolated shards,[212] human desires run amok, and Heavenly principle is lost. As a consequence, the learning of making bright one's bright virtue and loving the people is thrown into confusion and turmoil throughout the world. Now, in the past, there certainly were those who wanted to make bright their bright virtue throughout the world. Nevertheless, simply because they did not understand what it is to abide in the highest good and instead exerted their selfish heart-minds toward the achievement of excessively lofty goals, they were lost in vagaries, illusions,

---

208   Paraphrasing *Book of Songs, Mao # 260*, which in turn is quoted in *Mengzi* 6A6.

209   Citing the ideal described in the fifth section of the old text of the *Great Learning*; see Legge, *Li Chi*, vol. 2, p. 413.

210   Citing the well-known passage from the "Counsels of the Great Yu" chapter of the *Book of History*, which describes the difference between the wayward "human heart-mind" and the ideal "heart-mind of the Way"; see Legge, *The Shoo King*, pp. 61–62.

211   Quoting Zhu Xi. See note 112 in this part of the volume.

212   Wang is here criticizing an encyclopedic, scholastic form of scholarship that many neo-Confucians recognized as not adequate for moral knowledge. For a discussion, see my *Ethics in the Confucian Tradition*, pp. 77–80.

emptiness, and stillness and had nothing to do with the family, state, or world. The followers of the Buddha and Laozi are like this.[213] Now, in the past, there certainly were those who wanted to love the people. Nevertheless, simply because they did not understand what it is to abide in the highest good and instead dissipated their selfish heart-minds in what is base and trifling, they were lost in calculation, scheming, cleverness, and techniques and had nothing to do with the sincere expression of benevolence or compassion. The followers of the Five Despots and those who pursue worldly success are like this.[214] All of these mistakes arise from failing to understand what it is to abide in the highest good. And so, abiding in the highest good is related to making bright one's bright virtue and loving the people as the compass and square are related to what is round and square, as ruler and tape are related to long and short, and scale and balance are related to light and heavy. If what is round or square does not accord with the compass and square, it will deviate from its standard. If what is long or short does not accord with the ruler and tape, it will miss its measure. If what is light or heavy does not accord with the scale and balance, it will lose its balance. Those who [attempt to] make bright their bright virtue or love their people without abiding in the highest good will lose the root. And so, abiding in the highest good in order to make bright one's bright virtue and love the people—this is called the learning of the great person."

4. [Question:] " 'When knowledge abides in [the highest good], there is stability. When there is stability, there is calm. When there is calm, there is peace. When there is peace, there is deliberation. When there is deliberation, there is attainment.'[215] What about these lines?"

---

213   This is a typical neo-Confucian criticism of Buddhism and Daoism. Wang, though, admired certain followers of these two schools for their purity and dedication and held them in higher esteem than corrupt Confucians. See my *Ethics in the Confucian Tradition,* pp. 76–77.

214   For the Five Despots, see note 174 in this part of the volume. Those who pursue "worldly success" want to achieve status and profit by any means. These two form a natural group of self-interested miscreants.

215   This question continues to ask about the meaning of the next lines in the first chapter of the old text of the *Great Learning.*

[Master Yangming] replied: "It is only because people don't understand that the highest good is within their own heart-minds that they search for it on the outside. They mistakenly believe that each affair and every thing has its own fixed principle,[216] and so they search for the highest good within each affair and every thing. This is why they [become preoccupied with] disconnected fragments and isolated shards; confused and disheveled, they have no stable orientation. Now, once one understands that the highest good lies within one's own heart-mind and does not depend upon anything outside, then one's intentions will have a stable orientation and one no longer will suffer the misfortunes of being [preoccupied with] disconnected fragments and isolated shards and being confused and disheveled. Once one no longer suffers the misfortunes of being [preoccupied with] disconnected fragments and isolated shards and is no longer confused and disheveled, then one's heart-mind will not engage in wanton activity and one will be able to be calm. Once one's heart-mind no longer engages in wanton activity and one is able to be calm, then one's heart-mind will be relaxed and leisurely in its daily operation, and one will be able to be at peace. Once one is able to be at peace, then whenever a thought arises or an affair affects one, one's pure knowing will spontaneously inquire and explore as to whether or not this is the highest good, and so, one will be able to deliberate. If one is able to deliberate, then all one's decisions will be precise, all one's responses will be appropriate, and the highest good will thereby be attained."

5. [Question:] " 'Things have their roots and branches.'[217] A former scholar took 'making bright one's bright virtue' as the 'root' and 'renovating the people' as the 'branch'[218]—seeing these as two separate things opposing each other as inner and outer. 'Affairs have their conclusions

---

216   Quoting Zhu Xi; see note 112 in this part of the volume.

217   This continues with the next lines in the first section of the old text of the *Great Learning* . "Roots and branches" refers to what is primary and what is secondary, respectively. Wang's view insists on the fundamental, organic unity of "root" and "branch."

218   Here again, the "former scholar" is Zhu Xi. See his commentary to this portion of the *Great Learning* in the *Great Learning in Sections and Sentences*. Zhu modified the original text of the *Great Learning* and here read "loving the people" (*qin min* 親民) as "renovating the people" (*xin min* 新民). Wang insisted on following the original text.

and their beginnings.' The same former scholar took 'knowing to abide in [the highest good]' as the 'beginning' and 'attaining [the highest good]' as the 'conclusion'— seeing these as a single affair connected like head and tail. If we follow your explanation [of the text] and read 'renovating the people' as 'loving the people,' then isn't there a problem with this explanation of roots and branches?"

[Master Yangming] replied: "This explanation of roots and branches in general is correct. If we read 'renovating the people' as 'loving the people' and say that 'making bright one's bright virtue' is the 'root' and 'loving the people' is the 'branch,' this explanation cannot be considered wrong. But we simply must not separate branch and root and regard them as two separate things. Now, the trunk of a tree can be regarded as its 'root' while the tips of the limbs can be regarded as its 'branches.' [But] it is only because the tree is a single thing that these can be called its 'roots' and 'branches.' If you say that the trunk and the tips of the limbs are separate things altogether, then how can you talk about these purportedly separate things as [related] 'roots' and 'branches?' The meaning of the phrase 'renovating the people' is different from the meaning of 'loving the people,' and so the work of making bright one's bright virtue naturally is seen as something distinct from 'renovating the people.' [But] if one understands that making bright one's bright virtue is loving the people and that loving the people is how one makes bright one's bright virtue, then how could one separate making bright one's bright virtue and loving the people and regard them as two separate things? The real problem with this former scholar's explanation is that he did not understand that making bright one's bright virtue and loving the people are fundamentally a single affair, and so he came to regard them as two separate things. This is why, even though he understood that roots and branches should be seen as one thing, he could not avoid separating them into two things."

6. [Question:] "I see how the section of text that begins with 'The ancients who wished to make bright their bright virtue throughout the world . . .' and that runs through 'first . . . cultivated themselves' can be understood on your explanation of making bright one's bright virtue and loving the people. But may I ask about the sequence of spiritual training

and manner in which one should put forth effort that is described in the section beginning with 'Those who wished to cultivate themselves' and that runs through 'the extension of knowledge lies in rectifying one's thoughts [about things]?' "[219]

[Master Yangming] replied: "This section of the text offers a complete and detailed description of the effort needed to make bright one's bright virtue, love the people, and abide in the highest good. Now, we can say that 'self,' 'heart-mind,' 'thoughts,' 'knowledge,' and 'things' describe the sequence of spiritual training. While each has its own place, in reality they are but a single thing. We can say that 'rectifying,' 'extending,' 'making sincere,' 'correcting,' and 'cultivating' describe the spiritual training used in the course of this sequence. While each has its own name, in reality they are but a single affair. What do we mean by 'person?' It is the way we refer to the physical operation of the heart-mind. What do we mean by 'heart-mind?' It is the way we refer to the luminous and intelligent master of the person. What do we mean by 'cultivating the self?' It is the way we refer to doing what is good and getting rid of what is bad. Is the physical self, on its own, able to do what is good and get rid of what is bad, or must the luminous and intelligent master of the person first want to do so and only then will one physically start to do what is good and get rid of what is bad? And so, those who want to cultivate themselves must first correct their heart-minds.

"Now, the heart-mind in its original state is the nature. Since the nature is only good, the heart-mind in its original state is wholly correct. Why, then, must one make an effort to correct it? Since, as noted above, the original state of the heart-mind is wholly correct; it is only when thoughts and ideas begin to stir that there is that which is not correct. And so, those who wish to correct their heart-minds must correct their thoughts and ideas. Whenever they have a good thought, they must

---

219   This question probes Wang's understanding of the next portions of the *Great Learning*, the second and third sections of the old text; see Legge, *Li Chi*, vol. 2, pp. 411–12. The term *gewu* 格物 translated here as "rectifying one's thoughts [about things]" represents a distinctive feature of Wang's interpretation of this text and of self-cultivation more generally. The orthodox view, represented by Zhu Xi, understands this term as the "investigation of things." For a discussion of these different readings, see my *Ethics in the Confucian Tradition*, pp. 97–99 and elsewhere.

really love it in the same way that they love a beautiful color. Whenever they have a bad thought, they must really hate it in the same way that they hate a bad odor.[220] Then, all of their thoughts will be sincere and their heart-minds can be rectified.

"However, one's thoughts give rise to what is bad as well as to what is good. If one does not have a way to make clear the difference between these two, the true and the deviant will become confused with each other and mixed together. Then, even those who wish to make their thoughts sincere will be unable to do so. And so, those who wish to make their thoughts sincere must fully extend their knowledge. To fully extend (zhi 致) means to reach to the full extent (zhi 至), like the zhi 致 that appears in the line 'Mourning reaches to (zhi 致) the full extent (zhi 致) of grief.'[221] The Book of Changes says, 'Reach to (zhi 至) the full extent (zhi 至) of what one knows.'[222] [In the latter passage,] 'the full extent of what one knows' is a matter of knowing. 'Reaching to the full extent' is fully extending. To fully extend one's knowledge is not like the so-called filling out and broadening of what one knows that later scholars talk about.[223] It is simply to extend fully the pure knowing (liangzhi 良知) of my own heart-mind.[224] Pure knowing is what Mengzi was talking about when he said, 'All human beings possess the heart-mind that knows right and wrong.' The heart-mind that knows right and wrong knows without deliberation and is able to act without learning.[225] This is why it is called pure knowing. This is the nature with which Heaven has endowed me, my heart-mind in its original state, which spontaneously is clear, luminous, bright, and aware.

---

220   These memorable examples appear in the fifth section of the old text of the *Great Learning*; see Legge, *Li Chi*, vol. 2, p. 413.

221   Quoting *Analects* 19.14.

222   Quoting the commentary on the first hexagram of the *Book of Changes*. Here and with the prior quotation Wang attempts to bolster his interpretation by supplying glosses on key terms supported by passages from the classics. The two terms involved are homophones and cognates.

223   Here, Wang is criticizing Zhu and his followers, who argued that one must augment and enlarge one's moral knowledge.

224   For Wang's appropriation of the term "pure knowing" from the *Mengzi*, see my *Ethics in the Confucian Tradition*, pp. 48–50.

225   For these qualities of pure knowing, see *Mengzi* 7A15.

"Whenever a thought or idea arises, on its own, my pure knowing knows. Is it good? Only my pure knowing knows. Is it not good? Only my pure knowing knows. It never has a need to rely on other people's opinions. This is why even those petty people who have done bad things and would stop at nothing, still, 'whenever they see a gentleman, will dislike these [aspects of themselves] and try to conceal their wickedness and display their good points.'[226] This shows the degree to which their pure knowing will not allow them to hide from themselves. Those who want to distinguish the good from the bad in order to make their thoughts sincere can only do so by extending fully the knowledge of pure knowing. Why is this? If, as a thought or idea arises, my pure knowing knows it is good, but I am not able to sincerely love it and later turn my back upon it and cast it aside, then I take what is good as bad and obscure my own pure knowing, which knows the good. If, as a thought or idea arises, my pure knowing knows it is not good, but I am not able to sincerely hate it and later follow and act upon it, then I take what is bad as good and obscure my own pure knowing, which knows what is bad. In such cases, though one says one knows, one still does not know. [Under such circumstances,] can one's thoughts be made sincere? Now, if one sincerely loves and hates what pure knowing [knows to be] good or bad, then one will not be deceiving one's own pure knowing, and one's thoughts can be made sincere.

"Now, does the desire to extend one's pure knowing refer to something shadowy and vague; does it imply remaining suspended in what is empty and incorporeal? [No!] It requires one to always be working at some concrete task or affair.[227] And so, extending one's knowledge must lie in rectifying one's thoughts [about things]. A thing or object (*wu* 物) is a task or affair (*shi* 事). A thought always arises in regard to some affair or other. The affair that is the object of a thought is called a thing. To rectify (*ge* 格) is to correct. It refers to correcting whatever is not correct and returning to what is correct. Correcting whatever is not correct means to get rid of what is bad. Returning to what is correct means to

---

226   The quotation paraphrases the fifth section of the old text of the *Great Learning*; see Legge, *Li Chi*, vol. 2, p. 413.

227   Wang here alludes to a teaching first seen in *Mengzi* 2A2 but which Wang interprets in his own distinctive way. For a discussion of this issue, see my *Ethics in the Confucian Tradition*, pp. 92–94, 100–101, 107–8.

do what is good. This is what it means to rectify. The *Book of History* says, '[The good qualities of Emperor Yao] reached (*ge*) [Heaven] above and [earth] below,'[228] '[Emperor Shun] reached (*ge*) the temple of the illustrious ancestors,'[229] and '[The king's ministers] rectified (*ge*) his errant heart-mind.'[230] The word *ge* in the expression *gewu* combines these two meanings [i.e., 'to reach (some thing)' and 'to rectify (the heart-mind)'].[231]

"Even though one sincerely wishes to love the good known by pure knowing, if one doesn't actually do the good in regard to the thing about which one is thinking, then some aspect of this thing has not yet been rectified and the thought of loving it is not yet sincere. Even though one sincerely wishes to hate the bad known by pure knowing, if one doesn't actually get rid of the bad in regard to the thing about which one is thinking, then some aspect of this thing has not yet been rectified; the thought of hating it is not yet sincere. Now, concerning the good that is known by one's pure knowing, if one actually does the good in regard to the thing about which one is thinking to the very utmost of one's ability and, concerning the bad that is known by one's pure knowing, if one actually gets rid of the bad in regard to the thing about which one is thinking to the very utmost of one's ability, then things will be completely rectified and what is known by one's pure knowing will not be diminished or obstructed in any way. [This knowledge] then can reach its ultimate extension. As a result, one's heart-mind will be pleased with itself, happy and without any lingering regrets; the thoughts that arise in one's heart-mind at last will be without a trace of self-deception and can be called sincere. This is why it is said that 'when thoughts [of things] have been rectified, knowledge is fully extended. When knowledge is

228 See the "Canon of Yao" chapter of the *Book of History* in Legge, *The Shoo King*, p. 15.
229 See the "Canon of Shun" chapter of the *Book of History* in Legge, *The Shoo King*, p. 41.
230 See the "Charge of Qiong" chapter of the *Book of History* in Legge, *The Shoo King*, p. 585.
231 Wang wants to combine these two meanings in order to make clear that the thoughts of the heart-mind that are to be rectified have objects outside the heart-mind; the process is not simply inward-looking but is directed out to events and affairs in the world.

fully extended, thoughts are sincere. When thoughts are sincere, the heart-mind is correct. When the heart-mind is correct, the self is cultivated.'[232]

"While one can say that there is an ordering of first and last in this sequence of spiritual training, the training itself is a unified whole that cannot be divided into any ordering of first and last. While this sequence of spiritual training cannot be divided into any ordering of first and last, only when every aspect of its practice is highly refined can one be sure that it will not be deficient in the slightest degree. This explanation of rectifying, extending, making sincere, and correcting helps us to understand the orthodox tradition (*zhengchuan* 正傳) of [the sage emperors] Yao and Shun and is the heart-mind seal (*xinyin* 心印) of Kongzi's approval."[233]

---

232   Quoting the fourth section of the old text of the *Great Learning*; see Legge, *Li Chi*, vol. 2, p. 412.

233   The language of this last line invokes terms and ideas of the Chan School, as seen in texts such as the *Platform Sutra*. The "orthodox tradition" of the Chan school was a mind-to-mind transmission "that does not lie in writing or words." It was affirmed through receipt of a "mind seal" between patriarchs, which in essence was the mind of the Buddha. Wang is saying that the true Confucian tradition is likewise a transmission of the heart-mind.

ESSENTIAL INSTRUCTIONS FOR STUDENTS AT LONGCHANG[234]

So many of you have followed me here that I fear I will not be able to offer all of you help. If, though, you guide one another in regard to the following four topics, this will address your concerns. The first topic is "Establishing a Commitment"; the second is "Diligent Study"; the third is "Correcting Errors"; and the fourth, "Encouraging Goodness Through Reproof." Please listen to each of these carefully and do not disregard what I have to say.

Establishing a Commitment

If one does not first establish a commitment,[235] one will never succeed in any affair in the world. The various skills of the hundred crafts all are founded upon a commitment, but students today are neglectful, remiss, indolent, and careless. They take the passing of years lightly and instead desire to stretch out the moment;[236] as a result, they accomplish nothing. This is all because they have not yet established a commitment. And so, if one is committed to becoming a sage, one will become a sage. If one is committed to becoming a worthy, one will become a worthy. Those without a commitment are like rudderless ships or horses without bits. Drifting aimlessly and dashing about wildly, where will they get to in the end?

---

234   Wang presented this set of instructions on four essential aspects of learning to the students who had followed him to Longchang 龍場, where he was banished as part of his punishment for offending the eunuch Liu Jin. They offer a succinct summary of Wang's approach to learning. For Wang's conflict with Liu Jin, see Tu, *Neo-Confucian Thought in Action,* pp. 95–99; for a discussion of the four aspects of learning, see pp. 142–46.

235   *Analects* 2.4 describes Kongzi's spiritual autobiography. It begins, "At fifteen, I established a commitment to learning" (*wu shi you wu er zhi yu xue* 吾十有五而志于學).

236   Quoting a line from the first year of Duke Zhao in the *Zuozhuan*; see Legge, *The Ch'un Ts'ew,* p. 579.

People used to tell a story: "Suppose that when you were good, your parents would be angry with you, your brothers would resent you, and your relatives and neighbors would despise and deprecate you; under such conditions, it is likely that you would not be good. If, though, when you were good, your parents would love you, your brothers would be delighted with you, and your relatives and neighbors would revere and trust you, under such conditions, what could prevent you from *not* being good and *not* being a gentleman? Suppose, though, that when you were bad, your parents would love you, your brothers would be delighted with you, and your relatives and neighbors would revere and trust you; under such conditions, it is likely that you would be bad. If, though, when you were bad, your parents would be angry with you, your brothers would resent you, and your relatives and neighbors would despise and deprecate you, under such conditions, why would you ever be bad or become a petty person?" If you gentlemen contemplate this story, you will understand how to establish a commitment.

Diligent Study

Once you have established a commitment to become a gentleman, you should devote your efforts to study. When studies are not pursued diligently, it is always because one's commitment still is not sincere. Those of you who have followed me in my wanderings should not regard sharp intelligence and quick wit as the highest [qualities of heart-mind]; reserve your highest regard for diligence and humility. You gentlemen should look among yourselves. If there are those who are empty but act as if they are full, are lacking but act as if they have plenty,[237] hide their inadequacies, are jealous of the good in others, boast of their merits, affirm their own views, and use inflated words to deceive others, even if the abilities and talents of these people are superior and exceptional, is there anyone among you who does not dislike and despise them? Is there anyone among you who does not look down on and deprecate them? If such people really tried to deceive others, would not these others just secretly laugh at them?

If there are those among you who are humble, modest, and self-restrained and conduct themselves well though lacking in ability, demonstrate sincere commitment and make earnest effort, study diligently and

---

237   Compare *Analects* 7.25.

are good at raising questions, praise the good in others, and take responsibility for their errors, acknowledge the strengths of others, and make clear their own shortcomings, are conscientious, trustworthy, joyful, and at ease, and are the same on the outside as they are on the inside, even if the abilities and talents of such people are common and dull, is there anyone among you who does not acclaim and admire them? If such people really conduct themselves well though lacking in ability and do not seek to put themselves above others, would not those who earlier considered them lacking in ability revere and praise them? If you gentlemen contemplate this, you will understand how to devote your efforts to study.

Correcting Errors

Even great worthies cannot avoid committing some errors; nevertheless, this in no way detracts from their being great worthies, because they are able to correct their errors. And so, what we esteem is not being without errors but being able to correct one's errors. You gentlemen think about this for yourselves; in the course of your normal day, are there occasions when in your conduct you have been deficient in regard to humility, modesty, conscientiousness, or truthfulness? Have you been inadequate in terms of filial piety or friendship or succumbed to fraudulent, deceitful, mean, or stingy habits? I doubt that any of you have reached such a state, but if unfortunately any of you have, it will be because you unknowingly have walked down the path of error and earlier did not have the benefit of talking and practicing with teachers and friends and receiving their guidance and encouragement. I ask you gentlemen to turn and reflect upon yourselves. If there is the rare one among you who is tending in this direction, you absolutely must bitterly regret your mistake. Nevertheless, you should not become dissatisfied with yourself over this and allow it to weaken your resolve to correct your errors and follow what is good. If one day, people can completely wash away their old stains, even if they were bandits or thieves in the past, this in no way detracts from their being gentlemen today. However, should you say, "I used to be like that in the past, but today, even though I have corrected my errors and follow the good, no one trusts me," but you have not atoned for your former errors and instead shrink back in shame and willingly remain in a polluted state, I have absolutely no hope for you!

Encouraging Goodness Through Reproof

To encourage goodness through reproof is the way of friends, but you must present such reproofs conscientiously and lead others well. You must be exceedingly conscientious and loving and as accommodating and flexible as you can be, so that you get others to listen and follow, to understand and reform.[238] If you move them without inciting anger, you are doing well. If you begin by suddenly and thoroughly exposing their errors and wickedness, disparaging and reviling them in ways they cannot endure, you will only succeed in eliciting feelings of deep shame and heated resentment. Even though they may desire to comply and follow along with you, under such circumstances, they will be unable to do so. You will only stir them up and lead them to do what is bad. And so, whenever someone points out another's shortcomings or attacks their hidden weaknesses only to make a display of their own personal uprightness, this should never be called encouraging goodness through reproof.[239] Nevertheless, while correcting faults is something I should not do to others, it is something others can do to me,[240] for all those who attack my failings are my teachers.[241] How could I not receive such admonitions joyfully and take them to heart?

I have yet to attain any real insight into the Dao, and my study of it remains crude and inept. You gentlemen have made a mistake following me up to this point. When I think of this throughout the course of each night, I realize that I have yet to reach the point where I avoid doing what is *truly* bad—much less the point where I merely avoid making simple errors! People say that the proper way to serve a teacher is to "neither oppose your teacher nor cover up your teacher's faults."[242] But they go on to say that you should not admonish your teacher, and this

238   Compare *Analects* 4.26 and 12.23 on how to remonstrate with friends.

239   The idea expressed here is very similar to one of the four things that Zigong disliked. See *Analects* 17.24.

240   Wang's language here is highly reminiscent of the so-called Confucian Golden Rule. Compare *Analects* 12.2 and 15.24.

241   This is similar to something we find in *Xunzi*, chap. 2: "Those who disagree with me and are correct are my teachers."

242   The quotation is from the "Tan Gong" chapter of the *Book of Rites*. For a translation, see Legge, *Li Chi*, vol. 1, p. 121.

is wrong! The way to admonish your teacher is to be upright without reaching the point of opposition and to be accommodating without reaching the point of covering up faults. If I am right about something, such an approach will make clear what is right; if I am wrong about something, it will allow me to eliminate what is wrong. This shows how "teaching and learning support each other."[243] You gentlemen should begin your practice of *encouraging goodness through reproof* with me!

---

243   The quoted matter is from the "Record of Learning" chapter of the *Book of Rites*. For a translation, see Legge, *Li Chi,* vol. 2, p. 83.

POETRY

Gold Mountain[244]

Gold Mountain[245] is a dot, the size of one's fist;
Bursting through Heaven, reflected in the Yangzi.
Drunk, I lean upon the moon, resting on Mystery Heights Pavilion,[246]
The sound of a jade flute rattles the dragon, asleep in his cave.[247]

The Moon Obscuring Mountain Lodge[248]

The mountain is near; the moon is far away; so we feel the moon is small,
And we say the mountain is larger than the moon.
If human eyes were as large as Heaven,
We would see the mountain is small and moon immense!

---

244   This and the following poem are not included in Wang's complete works but are found in his *Chronological Biography, sui* 11. They were written when Wang was around ten years old. Wang composed the first verse extemporaneously purportedly to help his grandfather who was trying unsuccessfully to come up with a verse of his own. For a discussion, see Tu, *Neo-Confucian Thought in Action,* pp. 22–24.

245   Gold Mountain is located in Zhenjiang 鎮江 County in present-day Jiangsu Province. Originally, it was on an island in the middle of the Yangzi River, but because of efforts to reclaim the land beneath the riverbed, it now lies on the south bank of the Yangzi. Gold Mountain Temple is located on the top of this mountain.

246   Mystery Heights Pavilion was located at the highest peak of Gold Mountain.

247   This might be taken as referring to one of the cave grottoes on Gold Mountain or simply as an allusion to various literary precedents.

248   A friend of Wang's grandfather was impressed with Wang's first verse but asked that he compose another, on the spot, on the theme of "The Moon Obscuring Mountain Lodge." "Mountain lodge" (*shanfang* 山房) might refer to Mystery Heights Pavilion.

Moonlit Evening (Two Poems)

Written while singing with my students on Heaven's Spring Bridge [249]

(Number One)

For ten thousand leagues, the mid-autumn moon shines in the clear sky.
Over the four mountains, light clouds suddenly gather.[250]
But in an instant, the mist flies away on the wind,
Leaving the moon shining, as before, in the blue heavens.
If you believe that pure knowing is fundamentally unsullied,
How could external things ever stand in its way?
This night, this old man sings wild songs;[251]
Transformed into Heavenly melodies, they fill the great void!

(Number Two)

Throughout mid-autumn, this bright moon shines.
Where else could I find such a collection of talent?
What a pity that learning was cut off for one thousand years![252]
Be not remiss as you pass the years of your life young men!
Still suspicious of Zhu Xi's shadows and echoes,[253]

---

249 These poems were written in 1524 while Wang was celebrating the Mid-Autumn Festival. The setting, with the elder Wang enjoying a stroll along the river in the company of his disciples, is reminiscent of *Analects* 11.25; the second verse ends paraphrasing lines from this passage. This bridge is also the site where Wang later expounded his famous "Four Sentence Teaching." For a translation and discussion, see Chan, *Instructions for Practical Living*, pp. 241–46.

250 The "four mountains" or "mountains of the four directions" simply refers to mountains throughout China.

251 Here, and in the final line of the following verse, we find Wang using the word "wild" (*kuang* 狂) in a positive sense, meaning something like "ardor" or the like. The original source of this idea, which Wang developed and deployed throughout his work, is *Analects* 13.21. For a study of this aspect of Wang's philosophy, see Julia Ching, "Wang Yang-ming (1472–1529): A Study in 'Mad Ardor,'" *Papers on Far Eastern History* 3 (March 1971): 85–130.

252 This refers to the roughly one thousand years between the death of Mengzi (391–308 B.C.E.) and the revival of the learning of the heart-mind by Zhou Dunyi.

253 Wang criticized Zhu for neglecting the heart-mind and getting lost in the attempt to explore the principles of things. According to Wang, the heart-mind is principle and so what occupied Zhu's attention were no more than shadows and echoes.

Ashamed to do the fragmentary and disjointed work of Zheng Xuan,[254]
Setting aside his lute, while its strings still quivered in the spring breeze,
Dian—the wild one—understood how I feel![255]

Sitting in the Night[256]

Sitting alone in the courtyard under the new light of the autumn moon,
Where else between Heaven and earth could one enjoy greater leisure?
My loud song is in tempo with the pure wind and with it fades away;
My quiet thoughts follow the flowing waters of spring.
The thousand sages possessed no secret beyond what can be found in
the heart-mind.
The only use for the six classics is to wipe away the dust upon the
mirror.[257]
Feel sorry for those disturbed by dreams of the Duke of Zhou[258]
Who cannot maintain their clarity amid the poverty of a narrow lane.[259]

---

254   Zheng Xuan 鄭玄 (127–200) was a famous commentator of the Han dynasty.
Wang, though, looked askance at commentarial work as lacking in proper focus, tending
toward the collection of disconnected facts and leading nowhere.

255   These last two lines, as well as other features of these two poems, draw upon
Analects 11.25, in which Kongzi asked each of four disciples to express his own aspiration. Kongzi proclaimed that he was with Dian—who wanted, in the early spring, to
bath in the Yi River, enjoy the breeze at the altar of rain, and return home singing in
the company of several young men.

256   This poem was written sometime in 1524.

257   Wang borrows the image of the heart-mind as a pure mirror from the spirit verse
competition between Hui Neng and Shen Xiu in the Chan Buddhist classic the *Platform
Sutra*. See the selections from and introduction to this work contained in this volume.

258   In *Analects* 7.5, Kongzi bemoans the fact that it has been so long since he dreamed
of the Duke of Zhou. Wang here refocuses this idea, claiming that people need not look
to the sages for guidance; they are better served cultivating and following their own
heart-mind, which, as is clear from the next poem, contains a sage within.

259   This is an allusion to *Analects* 6.9, which describes how Kongzi's favorite disciple,
Yan Hui, did not allow material deprivation to affect his joy.

Four Verses on Pure Knowing Written for My Students[260]

(Number One)

Kongzi lies within the heart-mind of each and every person,
But he is hidden and lost by the suffering caused by sights and sounds.[261]
In this very moment, he points to your true face.[262]
It is none other than pure knowing—doubt no more!

(Number Two)

I ask you, sir, what keeps you unsettled each day?
You misdirect your efforts on a world of vexation and trouble.
Do not say that the school of the sages lacks an esoteric teaching.[263]
The two words "pure knowing" unify all things!

(Number Three)

Everyone has within an unerring compass;[264]
The root and source of the myriad transformations lies in the heart-mind.
I laugh when I think that, earlier, I saw things the other way around;
Following branches and leaves, I searched outside![265]

---

260   These were written sometime in 1524.

261   The idea is that the things of the world and the desires we form in response to them distract us and obscure the spontaneous intuitions of pure knowing.

262   This line shows considerable Chan Buddhist influence. The idea of *pointing to one's original face* and doing so *in the moment* are classic Chan themes. Compare the final line in the poem "Written at Goose Lake to Rhyme with My Brother's Verse" by Lu Xiangshan, contained in this volume.

263   Literally, a "verbal secret" (*kou jue* 口訣), i.e., an orally transmitted esoteric teaching like that characteristic of Chan Buddhism and made famous in the *Platform Sutra*.

264   The analogy is to a north-pointing, navigational compass.

265   "Branches and leaves" refers to the fragmentary and disjointed kind of scholarship Wang often criticizes, which takes one away from the "root" of understanding: the heart-mind.

(Number Four)

Lacking sound or scent—the moment when one understands on one's own,[266]
This is the foundation for all within Heaven and earth!
Those who abandon their own limitless treasury
Go door-to-door with alms bowl in hand—like a beggar!

Response to Someone Who Asked about Pure Knowing (Two Verses)[267]

(Number One)

Pure knowing is what one knows for oneself;
Apart from this, there is no knowledge.[268]
Who does not have pure knowing within?
Yet, who has attained pure knowing?

(Number Two)

Yet, who has attained pure knowing?
If you feel pain or an itch, you will know it!
If you ask others about feeling pain or an itch,
They will tell you: If you feel pain or an itch, there is no need to ask!

---

266   Compare *Doctrine of the Mean* 33.6, "The workings of high Heaven are without sound or scent," which quotes *Book of Songs, Mao* # 235. Understanding on one's own (*duzhi* 獨知) is reminiscent of the idea that the gentleman is watchful over his inner self (*shen qi du* 慎其獨). See the fifth section of the old text of the *Great Learning*; see Legge, *Li Chi,* vol. 2, p. 413.

267   This piece was written sometime in 1524.

268   Wang, in his ethical philosophy, relied on a distinction between ordinary knowledge and real knowledge. The former was what we might call common or everyday knowledge, more like hearsay; the latter required first-person experience and involved appropriate feeling as well as knowing. Compare note 26 in this part of the volume.

Response to Someone Who Asked about the Way[269]

When hungry—eat!
When tired—sleep![270]
This is self-cultivation;
It is an enigma within an enigma.[271]
When you explain this to the people of the world,
They are confused and refuse to believe.
Instead, they search for immortality beyond the physical body.

On Longevity

Vainly, I used to long for immortality,
But lacking the means to afford the great elixir,
I searched throughout the famous mountains,
Until my temples sprouted only silver, silken threads.
My frail form bound by this one thought,
Each day I moved farther from the Way.
In middle age, suddenly, I experienced an awakening.[272]
The Pill of Nine Returns lies here within me![273]
I have no need for furnaces or tripods,
No use for Inner or Outer alchemy.
There is no beginning and no end,
How much less life and death?
Those wandering masters of method,
Their subtle expressions only increased my doubts.

---

269 This poem was written sometime in 1524.

270 Quoting *Transmission of the Lamp,* chap. 5.

271 This is an allusion to the final line of the first chapter of the *Laozi.*

272 Wang's initial enlightenment occurred in 1508, when he was in his mid-thirties.

273 This line and the following two lines contain a number of references to Daoist techniques for longevity. For a good introduction to these, see Russell Kirkland, *Taoism: An Enduring Tradition* (New York: Routledge, 2004).

In a most confused fashion, those old men
Transmit techniques diverse and difficult.
Heaven and earth depend upon me!
What use is there in searching elsewhere?
The thousand sages all are passing shadows,
Pure knowing is my teacher!

SUGGESTED READINGS

General:

1. Berthrong, John. *Transformations of the Way*. Boulder, CO: Westview Press, 1998.
2. Chan, Wing-tsit, trans. *A Source Book in Chinese Philosophy*. Reprint, Princeton, NJ: Princeton University Press, 1973.
3. Chang, Carsun. *The Development of Neo-Confucian Thought*, vol. 1. New York: Bookman Associates, 1958.
4. Dumoulin, Heinrich. *India and China*. Vol. 1 of *Zen Buddhism: A History*. New York: Macmillan, 1988.
5. Fung, Yu-lan. *The Period of Classical Learning*. Vol. 2 of *A History of Chinese Philosophy*. Trans. Derk Bodde. Princeton, NJ: Princeton University Press, 1953.
6. Ivanhoe, Philip J. *Confucian Moral Self Cultivation*. Rev. 2d ed. Indianapolis: Hackett, 2006.
7. Taylor, Rodney. *The Religious Dimensions of Neo-Confucianism*. Albany: State University of New York Press, 1990.
8. Tillman, Hoyt C. *Confucian Discourse and Chu Hsi's Ascendancy*. Honolulu: University of Hawaii Press, 1992.

Platform Sutra:

1. Faure, Bernard. "The Concept of One-Practice Samadhi in Early Ch'an." In *Traditions of Meditation in Chinese Buddhism*, ed. Peter Gregory, 99–128. Honolulu: University of Hawaii Press, 1986.
2. _____. *The Rhetoric of Immediacy: A Cultural Critique of Chan/Zen Buddhism*. Reprint, Princeton, NJ: Princeton University Press, 1994.
3. Gomez, Luis O. "The Direct and the Gradual Approaches of Zen Master Mahayana: Fragments of the Teachings of Mo-ho-yen." In *Studies in Ch'an and Hua-yen*, ed. Robert M. Gimello and Peter N. Gregory, 69–167. Honolulu: University of Hawaii Press, 1983.
4. Gregory, Peter N., ed. *Sudden and Gradual: Approaches to Enlightenment in Chinese Thought*. Honolulu: University of Hawaii Press, 1987.

5. McRae, John R. *Seeing Through Zen: Encounter, Transformation, and Dialogue in Chinese Chan Buddhism*. Berkeley and Los Angeles: University of California Press, 2004.
6. Yampolsky, Philip B, trans. *The Platform Sutra of the Sixth Patriarch: The Text of the Tun-huang Manuscript*. New York: Columbia University Press, 1967.

Lu Xiangshan:

1. Cady, Lyman V. *The Philosophy of Lu Hsiang-shan*. Taipei: Pacific Cultural Foundation, 1939.
2. Ching, Julia. *The Religious Thought of Chu Hsi*. New York: Oxford University Press, 2000.
3. Huang, Siu-chi. *Lu Hsiang-shan: A Twelfth Century Chinese Idealist Philosopher*. New Haven, CT: American Oriental Society, 1944.
4. Hymes, Robert. "Lu Chiu-yuan, Academies, and the Problem of the Local Community." In *Neo-Confucian Education: The Formative Stage*, ed. William Theodore de Bary and Jonathan W. Chaffee, 432–56. Berkeley: University of California Press, 1989.
5. Ivanhoe, Philip J. "The Ethical Philosophy of Lu Xiangshan." In *Neo-Confucian Philosophy*, ed. John Makeham. Dao Companions to Chinese Philosophy Series. New York: Springer, forthcoming. (This essay is similar in content to the Introduction to Lu's work in this reader except for a final section, titled "Contemporary Relevance," which will be of interest to those concerned with such issues.)

Wang Yangming:

1. Chan, Wing-tsit, trans. *Instructions for Practical Living and Other Neo-Confucian Writings by Wang Yang-ming*. New York: Columbia University Press, 1963.
2. Ching, Julia, trans. *The Philosophical Letters of Wang Yang-ming*. Columbia: University of South Carolina Press, 1973.
3. _____. *To Acquire Wisdom: The Way of Wang Yang-ming*. New York: Columbia University Press, 1976.
4. Hauf, Kandice. "'Goodness Unbound': Wang Yang-ming and the Redrawing of the Boundary of Confucianism." In *Imagining Boundaries: Changing Confucian Doctrines, Texts, and Hermeneutics*, ed.

Kai-wing Chow, On-cho Ng, and John Henderson, 121–46. Albany: State University of New York Press, 1999.

5. Henke, Frederick Goodrich, trans. *The Philosophy of Wang Yang-ming.* Reprint, New York: Paragon Books, 1964.

6. Ivanhoe, Philip J. "'Existentialism' in the School of Wang Yangming." In *Chinese Language, Thought, and Culture: Nivison and His Critics,* ed. Philip J. Ivanhoe, 250–64. La Salle, IL: Open Court, 1996.

7. _____. *Ethics in the Confucian Tradition: The Thought of Mengzi and Wang Yangming.* Rev. 2d ed. Indianapolis: Hackett, 2002.

8. Nivison, David S. "Comments on P. J. Ivanhoe's Paper." In *Chinese Language, Thought, and Culture: Nivison and His Critics,* ed. Philip J. Ivanhoe, 336–41. La Salle, IL: Open Court, 1996.

9. Tien, David W. "Warranted Neo-Confucian Belief: Knowledge and the Affections in the Religious Epistemologies of Wang Yangming (1472–1529) and Alvin Plantinga." *International Journal for Philosophy of Religion* 55:1 (2004): 31–55.

10. _____. "Wang Yangming and the Basis of Self-Cultivation." In *Neo-Confucian Philosophy,* ed. John Makeham. Dao Companions to Chinese Philosophy Series. New York: Springer, forthcoming.

11. Tu, Wei-ming. *Neo-Confucian Thought in Action: Wang Yang-ming's Youth (1472–1509).* Berkeley: University of California Press, 1976.

INDEX

A Record for Reflection (*Jinsilu* 近思錄), 29n3, 117n35–36, 118n38, 118n41, 120n47, 153n166

abiding in the highest good (*zhi yu zhi shan* 止於至善). *See* highest good

Amitābha, 17

Angle, Steve, 105n13

Aristotle, 10

being watchful over oneself (*shen qi du* 慎其獨), 164, 182n266

benxin (本心). *See* original heart-mind

benxing (本性). *See* original nature

Berkeley, Bishop, 34, 108

biography, xi, 3, 4, 30, 32, 33, 89, 102, 104, 173n235, 178n244

Bodhidharma, 15

bodhisattva, 17, 26, 53

body (*ti* 體), 9, 10, 15–17, 107, 162n203, 162n205, 163n206 (*see also* one body)

Book of Changes (*Yijing* 易經), 31, 40–41, 45–46, 47n41, 49–50, 54n87, 56–59, 61, 62n120–21, 65, 68–70, 77n204, 78n209, 79–81, 96n282, 133n96, 150–51, 157, 159n192, 169

Book of History (*Shujing* 書經), 53n84, 56, 58, 62n124, 66n142, 68, 72, 75n194–95, 77n204, 78, 83n232, 89n254, 90n256–57, 118n39, 120n52, 121n53–4, 130n81–2, 133n95, 135n101, 136n107–08, 137n114, 143, 148n154, 151, 154, 157, 164n210, 171

Book of Music (*Yuejing* 樂經), 77n204, 151, 157

Book of Rites (*Liji* 禮記), 50n76, 51n76, 53n84, 56n94, 57n99, 73n186, 75n194, 77, 80n216–17, 125n66, 127n72, 130n81, 133n92, 135n101, 135n104–05, 136n111, 138n118, 139, 141n126, 151, 157, 158n184, 158n186–87, 159n196, 160n197, 160n200, 163n207, 164n209, 168n219, 169n220, 170n226, 172n232, 176n242, 177n243, 182n266

Book of Songs (*Shijing* 詩經), 54n87, 55n93, 60, 63n126, 64, 66, 77n204, 78n209, 81n219, 151, 157, 158n185, 158n187, 164n208, 182n266

bright virtue (*ming de* 明德), making bright one's bright virtue (*ming ming de* 明明德), 134, 136–37, 146–47, 160–68

Brown, Miranda, 34n15

Buddha, 4n4, 9, 18, 23, 26, 54, 165, 172n233

Buddha-nature (*foxing* 佛性), 4, 5, 10, 15n25, 16, 20, 22n37, 23, 25

Buddhism, xi, 3–6, 7n10, 8, 10, 14n22, 15, 17, 21n34, 52, 55, 86, 95, 97n285, 119, 120, 133, 149n157, 165n213, 181n263

Cady, Lyman V., 29n1

chan (禪). *See* meditation

Chan Buddhism, 3, 5, 6n9, 7–10, 12, 16n26, 17, 21, 42, 97n285, 117n32, 119, 172n233, 180n257, 181n262–63

Chan, Wing-tsit, 11n16, 20n32, 29n3, 56n97, 101n1, 102n3, 105n13, 109n19, 110n.21, 113n25, 115n29, 117n35, 117n36, 118n38, 118n41, 120n47, 122n58, 123n61, 153n166, 179n249

Chang, Carsun, 29n1, 101n1, 105n13

Chang Yü-ch'üan, 104n11

chang zhi (常知). *See* ordinary knowledge

Chen Xiyi (陳希夷), 41, 60

Cheng Mingdao (程明道) (Cheng Hao 程顥), 61n117, 92n269, 117, 120, 123

Cheng Yichuan (程伊川) (Cheng Yi 程頤), xi, 32, 44n32, 50n76, 61n104, 117, 118n38, 118n41, 133n92, 134n100, 139n121, 144, 149, 153

Cheng-Zhu School, Learning of Principle (*Lixue* 理學), xi, 32, 78n207, 158n189

Ching, Julia, 29n2, 37n22, 101n1, 105n13, 179n251

Chuanxilu (傳習錄). *See A Record for Practice*

Chunqiu (春秋). *See Spring and Autumn Annals*

cixin (此心). *See* this heart-mind

Classic of Filial Piety (*Xiaojing* 孝經), 48n51, 158n187 (*see also* filial piety)

classics, 7, 31, 36, 39, 41–42, 71–72, 77, 89n250, 150–56, 157, 169n222, 180

Collected Commentaries on the Book of Songs (*Shi jizhuan* 詩集傳), 158n181

Collected Comments on the Four Books (*Sishujizhu* 四書集註), 137n116, 149n155, 157n181

Collected Comments on the Mengzi (*Mengzi jizhu* 孟子集註), 143n131

Comprehending the Book of Changes (*Tongshu* 通書), 41, 56–57, 61

Confucius. *See* Kongzi

Craig, Edward, 9n15

Crisp, Roger, 33n14

Da Dai Liji (大戴禮記). *See Rites of the Elder Dai*

Dao (*dao* 道). *See* Way

dao wen xue (道問學). *See* pursuing inquiry and study

Daodejing (道德經), *Laozi*, 41, 60, 65n137–38, 182n271

Daoism, 5, 6n9, 7n9, 10, 12, 23n25, 38, 41–42, 51, 60n112, 60n113, 65, 71n168, 71n170, 86, 133, 149n157, 165n213, 183n273

daoxin (道心). *See* heart-mind of the Way

Daxue (大學). *See Great Learning*

Daxue huowen (大學或問). *See Some Questions on the Great Learning*

Daxue wen (大學問). *See Questions on the Great Learning*

Daxue zhangju (大學章句). *See Great Learning in Sections and Sentences*

delusion, 6, 11, 14, 16, 18, 20, 22, 24, 37

dharma, 14, 16, 18n30, 19, 21–23, 54n88

dhyāna. See meditation

Diamond Sutra, 4

(*ding* 定). *See* meditative stability

Dingxingshu (定性書). *See* Letter on Calming One's Nature

Dippman, Jeffrey, 12n19

Discipline of the Bodhisattva, 26

Doctrine of the Mean (*Zhongyong* 中庸), 50n74, 51n76, 54n87, 63n129, 64n103, 66, 73n187, 75n196, 78n209, 80, 81n222, 83n231, 96n280, 117n37, 119n46, 121n55, 123n63, 126n68, 127n69, 127n72, 129, 133n93, 135n101, 139n122, 144n135, 144n137, 144n139, 145n140, 146, 148n153, 149n155, 154n170, 159n191, 159n193, 160, 182n266

Doctrine of the Mean in Sections and Sentences (*Zhongyong zhangju* 中庸章句), 149n155

Duke of Zhou (*Zhou Gong* 周公), 150–51, 155, 180

dunwu (頓悟). *See* sudden enlightenment

dhyāna. See meditation

E hu si (鵝湖寺). *See* Goose Lake Temple

Elements of Learning (*Xiaoxue* 小學), 117

empty talk (*kong yan* 空言), 58n100

enlightenment, 6–8, 13, 14n23, 16–17, 19–21, 37, 53, 79, 107, 137, 183n272 (*see also* sudden enlightenment)

Er Cheng yishu (二程遺書). *See Extant Works of the Two Cheng [Brothers]*

Er Cheng yulu (二程語錄). *See Recorded Sayings of the Two Cheng [Brothers]*

errors, faults, or shortcomings, 57–58, 81–82, 90, 120–21, 173, 175–76

Explanation of the Diagram of the Supreme Ultimate (*Taiji tushuo* 太極圖說), 41, 56–57, 61

"Explanations of the Trigrams" (*Shuogua* 說卦), 69n163, 70n164, 159n192

Extant Works of the Cheng [Brothers] from Henan (*Henan Chengshi yishu* 河南程氏遺書), 104n10, 117n35–36, 120n47, 149n156, 153n166

Extant Works of the Two Cheng [Brothers] (*Er Cheng yishu* 二程遺書), 44n32

extending knowledge (*zhi zhi* 致知), 106–08, 125–26, 144, 147, 153n166, 168, 170–72 (*see also* extending pure knowing)

extending pure knowing (*zhi liang zhi* 致良知), 106–108, 113, 118n44, 126, 128–30, 169–70 (*see also* extending knowledge)

Fifth Patriarch, 4, 14, 16, 20–21

filial piety (*xiao* 孝), 47, 137–39, 141, 163, 175 (*see also Classic of Filial Piety*)

five agents (*wuxing* 五行), 56n97

five senses, 53, 72

four sprouts (*siduan* 四端), 48, 73,

Foxing (佛性). *See* Buddha–nature

function (*yong* 用), 9–12, 17, 19, 22–23, 25, 37, 107, 137n115, 162n204–5, 163n206

gang (剛), 50, 69

Gao Yao (皋陶), 76, 83, 121n54

gewu (格物). *See* investigating things/rectifying thoughts

(*gong* 公) and (*si* 私). *See* public and private

gongfu (功夫). *See* spiritual effort/ spiritual task

Goose Lake Temple (*E hu si* 鵝湖 寺), 29, 38, 42, 96n278

Graham, A. C., 9n15, 61n117, 71n168

Great Appendix to the Book of Changes (*Xici zhuan* 繫辭傳), 40, 47n41, 50, 53n82–83, 54n87, 58–59, 62n96n282, 120, 65, 68n157, 69n161, 70, 74n189, 118n43, 127n70

great compassion (*mahākaruna*), 5

Great Learning (*Daxue* 大學), 50n76, 51n76, 57, 67, 73n186, 75n194, 80, 106–07, 114n28, 125n66, 127n, 72, 130n81, 132, 133n92–93, 134, 135n101, 135n104–5, 136–37, 139n121, 141, 143n127, 146, 147n147, 158n189, 159n190, 160–72, 182n266

Great Learning in Sections and Sentences (*Daxue zhangju*

大學章句), 137n116, 160n199, 166n218

Gregory, Peter N., 5n6

Gu Weixian (顧惟賢), 140

Han Yu 韓愈 (Changli 唱黎), 71n172, 149

Hartman, Charles, 71n172

health (metaphor for spiritual achievement), 10–11, 114, 130–31

heart-mind (*xin* 心), xi, 15n25, 32–39, 42, 45, 48–50, 54, 62, 70–73, 74n190, 75, 78, 84–86, 89–90, 91n263, 92, 93n271, 96, 102, 105–114, 117, 119–121, 127, 132, 133n95, 137–40, 143–49, 153, 156, 161–62, 164–66, 168–69, 171–72, 174, 179n252–53, 180 (*see also* human heart-mind *and* heart-mind of the Way)

heart-mind of the Way (*daoxin* 道心), 38, 41, 133n95, 148–49, 164n210

Hegel, G. W. F., 36

Henke, Frederick G., 101n1, 105n13, 109n19

Henan Chengshi waishu (河南 程氏外書). See *Outer Works of the Cheng [Brothers] from Henan*

Henan Chengshi yishu (河南程氏 遺書). See *Extant Works of the Cheng [Brothers] from Henan*

highest good (*zhi shan* 至善), 80, 136n111, 137, 139–40, 143, 163–68

Hongren (弘忍), 4, 6, 7

honoring the virtuous nature (*zun de xing* 尊德性), 39, 159

Hu Shi, 21

Huainanzi, 134n99
Huang Chengfu (黃誠甫), 129
Huang Siu–chi, 29n1
Huang Zongxian (黃宗賢),
    75n194, 118, 128, 140
(*hui* 惠) *see* insight
Huineng (惠能), 3–4, 6, 8–9,
    15–16, 20–21
human heart-mind (*renxin* 人心),
    32, 36–39, 41, 78, 84, 90, 92,
    96, 111, 114, 121, 133n95,
    148–49, 164n210
Hursthouse, Rosalind, 33

idealism, 34, 114
insight (*prajñā*) (*hui* 惠), 8–10,
    14–19, 97n285
investigating things/rectifying
    thoughts (*gewu* 格物), 62, 80,
    107–08, 113, 125, 127n74, 132,
    136n112, 143–44, 146–47, 159,
    168, 170–72

Jingde chuandenglu (景德傳燈錄).
    See *Transmission of the Lamp*
Jinsilu (近思錄). *See A Record for
    Reflection*
Jizi (箕子), 76
Ju Boyu (蘧伯玉), 81, 120

Kant, Immanuel, 111–12
karma, 19–21, 23, 54n90
kong yan (空言). *See* empty talk
Kongzi (孔子), 24n40, 31–32,
    46–48, 50n76, 57–58, 59n107,
    60, 63n125, 63n126, 67, 71,
    81, 84–85, 88–89, 90n255,
    90n258, 92, 96n284, 120–21,
    125, 131–32, 134n97, 136, 143,
    149n157, 150–158, 172,
    173n235, 180n255, 180n258–9,
    181

Kongzi Jiayu (孔子家語). *See
    Sayings from Kongzi's School*

Laozi (老子), 60–61, 65, 71,
    77–78, 165
Laozi. *See Daodejing*
Learning of Principle (*Lixue*
    理學). *See* Cheng-Zhu School
Learning of the Heart-mind
    (*Xinxue* 心學). *See* Lu-Wang
    School
Letter on Calming One's Nature
    (*Dingxingshu* 定性書), 117n32,
    123
(*li* 理). *See* principle
liangzhi (良知). *See* pure knowing
Liezi (列子), 12n19, 71
Liji (禮記). *See Book of Rites*
Littlejohn, Ronnie, 12n19
Liu Jin (劉瑾), 101, 173n234
Liu Yuandao (劉元道), 117n32,
    122, 131n85
Liu Zicheng (劉子澄), 117n34
loving the people (*qin min* 親民),
    134–36, 162–65, 166n218,
    167
Lu Jiuling (陸九齡) (Fuzhai復齋),
    29, 38
Lu Jiushao (陸九紹) (Suoshan梭
    山), 29, 38, 40–41, 52, 55n92,
    56–57, 58n103, 59, 61n118
Lü Zuqian (呂祖謙), 29n3, 38
Lu-Wang School, Learning of the
    Heart-mind (*Xinxue* 心學), xi,
    3, 32

mahākaruna. *See* great compassion
Mahāyāna Buddhism, 4n5, 5n6
making bright one's bright virtue
    (*ming ming de* 明明德). *See*
    bright virtue
McDowell, John, 109n20

meditation (*dhyāna*) (*chan* 禪),
8–9, 22n36, 24–25, 117, 122
meditative stability (*samādhi*) (*ding*
定), 8, 9, 10, 17, 19, 25, 117
Mencius. *See* Mengzi
Mengzi (孟子), 4n4, 8n11, 32,
45, 47–50, 55n91, 56, 62, 65,
66n141, 72–74, 81, 83, 85–87,
91, 125, 135, 137n113,
143n132, 154, 159n196,
161n202, 169, 179n252
Mengzi jizhu (孟子集註). *See*
Collected Comments on the
Mengzi
ming de (明德). *See* bright virtue
ming ming de (明明德). *See*
making bright one's bright virtue
mirror (metaphor for the mind),
6, 15–16, 25, 119, 128, 180
Morgan, Evan, 134n99
Mozi (墨子) (Mo Di 墨翟), 65,
81n220, 86n244
Mu Bozhang (穆伯長), 60

Nivison, David S., 47n47,
111n22, 113n27, 157n179

Olberding, Amy, 31n7
one body (*yiti* 一體), 10, 17, 112,
115, 161–3 (*see also* body)
ordinary knowledge (*chang zhi* 常
知), 113, 182n268
original heart-mind (*benxin* 本心),
15–16, 20, 26, 49–50, 105, 120,
138n117
original nature (*benxing* 本性), 10,
12, 14, 20, 23, 25
Outer Works of the Cheng [Brothers]
from Henan (*Henan Chengshi*
waishu 河南程氏外書),
92n269, 118n41
Ouyang Xiu (歐陽修), 32n9

Pang Yun (龐蘊), 25n42
Peng Guoxiang, 31n7
perfection of wisdom (*prajñā*
pāramitā), 8
poetry, 6–7, 14–16, 38, 39n25,
42, 47n45, 74n191, 84n236,
90n260, 93–97, 104, 178–84
prajñā. See insight
prajñā pāramitā. See perfection of
wisdom
principle (*li* 理), 12, 32–38, 40, 42,
45–49, 55–59, 61, 63–70, 73–82,
89–92, 105–10, 111n22, 112–14,
118, 128, 136–40, 143n127,
144n133, 146–49, 153–55, 157,
159, 164, 166, 179n253
public (*gong* 公) and private (*si*
私), 52
pure knowing (*liangzhi* 良知), 11,
49, 91, 94n274, 105–08, 110,
112–15, 118n44, 126–130, 147,
163, 166, 169–171, 179,
181–82, 184
pursuing inquiry and study (*dao*
wen xue 道問學), 39, 159

qi (氣). *See* vital energy
Qian Dehong (錢德洪), 160
qin min (親民). *See* loving the
people
Questions on the Great Learning
(*Daxue wen* 大學問), 114n28,
143n127, 160–172

Rabten, Geshe, 23n39
real knowledge (*zhen zhi* 真知),
113, 141–42, 182n268
Record of Learning (*Xueji* 學記),
53n84, 177n243
Recorded Sayings of the Two Cheng
[Brothers] (*Er Cheng yulu*, 二程
語錄), 118n42

Record for Practice (*Chuanxilu* 傳習錄), 11n16, 20n32, 62n123, 101n1, 102n3, 103n4–5, 109n19, 110n21, 113n25, 115n29, 122n58, 122n60, 125n66, 127n73–74, 131–60

Records of the Historian (*Shiji* 史記), 58n100

rectifying thoughts. *See* investigating things/rectifying thoughts

renovating the people (*xin min* 新民), 80, 134–36, 166–67

renxin (人心). *See* human heart-mind

right practice, 9, 18–19, 24

Rites of the Elder Dai (*Da Dai Liji* 大戴禮記), 80n215

Rites of Zhou (*Zhouli* 周禮), 77n204, 151

rou (柔), 50, 69

samādhi. *See* meditative stability

Sariputra, 19

Sayings from Kongzi's School (*Kongzi Jiayu* 孔子家語), 75n193, 133n96

Schirokauer, Conrad, 34n15

self (notion of), 5, 6, 9, 11–12, 14–15, 17–18, 23, 36–39, 46, 74–75, 106, 113–14, 117, 144–45, 148, 159, 168, 172, 182n266

self-deception, 7, 21, 37, 171

selfish (desires, thoughts, etc.), 5, 10–12, 18, 23, 37, 50n74, 52n81, 106, 113, 119, 125, 127n73, 128, 130, 138, 140–41, 147, 152, 162, 164–65

shen qi du (慎其獨). *See* being watchful over oneself

Shenxiu (神秀), 6

Shi jizhuan (詩集傳). *See* Collected Commentaries on the Book of Songs

Shiji (史記). *See* Records of the Historian

Shijing (詩經). *See* Book of Songs

Shujing (書經). *See* Book of History

Shun (sage emperor), 47, 55, 63, 76, 90, 91n264, 120, 135–36, 151, 154n173, 155–57, 171–72

Shuogua (說卦). *See* Explanations of the Trigrams

siduan (四端). *See* four sprouts

Sima Qian (司馬遷), 58n100

Sishujizhu (四書集註). *See* Collected Comments on the Four Books

sitting in meditation, 19, 24–25, 117, 122

Sixth Patriarch, 3, 14

skillful means (*upaya*), 4n5, 5n6

Slote, Michael, 33n14

Some Questions on the Great Learning (*Daxue huowen* 大學或問), 136n112, 139n121

spirit verses, 6, 180n257

spiritual coach, 7, 13, 17

spiritual effort/spiritual task (*gongfu* 功夫), 11, 118–19, 121, 124n65, 125–26, 128, 147–48

spontaneity, 4, 7, 12, 23–24, 42, 94n274, 114, 159n196, 166, 169, 181n261

Spring and Autumn Annals (*Chunqiu* 春秋), 55, 58n100, 77n204, 151, 152, 153n164, 156

sudden enlightenment, (*dunwu* 頓悟), 5, 20, 33n13, (*see also* enlightenment) supreme ultimate (*taiji* 太極), 38, 40–42, 57–61, 64–68

Suzuki, Shunryu, 18

sympathy, 36, 130, 161

taiji (太極). *See* supreme ultimate

Taiji tushuo (太極圖說). *See Explanation of the Diagram of the Supreme Ultimate*

Tao, Julia, 12n19, 52n81

Taylor, Rodney, 117n32

teachers (role of), 5n7, 7, 13, 17, 20–21, 31, 44, 62–63, 80–81, 102–03, 132, 175–76, 184

therapeutic approach, 7, 31, 114

this heart-mind (*cixin* 此心), 48, 72–73, 90, 102, 138–40, 148

three acmes, 53, 74

ti (體). *See* body

Tien, David W., 3n1, 105n12

Tiwald, Justin, 75n193

Tongshu (通書). *See Comprehending the Book of Changes*

Transmission of the Lamp (*Jingde chuandenglu* 景德傳燈錄), 53n85, 183n270

Tu Wei-ming, 101n1, 105n13, 173n234, 178n244

ultimate-less (*wuji* 無極), 38, 40–41, 57–61, 64–65, 66n147, 68n155

unity of knowing and acting (知行合一), 9, 17n27, 103, 112–15, 123–26, 140–42, 144

upaya. *See* skillful means

viewing purity, 12, 19, 24

viewing the mind, 12, 19, 24

Vimalakīrti, 19

Vimalakīrti-nirdesa Sūtra, 18, 19, 23, 26

vital energy (*qi* 氣), 12, 34n15, 38–39, 50n56, 70, 85, 106, 113

Wang Anshi (王安石), 51

Wang Bi (王弼), 9

Wang Shunbo (王順伯), 51, 74n189

Wang Tong (王通). *See* Wenzhongzi

Way (Dao, *dao* 道), 10, 13, 14n24, 17–18, 22–24, 26, 35, 37–39, 40–42, 46–48, 50, 53–54, 59, 61–62, 66, 68–70, 73, 75–76, 78, 80, 82–85, 87n246, 88–89, 95, 96n283, 103, 105, 107, 113, 116–17, 121–22, 133, 134n97, 148–52, 155–56, 164n210, 176, 183

Wei Shiyue (魏師說), 127

Wenzhongzi (文中子), Wang Tong (王通), 149–50, 152

Williams, Paul, 5n6

Wright, Arthur F., 113n27

Wu Zisi (吳子嗣), 35n17, 74, 130n81

wuji (無極). *See* ultimate-less

wuxing (五行). *See* five agents

xiao (孝). *See* filial piety

Xiaojing (孝經). *See Classic of Filial Piety*

Xiaoxue (小學). *See Elements of Learning*

Xici zhuan (繫辭傳). *See Great Appendix to the Book of Changes*

xin (心). *See* heart-mind

xin min (新民). *See* renovating the people

Xu Ai (徐愛), 44n32, 103n4–5, 122n60, 131–32, 134n97–8, 159
Xuan Zong (玄宗) (Emperor), 48n51
Xueji (學記). *See* Record of Learning
Xunzi (荀子), 8n11, 88
Xunzi, 88n249, 132n89, 158n187, 176n241

Yampolsky, Philip B., 3n2, 26n45
yang (陽), 50, 56n97, 57, 59, 62, 68–70, 79–80
Yang Zhu (陽朱), 65, 81n220, 86n244
Yao (sage emperor), 47, 55, 76, 90, 120, 151n163, 154n173, 155–57, 171–72
Yijing (易經). *See Book of Changes*
yin (陰), 50, 56n97, 57, 59, 62, 68–70, 79–80
Ying Yuanzheng (應原忠), 118, 128n76
yiti (一體). *See* one body
yong (用). *See* function
Yu Kam-por, 12n19, 52n81
Yuejing (樂經). *See Book of Music*

Zeng Zhaizhi (曾宅之), 44
Zhang Taibo (章太博), 44
Zhang Xuecheng (章學誠), 71n.172, 111n22, 157n179
Zhang Zai (張載), 34n15
Zhao Ruqian (趙如謙), 50n69
zhen zhi (真知). *See* real knowledge
Zheng Xuan (鄭玄), 180
Zheng Zhaoshuo (鄭朝朔), 139
zhi liang zhi (致良知). *See* extending pure knowing

zhi shan (至善). *See* highest good
zhi xing he yi (知行合一). *See* unity of knowing and acting
zhi yu zhi shan (止於至善). *See* residing in the highest good
zhi zhi (致知). *See* extending knowledge
Zhongyong (中庸). *See Doctrine of the Mean*
Zhongyong zhangju (中庸章句). *See Doctrine of the Mean in Sections and Sentences*
Zhou Dunyi 周敦頤 (Lianxi 濂溪), 40, 56–57, 59–61, 178n252
Zhou Gong (周公). *See* Duke of Zhou
Zhouli (周禮). *See Rites of Zhou*
Zhu Jidao (朱濟道), 74
Zhu Xi (朱熹), xi, 29, 31, 32n10, 34n15, 37, 39n24, 42n28, 44n30, 50n76, 55, 61, 62n123, 65n135, 65n137, 65n139, 66n142, 96n278, 96n283, 104, 108n17, 117n34, 124–25, 127n72, 133n92, 134, 135n101–03, 136–37, 143–44, 146, 148, 154n172, 157n181, 160n199, 164n211, 166n216, 166n218, 168n219, 179
Zhu Zifa (朱子發), 60
Zhuangzi (莊子), 71
Zhuangzi, 7n10, 23n38, 25, 71, 78, 129n80
zun de xing (尊德性). *See* honoring the virtuous nature
Zuozhuan (左傳), 66n144, 153, 173n236